Praise for Nancy I. Sanders and *] to Write Beginning Readers and C...*

As an experienced educator, I can vouch for the fact that if you want to learn how to write beginning readers and chapter books, you won't find a more outstanding teacher than Nancy. She knows how to break a complex task down into doable components, and in her book *Yes! You Can*, she's there each step of the way, sharing her experiences, expertise, and can-do encouragement, to help you succeed in reaching your goals.
-Evelyn B. Christensen, Ed.D., Educator and award-winning author of over 40 books
www.evelynchristensen.com

Most books on children's writing deal with picture books or children's novels. Here at last is a book that deals specifically with how to write beginning readers and chapter books--a very specialized segment of that market. The inside scoop from a writer who has already proved she knows the children's market with her previous book on the subject.
-Sally E. Stuart, Founder of *Christian Writers' Market Guide*
www.stuartmarket.com

This exciting new book from Nancy I. Sanders is a comprehensive blueprint for anyone who wants to write beginning readers and chapter books. Nancy offers tips for new writers as well as tips for seasoned professionals in each section of the book. She also includes fun exercises specifically designed to help anyone learn to write beginning readers and chapter books that get published! Nancy could have called this book *Everything You Need to Know about Writing Beginning Readers and Chapter Books* because she seems to have covered everything anyone needs to know if they're serious about writing these types of materials for publication. This is a must-have resource for any children's writer's professional library!
-Suzanne Lieurance
Children's Author, freelance writer, writing coach
www.suzannelieurance.com
www.workingwritersclub.com

Yes! You Can

Learn How to Write

Beginning Readers
and
Chapter Books

NANCY I. SANDERS

Copyright © 2012 Nancy I. Sanders

ISBN-13: 978-1478168225

ISBN-10: 1478168226

Cover image © Nancy I. Sanders:

Quilt handmade by Nancy I. Sanders, with author's cat Pitterpat

If one can, anyone can.

If two can, you can, too!™

Titles in this Series

Yes! You Can Learn
How to Write Children's Books,
Get Them Published, and
Build a Successful Writing Career

Yes! You Can Learn
How to Write Beginning Readers
and Chapter Books

www.YesYouCanLearn.wordpress.com

Dedication

This book is dedicated to Mrs. Ross, my first grade teacher in Everett Elementary School, Everett, Pennsylvania. Mrs. Ross taught me to read with *Dick and Jane*, but most of all, she introduced me to a lifetime of joy by giving me the gift of reading.

Acknowledgements

Once again, Tina M. Cho has helped edit and critique this book each step of the way. Tina, how blessed I've been to receive your constructive and encouraging feedback on this book especially since you were a kindergarten teacher for over ten years! Thanks, too, for your junior editor, Anna, who helped spot typos as she stood by your shoulder, and for Isaac, whose many escapades into the world of books brightened my days as you shared them with me. What a thrill it was the day (right in the middle of writing this manuscript) when you told me you just landed your first book contract for a series of 16 beginning reader picture books! Congratulations! May God richly bless you with a successful writing career.

I also want to thank my editors over the years who have helped me grow as a writer and worked with me to develop books and stories for the beginning readers and chapter books market. A special thank you to Ruth Geisler at Concordia Publishing House, Deborah Schecter at Scholastic Teaching Resources, Sharon Coatney at Libraries Unlimited, and Dr. Raymond White with Downey Child Care Center.

I am also deeply indebted to Eve Heidi Bine-Stock at E & E Publishing. Yes! I treasure your input and value your insight.

And as always, words cannot express my thanks to my best friend, my husband Jeff. Happy anniversary, honey! It's been a wonderful 30 years together. I'm looking forward to the new season God has planned for our lives and for our family. Thank you for encouraging me to write this book and cheering me on along the way!

TABLE OF CONTENTS

INTRODUCTION

Welcome to the world of beginning readers and chapter books! It's a world of sunshine and flowers, puppies and kittens, little hard seeds that grow into giant juicy watermelons, and clumsy caterpillars that change into delicate butterflies. It's the world of children as seen through the eyes of a child. It's a delightful world, and it's filled with fun and surprises. It's a world that you can be part of if you like to write for kids!

The world of beginning readers and chapter books is a wonderful place to be if you are a children's writer. Whether just starting out on your journey as a writer, or with many years and numerous publications under your belt, I want to welcome you here. Let's explore it together, learn about its challenges and rewards, and grow together by polishing our writing skills.

Perhaps you are new to this world. Maybe you've got a foggy idea of what this world is all about, but you're not quite sure. You may wonder exactly what beginning readers and chapter books are. In a nutshell, beginning readers and chapter books are the first books children learn to read all by themselves. They are the bridge between picture books that others read to them, and middle grade novels that they can read on their own. Beginning readers and chapter books have carefully chosen vocabulary words and short sentences that help children in early elementary school acquire the skills they need to read all by themselves. These books are known as "leveled" reading, or reading material that is geared for children in specific grade levels in school.

The beginning readers and chapter books market isn't limited to books for students in kindergarten or first grade, however. Today's market is multi-dimensional and ever expanding to reach beyond elementary school and equip struggling readers even at the junior high and high school levels. Fluid and changing to meet the needs of today's educational objectives, leveled readers can now be found in an amazing array of formats such as Readers Theatre plays and reproducible mini-books. Because there are no clearly defined boundaries in this market, here in this book, *Yes! You Can Write Beginning Readers and Chapter Books* we'll discuss material that is geared to leveled reading in any market and at any age.

Even if you've never heard the terms "beginning readers" or "chapter books" before, you can join this exciting world with the dreams of writing for this delightful market. By taking steps to understand the parameters of this world and practicing specific exercises to hone and polish your writing abilities, you can acquire the skills needed to start seeing your dreams come true.

So come on! Join the journey! Step along in stride with the countless numbers of children's authors who have discovered the joys of writing beginning readers and chapter books. They learned how to experience success in this market, one step at a time. You can, too!

PART I

The World of

Beginning Readers

and

Chapter Books

Chapter 1

A WORLD ALL ITS OWN

1.1 A Place of Wonder and Delight

The world of beginning readers and chapter books is a place filled with wonder and delight! It's the world of very young children, whose entire existence is centered on exploration, play, imagination, and tender love. It's the exciting place where precious young minds discover the mystery and joy of the written word. As a children's writer, it's a place where you can join the dance of the beginning of life, all over again.

Picture the image of a little baby taking her first step. Arms spread wide, a delighted grin on her slobbery face, eyes aglow with the thrill of discovery, she takes a step. Then another! Suddenly, the whole world opens up before her to explore.

It's the same when a child first discovers that the black marks on paper have meaning. Suddenly, a fuzzy shape gels and is recognized. It is a letter, and that letter makes the same sound each time it appears in a favorite story. Cuddled up on Grandma's lap, listening to the music of her voice as she reads the story aloud again and again, following along first with the pictures and then with those little black marks on the page, a thrill runs through the child's heart as he identifies the shape of a letter and sees it again and again on the different pages of the book.

Eyes bright with excitement, he identifies another letter. Then another! Soon he can read entire combinations of letters and knows they form a word. He learns more words. Then more! Suddenly, the whole world opens before him. He can read!

The world of beginning readers and chapter books is chock full of fun! Children's writers get to invent new word concoctions that help emerging readers master the power of words. Children's writers get to create new recipes of tasty word combinations that satisfy reader's appetites to learn important reading skills, while tickling their taste buds and enticing them to read even more.

Beginner's Tip

Go to your local library and explore the beginning readers section. In most libraries, these books are shelved in their own location, separate from the picture books, nonfiction, and middle grade or young adult novels. If you don't know where to look, ask the children's librarian for help. These books include titles such as the classics *Green Eggs and Ham* by Dr. Seuss and the *Frog and Toad* series by Arnold Lobel. Check out at least 10 beginning reader books to take home.

Professional Track

Sometimes we get so busy with deadlines and writing projects that we lose touch with the world of children. Go on a scavenger hunt at your local library. Visit the children's section and *sit*. Stay there until you find these three things: a child who laughs out loud while listening to a story, a child who snuggles close while someone reads a story aloud, and a child who hands a book to someone and asks for it to be read aloud. Be sure to enjoy the pleasure of each magical moment. When you're done, gather at least 10 beginning reader books and check them out to take home.

Strengthen Your Writing Muscles

Write down your earliest memory of reading on your own, whether it was learning to identify new words in an exercise at school or the earliest book you remember reading all by yourself. Describe how you felt while you were reading. Were you aware of the world of books, or did you simply get caught up in one single story at the time? As you write, try to capture the joy and wonder of the experience through the eyes of your inner child.

1.2 A Ripe Field of Opportunity

If you're weighing a decision whether or not to write for the beginning readers and chapter books market, I want to encourage you to give it a try. When I first started writing for this market, I knew nothing about word lists or controlled vocabulary. Yet, as I began to write beginning readers for educational publishers, I discovered to my surprise that I enjoyed it. If you're drawn to this market enough to read this book, go ahead and give it your best! You can try it on for size.

Chances are, though, that you'll hear at some writer's event or from some editor that the field of beginning readers and chapter books is a closed market. In comparison to the literally untapped beginning readers market in the mid 1900s with the advent of *The Cat in the Hat*, this is most certainly true. Since then, many publishers have established entire lines of trade books in their beginning readers series.

However, my husband Jeff has been teaching elementary school in southern California for over 25 years. I keep my ear close to the ground when it comes to following educational trends. From the educator's perspective, they're always being pushed to use new cutting edge material in their classrooms. The domino effect is that publishers are therefore motivated to meet this need and will continue to publish new materials teachers can use in their classrooms, even during tough economic times.

A concrete example of this is the fact that my teacher's book of reproducible mini-books for pre-emergent readers hit the scene during a major economic crunch. Fellow authors as well as big name publishers bemoaned the devastating effect in lack of sales that year. Yet when I received my royalty check that same year for *25 Read and Write Mini-Books that Teach Word Families*, I discovered sales had skyrocketed and I had a big fat royalty check to prove it. Teachers were still buying new beginning readers, even in tough times.

Yes, the trade picture book market for beginning readers (the full color ones you find in racks at the big chain bookstores such as *The Cat in the Hat*) is much tighter with stiffer competition and is harder to break into than earlier years. Yet more and more publishers are attempting to fill the educator's need for material for beginning readers in a variety of formats and in a continuous flow of new products. If you want to break into the beginning readers and chapter books market and hit a dead end with one publisher or with one type of format, change your course. Research different publishers, look for different markets, and explore different beginning reader formats. Openings *are* there and will continue to be there, even for new authors in this field.

For instance, a couple of years ago, one writer shared in our local writing group of a new opportunity she had read about in the newspaper. A local Christian school was developing a reading curriculum and sent out a call for needed writers. A number of my writer friends hopped on board, most having never before written a beginning reader! Over the months ahead, following the school's guidelines, we wrote beginning readers from second grade through sixth grade, story after glorious story for a total of 30 books, each anthology containing a large number of stories written for each different reading level. And when the books were finally finished and all the material was written, the school decided to develop an entire new set of stories for oral reading at different levels. The exciting journey to write beginning readers started all over again!

If you have skills or an educational background in teaching, literacy, or English as a Second Language (ESL) training, the beginning readers and chapter market could be a fantastic place for you to succeed. It's even more open to writers already versed in the world of teaching children to read. As you step into creating material for this market, you might even find your elusive writer's voice that you've been searching for.

Test companies need new test material that children at various levels can read themselves. Teachers need new reproducibles such as read-aloud stories or Readers Theatre plays that they can distribute to students to practice essential oral reading skills. Online sites need new beginning reader material to enhance their Websites and entice educators to visit. Magazines need new stories that young readers can read by themselves. The field is ripe with opportunity for writers in this genre. To help determine if the field of beginning readers is a good fit for you as a children's writer, continue on to the following section.

Beginner's Tip

If you're not sure where to start, try taking two paths until you discover which one offers more success. Target both the trade book market and the educational market. (Trade book publishers are ones who produce fully illustrated beginning readers as stand-alone titles, or individual books children can read. Educational publishers produce material for teachers to use with students.) Write one manuscript for each market and then submit each manuscript to its target publisher.

Professional Track

Use your published success in another market to help build name recognition in this market so that when your beginning readers and chapter books eventually hit the scene, educators will already know your name and gobble up your books! To do this, beef up your blog, originally referred to as a Web log. Include beginning readers on your blog as freebies based on your already-published book. Invite teachers to download and use these freebies in their classroom. For instance, do you already have a picture book, nonfiction book for kids, or a middle grade novel published? Write Readers Theatre plays, a section of your book as a hi-lo reader for struggling students, or read-aloud stories all based on your book and post these as freebies on your blog.

Strengthen Your Writing Muscles

Google the term "word family" or visit the site of Hubbard's Cupboard and explore her delightful and fun printable Word Family Booklets at www.hubbardscupboard.org/printable_booklets.html. Make a list of words that all end in the same word family such as *–ay, –in,* or *–op*. Write a rhymed story using several words from the same word family.

1.3 The Perfect Fit

Throughout my experience as a writer, there have been times I have explored writing for a new market. At first it might feel like a struggle, but as I allow myself the freedom to work through challenges and make mistakes, I have come to make the delightful discovery that this market is a good match for my personality and creative writing talents. I want to encourage you to take the time to explore the world of beginning readers and chapter books. Don't give up at the first roadblock. Work through the challenges within your own comfort zone until you see a measure of success. You might be delightfully surprised that you can write for the beginning readers and chapter books market. It might be the perfect fit!

Over the years, I have led various different writers' groups and critique groups. I have seen with my own eyes children's writers who have longed to get published but have had no success. They may have struggled writing picture books. They might be disappointed that they aren't a master storyteller in the YA, or young adult, market. Yet when they have attempted to write for the beginning readers and chapter books market, for the very first time they experience the thrill of getting their manuscripts accepted and receiving assignments to write even more.

The world of beginning readers and chapter books is a world filled with structure. Often editors provide a grade-level word list for a specific project, and the writer must use only words from this list in the stories. Even the sentence length at each level is carefully controlled since children learning to read can only handle a certain number of words in each sentence for easy comprehension. Sometimes the number of characters, or individual letters typed on each page, has to be a specific amount. This is usually because the font size of the text in the earliest levels is larger and easier for pre-readers to read, so the publisher has to make sure it can actually fit on the page of the book.

Some authors discover that they thrive in this type of environment. They like being able to choose words from a list to put in their story rather than trying to think of words on their own. They like the tight parameters and careful guidelines that have to be followed. If they felt like they were floundering in a vast world of too many ideas to choose from, too many plots to pick, and too many avenues to take in the world of picture books, middle grade novels, or young adult novels, the tight structure of the world of beginning readers and chapter books appeals to them as nothing else has before.

Before I started writing for this market, I had no idea I would thrive in it. To be honest, the idea of all that structure rather frightened me at first. I felt unsure of myself, especially since I wasn't a teacher or a reading specialist. I'm glad that I didn't avoid this market because of these insecurities, however. As I started writing more and more beginning readers, I discovered things about myself as a writer that I'd never known before. I discovered I could take this type of structure and run with it to create fresh new stories and offer publishers a fresh new approach to take to reach struggling readers at various levels.

I didn't make these discoveries until I'd written quite a few stories for beginning readers. If I had quit while I was still struggling to get solid footing, I would have missed the thrill of discovering one of my strengths as a writer. That's why I want to encourage you to spend time writing for this market. Write enough beginning readers until you feel like you have a grasp of the basic structure and can move around comfortably in this world. Then keep on writing. Once you get past learning how everything works, you'll be able to determine whether or not this is a world you want to work in. If you feel like you want to give it a try, but you're just not sure how to get started, read the next section. I'll show you how to take your very first step in the beginning readers and chapter books market.

Beginner's Tip

Don't worry too much about structure, sentence length, or vocabulary at first. Just write the first draft of your story and let the words flow. When done, you can then go back and work on your manuscript to make the sentence length and vocabulary words fit the reading level you're targeting.

Professional Track

If you've written middle grade or young adult novels in a popular series for a packager, you know all about structure. The publisher handed you an entire story bible to follow while you were writing that manuscript! If you enjoyed that type of environment, dive right into this market. If you didn't enjoy it, you can breathe a sigh of relief. Instead of writing 40,000 words, many beginning reader stories are less than 1000 words. You can do it!

Strengthen Your Writing Muscles

Read three to five beginning readers by the same publisher in the same series at the same reading level. Write a one-sentence plot summary for each one. When finished, choose one of these plots and write a brand new story for that same level based on that plot summary.

1.4 Yes! You Can—but if You Feel You Can't

You're reading this book because you are attracted to the precious stories in this market. Perhaps you have a young child who giggles with delight when she reads her favorite beginning reader all on her own. Maybe you're an educator who understands the immense value these books have in the process of teaching children to read. Whatever your reasons, you want to write stories, wrap them up as a special gift in a published book, and watch children open up the treasures you're giving them to discover the love of reading. And even if you feel like this might be a tough market to crack, there are practical steps you can take to start seeing your dreams come true.

I taught about the Triple Crown of Success in my first book in this series, *Yes! You Can Learn How to Write Children's Books, Get Them Published, and Build a Successful Writing Career*. The basic concept of the Triple Crown of Success is that the key to building a successful writing career is to use three separate strategies to meet three separate goals. Over the course of my writing career, I've discovered that there are three main reasons people write:

1. For personal fulfillment.
2. To get published.
3. To earn income.

Most people write one manuscript to meet all three goals, as I explain in my first book. However, this often leaves writers with a high level of frustration, lack of published credits, fistfuls of rejection letters, not much of a reliable income from writing, and hardly any success to speak of.

The method I recommend in the Triple Crown of Success is to use three entirely different strategies to meet each one of these three goals. Basically, this means that most of the time, I recommend working on three entirely different manuscripts at the same time, one for each different goal.

The reason I'm mentioning the Triple Crown of Success at this point is to help you determine which goal to focus on as you're exploring the world of beginning readers and chapter books. If you're attracted to these delightful books but feel it might be too much to handle, I encourage you to start out by working in this market toward the goal of personal fulfillment.

Don't make the mistake and try to learn how to write beginning readers and chapter books in order to meet all three goals at once. Don't daydream about writing one single beginning reader manuscript to get published and earn income and also find personal fulfillment. If you do, you'll get frustrated very quickly and probably stop writing for this market completely.

If you are brand new to this market and unsure whether you can write successfully for this market, use other manuscripts for the goal of getting published. Work on still other writing projects for the goal of earning income. Meanwhile, take your time to learn and explore and practice writing beginning readers for the goal of personal fulfillment until you feel confident enough that you can start pitching ideas and landing contracts to write beginning readers for income. You'll learn step-by-step methods to take along this journey as you continue to read through the chapters in this book.

Also in my first book, *Yes! You Can Learn How to Write Children's Books, Get Them Published, and Build a Successful Writing Career*, I share helpful time-management strategies in my model, the Writer's Pyramid. Familiarize yourself with how the Writer's Pyramid works and schedule time to learn the skills for this market and write sample beginning reader manuscripts during the hours each week or month allocated for the goal of writing for personal fulfillment. Watch your confidence grow!

As in my first book, I recommend that if you want to earn income as a children's writer, you should learn how to pitch queries, submit proposals per request of an editor, and land book contracts or assignments before you write the manuscript. You'll find detailed instructions about how to achieve this in my first book. The emphasis in this book is the same. If you want to earn income writing beginning readers and chapter books, I recommend that you learn how to pitch your ideas to an editor and land a contract or assignment before you write the manuscript. Here, in the chapters of this book, I explain how to do this specifically in the beginning readers and chapter books market.

When I wrote my very first book of reproducible beginning reader math plays for teachers, I pitched the idea to an editor at Scholastic Teaching Resources. She requested a proposal and I submitted one. Then I landed the contract to write the book. My dear friend and writing buddy Sheryl Ann Crawford co-wrote the book with me. We didn't write the entire book first and then try to send it on its rounds of submissions. Even though neither of us had written beginning readers before, we landed the contract first and then wrote the book.

If you feel confident to do the same, you can try doing this, too! If you're still not sure, keep following my suggestions here in this book until your confidence grows. There is a quote that appears in the front of this book. It's also in the front of my first book in this series. I place this quote front and center in these books because I absolutely believe it is true:

If one can, anyone can.

If two can, you can, too! ™

If I can land a contract to write a book for the beginning readers market, anyone can. I'm not an educator or reading specialist. I didn't have a lot of experience at the time in the beginning readers market. But I'm not the only one who does this. I know other writer friends who land book contracts or assignments to write beginning readers before they write the manuscript. If two can do this, you can, too!

Beginner's Tip

If you lack confidence in your writing abilities in general, start writing regularly for periodicals that pay little if anything at all. Submit articles to your church newsletter, local community magazines, or free online resources for children. You'll work with editors, see your name in print, and start building published credits. Writing frequently for the no-pay/low-pay market is a great way to boost your confidence as a writer.

Professional Track

Explore your publisher's Website(s) to see if they publish a line of beginning readers. If so, start working toward the goal of pitching an idea to write a manuscript that would fit into their beginning reader product line. If your publisher doesn't have beginning readers, try searching for a publisher who does and who also publishes products similar to the types of manuscripts you've already had published. Try breaking into this new publisher in your area of expertise. Then, after you become one of their authors, try to break into their line of beginning readers.

Strengthen Your Writing Muscles

Many beginning readers use school as the setting for the story. Make a list of five memories from your childhood that happened during elementary school. (Or think of five school events in the lives of elementary-age children you know.) Try to think of at least one humorous incident to add to the list. When finished, choose one event from the list. First write about that incident as if you were telling the memory to one of your adult friends today. Then rewrite it as if you were telling it to a child. Take one step further and try writing it as a beginning reader.

Chapter 2

THE HISTORY OF BEGINNING READERS AND CHAPTER BOOKS

2.1 Before Beginning Readers

Many reading specialists, educators, and literacy advocates have a basic knowledge of the history of beginning readers. Even if you've never researched this topic, however, as a children's writer it's important to become familiar with how this market came into existence. This brief background will provide you with a working knowledge of the world of literacy and how it relates to young children so that you can step more successfully into the line of authors who provide reading material for this target group.

In the early 1900s, Edward W. Dolch conducted research on the topic of teaching children to read. He created a list of words that were commonly found in roughly 50-75% of the material read by students. Many of these words cannot be easily sounded out or illustrated to provide clues for children who are beginning to read. Dolch developed a theory that essentially stated if children learned to memorize a basic list of words by sight, it would help them better master the skill of reading.

Dolch compiled a list of 220 words that included words such as pronouns, adjectives, and prepositions. These words are known as *sight words* or *high-frequency words.* These terms reflect Dolch's theory that young children encounter the words on this list frequently in the material they're reading, along with his belief that children should memorize these words in order to recognize them by sight rather than by sounding them out or figuring them out based on the pictures accompanying the text.

Dolch's list of 220 words includes words such as: a, about, after, again, all, always, am, an, and, any, are, around, as, ask, at, ate, away. He also developed a list of the most common 95 nouns found in material young children read. In 1948, he published these lists in his book, *Problems in Reading.* His theory and research revolutionized the way educators taught reading to the very young. His basic word lists are still in use today in classrooms across the nation, although some of the words have become outdated. To update Dolch's list of sight words for today's culture, a new list has been developed by Edward B. Fry and Jacqueline E. Kress in their book, *The Reading Teacher's Book of Lists*.

Beginner's Tip

Don't feel stressed if you don't entirely feel comfortable navigating through information about Dolch's lists or various educational lingo. Teachers learn about topics such as this in university-level courses. Just start familiarizing yourself with a basic knowledge of the history behind beginning readers. As you start writing for this market, you will grow more familiar with how this all fits together.

Professional Track

Learn more about Dolch and his theory. Write articles based on your research and submit them to teacher's magazines or websites. Start building name recognition among teachers as early as possible to help increase sales when you publish books in this market.

Strengthen Your Writing Muscles

Do a freewriting exercise comparing learning how to read with learning how to write beginning readers. Begin with this prompt: Learning how to read is similar to learning how to write beginning readers because…

2.2 *Beginning Readers are Born!*

In the late 1950s, Theodore Geisel, beloved children's author known to most as Dr. Seuss, took Dolch's list of 220 high-frequency words and his list of 95 common nouns. He wrote and illustrated a simple rhyming picture book incorporating Dolch's lists in his text, and published it in 1957 with Random House. *The Cat in the Hat* hit the scene, and beginning readers were born.

Up until that time, most educators were using basal readers to teach reading in early elementary grades. A basal reader is a textbook used to teach reading. Stories in these textbooks with characters such as Dick and Jane and Spot were used by educators to teach children to read based on an approach that introduced new words steadily and repeated these words often.

In contrast, *The Cat in the Hat* was a trade picture book and not a textbook. For the first time in history, children could hold a picture book in their very own hands and learn how to read based on Dolch's theory and lists of sight words and common nouns. Random House used *The Cat in the Hat* as the launch of a new line of picture books and called their series, Beginner Books.

Soon other publishers jumped on board the beginning reader phenomena, each publishing their own line of beginning readers. Each publisher created its own series with its own catchy name and with its own unique levels of reading. A new award was even created called the *Geisel Award* in memory of Theodore Geisel (Dr. Seuss), the creator of beginning readers. This prestigious award is given out annually by the American Library Association to honor the author(s) and illustrator(s) of the most distinguished book for beginning readers published the previous year.

As more and more demands are put upon educators to develop strong readers, or students who score high test scores, beginning readers have developed over the years to meet this ever-growing need. To learn more about today's market for beginning readers, read the following section.

Beginner's Tip

Read a picture book such as Jane O'Connor's *Fancy Nancy* and compare it to a beginning reader such as *The Cat in the Hat.* Picture books such as *Fancy Nancy* are meant to be read aloud by an adult to the child, and therefore have no limit to the vocabulary words they use as long as the concept is presented to children in a way they can understand. In direct contrast, beginning readers such as *The Cat in the Hat* are meant to be read by children themselves. Beginning readers therefore have carefully chosen vocabulary words and sentence structure found within their text.

Professional Track

Because many publishers want to publish beginning readers in a variety of formats, consider developing your own leveled reading system and pitch an idea to a publisher for a brand new series. Research existing levels of beginning readers and come up with your own unique strategy.

Strengthen Your Writing Muscles

Choose words from both Dolch's lists of 220 sight words and 95 nouns, and write a short story for a child in kindergarten or first grade. Write the entire story only using words from these lists. Search online for both lists or use the ones found at this site: Mrs. Perkins' Dolch Words at www.mrsperkins.com/dolch.htm.

2.3 Types of Leveled Readers

Today's market for beginning readers and chapter books is multi-dimensional. Ever expanding, it now reaches ages beyond kindergarten and first grade to encompass struggling readers even at the junior high and high school levels. Ever changing, beginning readers and chapter books in today's market can be found in a variety of formats including Readers Theatre plays and reproducible mini-books. As a children's writer, you can plug into this exciting market by finding your place as a contributor of reading material.

Publishers and librarians classify beginning readers differently. Publishers classify beginning reader books as picture books since most are illustrated in full color. You will therefore find information about beginning readers in a publisher's catalog or writer's book under the category of picture books. However, in most libraries, beginning reader books are separated from picture books and shelved in their very own section.

Beginning readers aren't limited to the trade picture book market, however. Yes, you'll find beginning readers in the trade picture book market that produces fully illustrated paperback and hardback books for children. But you'll also find beginning readers in the educational market that produces textbooks and test material as well as black and white reproducibles, or worksheets that can be photocopied and distributed to students for classroom use. You'll find beginning readers in magazines and in other markets such as the ESL (English as a Second Language) market with printed material that teaches English skills to students whose primary language isn't English.

As more and more educators work with students even on up through high school to learn solid reading skills, more and more publishers are expanding the concept of beginning readers and are starting to produce leveled reading material on up through junior high and high school.

Whether in the trade picture book market, the educational market, the magazine market or other markets, most publishers develop their own reading levels within their unique product line. For one of my books, I had the privilege of developing the reading levels from the ground up. I had chatted with one of my editors in the educational market regarding the publisher's need to develop books for struggling middle grade readers. As a result of this conversation, I pitched an idea for a Readers Theatre math book based on a reading level I developed from researching existing series of beginning readers. A book contract was offered, and I wrote the book *Hello Hi-Lo: Readers Theatre Math* (Libraries Unlimited, 2010). It has leveled reading scripts for grades 4 though 8 and teaches important middle grade math skills in each different play.

No matter which reading levels a publisher determines for its own product line, however, there are general levels most beginning readers and chapter books are categorized in. Here is a generalized breakdown of what these include:

Pre-emergent Readers

This level is also known as pre-readers, nonreaders, or guided readers. The target audience for these readers includes children in preschool (those who are preparing to enter kindergarten), kindergarten, and first grade who do not yet know how to read. Sometimes this level will be classified as PreK-1. This label means "pre-kindergarten to first grade." The goal in many schools today is to help children learn how to read by the end of kindergarten, but some children learn by the end of first grade.

Material presented to children at this level is very simple. A book might feature one word on each page, accompanied by an illustration that provides picture clues for the decoding of the word, whether through sight recognition of the word or sounding it out phonetically where the child utilizes a basic understanding of the sounds each letter makes. Thus, one page might show a picture of a cat and have the word *cat* printed on the page.

Material is organized and presented in such a way as to help children learn the basic building blocks of reading skills while also gaining confidence in acquiring these essential skills. For instance, a book might contain words within the same "word family" that all have the same ending –*at* such as *cat, hat, mat, bat*. Or, a book might contain words that are grouped together according to theme such as *cat, dog, cow, pig*. Or, a book might contain words that all begin with the same letter of the alphabet such as *ball, bat, barn, bird*. Some material at this level groups words in simple phrases and basic patterned or repetitive sentences in order for children to learn that words are put together in a meaningful way to convey information. Some teachers refer to these as little guided reading books, and for our purpose here as writers, we can include these in the category of pre-emergent readers. The variety of presentations is endless, but the goal in each pre-emergent reader is the same: to teach non-readers how to take the first steps toward reading.

Emergent Readers

This level is also known as beginning readers. The target audience for these readers includes children in kindergarten and first or second grade who have already acquired some reading skills. Sometimes this level will be classified as Grades K-1 or Grades K-2. This label means "kindergarten to first grade" or "kindergarten to second grade." The goal in most schools today is to develop solid readers step-by-step throughout the kindergarten and first grade or second grade experience.

Even though there are some preschoolers who know how to read and can therefore be classified as emergent readers, publishers usually do not lump preschoolers in this group since state and national standards do not require educators to teach preschoolers to be fluent, or strong, readers. (Educators are required to teach students according to the standards of the state they teach in as well as national standards for all schools. States have also adopted Common Core State Standards. To learn more about these standards and how they relate to beginning readers and chapter books, read *Section 3.2 State and National Standards.*)

Stories in emergent readers are simple. Vocabulary reflects the vocabulary being taught to students in the lower elementary grades. Material is organized and presented in such a way to help children practice the reading skills they've already acquired while building on those skills to increase fluid reading, or the ease in which they read, as well as comprehension of the material. For instance, simple and short repetitive sentences are used at this level such as: *The bird had a cap. The bird had a bat. The bird hit the ball.* The goal in each emergent reader is the same: to guide children forward to practice and acquire the reading skills needed so that they can read on their own.

Easy Readers

This level is also known as independent readers. The target audience for these readers includes children in early elementary grades who have already acquired basic reading skills and are learning to read on their own. This level usually includes up to third grade, but does not typically target upper elementary students in grades 4 through 6, although struggling readers in upper elementary may choose to read books classified in this level. Often however, older students tend to avoid books at this level because they might feel that their peers think they're reading books for "babies" since many children read much more advanced books by fourth grade such as middle grade novels.

Since easy readers typically target students in third grade and younger, the themes and topics they cover address interests of children this age and usually don't appeal to older kids. This reading level targets students who are just gaining the confidence to read their first books all by themselves. Stories are more complicated than in earlier levels, but not too complex. The goal in easy readers is to help children gain confidence in reading skills rather than in attempting to teach them to comprehend complicated story plots. Some publishers stop their product line at this level and do not write beginning readers for older readers.

Material is organized and presented in such a way that children become more familiar with the more formal structure of written stories such as paragraphs, sentences of different lengths, and a strong story arc or arch with a beginning, middle, and end. The goal in each easy reader is the same: to teach children to read independently and read with ease.

Advanced Readers

This level is also known as proficient readers. These books usually contain short chapters, longer sentences, more advanced controlled vocabulary, and more complicated stories than earlier levels. Advanced readers usually target middle elementary students in grades 3 and 4, so subjects cover topics taught at these grade levels such as United States history, multicultural awareness, and science topics such as light or heat. Many titles of advanced readers are nonfiction. Some publishers classify their advanced readers according to different genre such as *Mystery* or *Sports*.

Material is organized and presented in such a way to help children feel they have the confidence to read books for older audiences, even if in actuality they are not quite ready to tackle an entire middle grade novel by themselves. The goal in each advanced reader is the same: to build confidence in reading grade-level material and guide children toward reading books independently that do not contain controlled vocabulary or structured sentences.

First Chapter Books

The difference between an advanced reader and a first chapter book is that most books classified as advanced readers are usually in a series of beginning readers and have a similar look, feel, and cover size (or trim size) as all the other books by that publisher in the earlier levels of the series. A first chapter book, however, usually has the look, feel, and cover size of a middle grade (MG) novel. First chapter books bridge the gap between beginning readers and middle grade novels. The entire length of a first chapter book can be the same as one single chapter in a novel.

First chapter books are at the highest level of beginning readers. These include the first books children read independently that have chapters. For some publishers, the word count for a first chapter book is comparable to a chapter in a novel.

Material is organized and presented in such a way to help children cross the bridge from beginning reader to middle grade novel. The goal in each first chapter book is the same: to teach children to love reading while giving them the skills and confidence to read entire novel-length books on their own.

Hi-lo Readers

This level is also known as high interest/low readability readers. Because so many children struggle with learning challenges and still can benefit from beginning readers in upper elementary, this level was created to help meet this need. These books target upper elementary students in grades 4 through 6 as far as content is concerned. This means that the subjects found in hi-lo readers cover topics taught in upper elementary and middle grades. However, the readability, or reading level, of the text is below grade level in that it could be read by many independent readers in second or third grade. Publishers take extra care to package a hi-lo reader that looks and feels like it's for older kids so that these students don't feel embarrassed reading these books. However, the sentence structure and vocabulary words found in hi-lo readers were taught at an earlier elementary grade—it's just that some students have not yet mastered these essential reading skills even though they are in upper elementary.

Material is organized and presented in such a way to help older children feel good about themselves and experience a measure of confidence as they read. The goal in each hi-lo reader is the same: to teach children the building blocks of reading they didn't master in an earlier grade in an attempt to bring them closer to being able to read at their own grade level.

Once again, these are generalized categories of beginning readers in today's market. I only included a breakdown from preschool through sixth grade as this is the main target range even though some publishers today are producing leveled reading material on up through high school. Publishers each have developed their own unique approach to leveling their beginning readers and chapter books that will most likely overlap some of the categories I presented. However, the breakdown I provided here is to help you compare at a glance the different levels of beginning readers found in today's market, which grade level of students are in each target range, and what the goal of each level is regarding teaching reading skills.

Beginner's Tip

Gather a series of beginning readers by one publisher. Be sure to get at least one title from each level in their series. Read through the books and choose a favorite title from each level. Type out word for word one book from each level and save them in a file on your computer. Which level(s) felt more like a natural fit for you as you tried to write the different beginning readers?

Professional Track

In which children's markets or genres have you already experienced published success? Determine how you can utilize the writing skills you have already acquired to break into the beginning readers and chapter books market. Have you published nonfiction for older kids? Pitch a proposal to an editor for a nonfiction advanced reader. Have you published a children's novel? Submit a query to write a first chapter book. Do you have picture books in your list of published credits? Try your hand with pre-emergent or emergent readers.

Strengthen Your Writing Muscles

Read three books from three different levels in the same publisher's series. Then choose one of the books. Rewrite the story to fit in one of the other two levels instead. What key changes did you have to make?

Chapter 3

TOOLS OF THE TRADE

3.1 Reading Levels and Readability Lists

There are key reference books you'll want to purchase to have on your bookshelves. These books help take the guesswork out of reading levels and readability lists. They give you solid footing regarding vocabulary and choice of words at each grade level so you can have the tools you need to craft effective beginning readers and chapter books to guide children in the development of becoming fluid readers.

The standard in the industry is the *Children's Writer's Word Book* by Alijandra Mogilner. This book is a must-have for writers in the beginning readers and chapter books market. In the beginning of the book is an Alphabetical List of vocabulary words, each assigned its own grade level of readability from kindergarten up through sixth grade. For instance, we see in this list that the word *abacus* is a 5th grade word and the word *abandon* is a 4th grade word.

Following the Alphabetical List is a chapter-by-chapter section of each grade level from kindergarten up through sixth grade. The introduction to each grade level explains which subjects are taught in that grade level and how it affects vocabulary usage. For instance, even though kindergarten vocabulary lists contain simple and basic words such as *cat* and *car*, students learn about holidays in kindergarten, so more difficult words such as *Christmas* and *Easter* are also appropriate for this level of reading. Sentence structure and sentence length are also discussed, and examples are given. The end of each chapter includes a Word List of words that are taught at that grade level.

Following these chapters, there is a thesaurus. This thesaurus is indispensable when you want to use a certain word but it's not appropriate for the reading level you're targeting. This thesaurus lists related words with similar meanings and also gives the grade level for each. For instance, you might want to use the word *compassion* in your story, but you are writing for a first grade reading level. Look up the word *compassion* in the thesaurus. It says: ***Compassion 5th****: care K, pity 4th, sympathy 4th, tenderness 3rd, understanding 1st*. Since you're writing for a first grade reading level, you would choose the word *understanding* to use in your story.

Other references to help you learn more about readability levels and how reading is taught in the classroom include:

The Reading Teacher's Book of Lists by Edward B. Fry and Jacqueline E. Kress

Phonics from A to Z by Wiley Blevins

Building Fluency: Lessons and Strategies for Reading Success by Wiley Blevins

Teaching Phonics and Word Study in the Intermediate Grades: A Complete SourceBook by Wiley Blevins

If you are working with readability levels in the middle grades (grades four through eight), a key reference tool is Merriam Webster's *Intermediate Dictionary*. If a word is not listed in this dictionary, it shouldn't be included in stories written for a middle-grade readability level.

Another tool that many authors use comes built in with Microsoft Word and gives you the Readability Statistics of your text. If you highlight a portion of text and run the spell-check feature, after it is done checking the spelling, a small box pops up listing the Readability Statistics. Under Readability, it lists the Flesch Reading Ease and the Flesch-Kincaid Grade Level. Basically, this shows the reading level of that portion of text. For instance, if it scores a 6.2 on the Flesch-Kincaid Grade Level, students reading at grade level in the second month of sixth grade should be able to read it successfully.

Just a word of caution when using the Flesch-Kincaid Grade Level: It should not be your definitive measuring tool when working with reading levels in the elementary grades. It does not work entirely accurately when analyzing very short sentences, so doesn't work the best with many beginning readers. Even though I will use this tool as a reference, especially when evaluating long portions of text for the intermediate or high school leveled readers, I refer mainly to the *Children's Writer's Word Book* when writing beginning readers and chapter books for elementary students.

Yet another tool that is standard in both the publishing community and the world of educators is the Lexile® Measure. A rating system that utilizes a specific software program, the Lexile® Measure is twofold. It rates the reading level of a book's text and it is also used to measure the student's reading ability. Working together, it helps students find books to read that match their ability. To learn more about the Lexile® Measure and how it is being used today, visit the Website, The Lexile® Framework for Reading, at www.lexile.com.

Beginner's Tip

Start building your own personal research library to use as a reference while writing for the beginning readers and chapter books market. Make your first purchases include the *Children's Writer's Word Book*. Add a variety of beginning readers. Look for bargain deals at thrift stories, library used bookstores, and online used bookstores such as on Amazon.com.

Professional Track

Do you have an out-of-print children's book or children's magazine article that was published long ago? Use the *Children's Writer's Word Book* and mark the grade level of each word in a short section. Does it fit into a certain grade regarding its readability level? Could you perhaps tweak it, change the names of the characters, breathe new life into it, and get it published as a beginning reader or chapter book? Learn to recycle your published material in a variety of ways.

Strengthen Your Writing Muscles

Write a nonfiction story for children about the life cycle of a butterfly. (If unsure of the facts, check an encyclopedia.) After your story is finished, look up each word of the story in the Alphabetical List in the *Children's Writer's Word Book*. Mark the grade level of each word. Then use the thesaurus to change all the words in your story to be at a first grade reading level. (Your story may also contain words found on the Kindergarten Word List.) Shorten longer sentences by dividing them into two short sentences.

3.2 State and National Standards

The world of beginning readers and chapter books is the world of teachers, students, and schools. This world is monitored and governed by state and national requirements. The measuring stick all teachers must follow in every subject area that they teach are the guidelines found within the State and National Standards as well as the Common Core State Standards (CCSS). Whether or not you are an educator, and even if you have never heard of these standards before, you can quickly become familiar with the State and National Standards along with the Common Core State Standards so that you can write successfully for the world of beginning readers and chapter books.

For starters, visit the site Common Core State Standards Initiative at www.corestandards.org. Check out the mission statement of the Common Core State Standards on the home page. Browse through the site. Check out the FAQ page. Download the file of the CCSS for English Language Arts as well as the file of the CCSS for Mathematics. Scroll through both documents.

After you visit the site for the Common Core State Standards, take time to learn more about the National Standards. Search the Internet for the term "National Standards" or visit the site Education World® at www.educationworld.com/standards/. If you look at the link to the Table of Contents for the National Standards, you'll find that there are seven main topics or categories these standards include: Fine Arts, Language Arts, Math, Physical Education and Health, Science, Social Sciences, and Technology. Spend time browsing through the various topics and exploring the links. Basically, what you'll find is an explanation of what topics teachers are supposed to be teaching in their classrooms at certain grade levels and what concepts about each topic students are supposed to be learning in each grade in school.

For instance, let's explore the National Standards for Science. If you click on the Science link, you'll find links to different grade levels. Let's look at the link for grades K-4. These National Standards may be updated at any time, but at the time I am writing this book, there are seven key areas of Science students should learn about in grades K-4: Science as Inquiry, Physical Science, Life Science, Earth and Space Science, Science and Technology, Science in Personal and Social Perspectives, and the History and Nature of Science.

Let's look at the standard for Life Science. At the time I'm writing this book, there are three key areas the National Standards require that students should develop an understanding of while they are in kindergarten on up through fourth grade: 1) the characteristics of organisms, 2) life cycles of organisms, and 3) organisms and environments.

Just exactly what does this mean? And how does it affect you as a writer for the beginning readers and chapter books market? To gain a better understanding of this, let's compare this to the State Standards.

If you are writing a beginning reader or chapter book specifically for use in one state, you should look up the State Standards for that state. Usually, however, most publishers target a national audience. Therefore, they are usually most interested in the standards for either the state of California or the state of Texas. Both of these states tend to set the bar regarding what topics are taught in their schools. This means that if you write material that will meet the qualifications for California's or Texas's state standards, it will probably meet the standards required in any other state. For a point of reference, let's look at the State Standards for California.

On the Internet, search for the term "California State Standards," or once again, visit the informational and comprehensive site Education World® at www.educationworld.com/standards/. Click on the link to State Standards and select California. At the time I am writing this book, there are six topics or categories the State Standards for California include: English-Language Arts, Mathematics, Health Education, History-Social Science, Science, and Visual and Performing Arts.

As a point of reference, let's look once again at the standards for Science. Click on the link and scroll down on the new page to find the link for Science. Download the Science Content Standards. These are broken down according to grade level.

Let's look at the standards for first grade, and once again, examine the requirements for Life Science. At the time I'm writing this book, the State Standards for California require that students in first grade should develop an understanding that "Plants and animals meet their needs in different ways." First grade students should know: a) "different plants and animals inhabit different kinds of environments…" b) "both plants and animals need water, animals need food, and plants need light," c) "animals eat plants or other animals for food and may also use plants or even other animals for shelter and nesting," d) "how to infer what animals eat from the shapes of their teeth," e) "roots are associated with the intake of water and soil nutrients…." (Quoted from the *Science Content Standards for California Public Schools: Kindergarten Through Grade Twelve,* Adopted by the California State Board of Education, October, 1998.)

Once again, just exactly what does this mean? And how does it affect you as a writer for the beginning readers and chapter books market? To really gain a firm grasp and better understanding, it will help to dig one level deeper. Find out what teachers are actually teaching about Life Science in the first grade classroom.

There are a couple of different ways you can discover this. You can visit your local school district. Explain that you are a children's writer. Ask to view a copy of their School Standards. Many schools have notebooks of standards written by educators within their own district that spell out in easy-to-understand terms exactly what their teachers need to teach at each grade level in order to best meet the State and National Standards.

For instance, I have a copy of a local school district's Science Standards. Instead of using the term "Life Science," this school uses the term "Biological Science." In first grade, this school includes science lessons about topics such as animal homes, animals at night, bears, birds, amphibians, and reptiles.

You can also ask for a copy of a textbook. Some schools don't use textbooks for some subjects in the earlier elementary grades. But if they do have a textbook, ask to view the Science textbook. Look at the chapter headings as well as each topic covered within each chapter. You'll discover very specific Science topics that first graders learn such as the life cycle of a caterpillar, the birth of kittens and how they grow, and animals in a zoo. Each one of these lessons supports the State and National Standards.

Another way to find out what teachers are actually teaching about Life Science in the first grade classroom is to visit your local teacher's bookstore or a bookstore that sells books for teachers. If you don't have one locally, go online to Amazon.com. Look for teacher's books that offer the "Look inside the book" feature. You might need to do an Advanced Search under Books. Type in the name of a publisher who publishes books for teachers such as *Scholastic Teaching Resources*. Type in a key word such as *Science*. When a list of teacher's books comes up, look for one that shows actual pages of the book. Look inside the book and examine the table of contents.

For instance, my dear friend Sheryl Ann Crawford and I co-write a book for teachers to use in first and second grade called *25 Science Plays for Beginning Readers* (Scholastic Teaching Resources, 2000). In the table of contents, you'll find beginning reader plays for Life Science topics such as spiders, butterflies, hatching ducks, animal homes, animals at night, animals during winter, seeds, trees, and harvest time. Each of the plays in this book supports, or is coordinated with, the State and National Standards for teaching Life Science in the first grade.

The reason it is so important for writers in the beginning readers and chapter books market to understand and become familiar with the State and National Standards as well as the Common Core State Standards is because teachers are required to teach about topics listed in these Standards. Since beginning readers and chapter books target teachers as their main customer, most publishers are only interested in producing beginning readers and chapter books that teachers can use in their classroom.

For example, if a story is written at the first grade reading level but is about cells, first grade teachers can't really use that story. According to the National Standards, students in grades nine through twelve are supposed to learn about cells, not first graders.

An extra bonus for writers who understand and become familiar with the State and National Standards as well as the Common Core State Standards is that it gives us a ready-made list of topics to write about! When I worked on pitching the idea to Scholastic Teaching Resources and submitting the requested proposal for the book of *25 Science Plays for Beginning Readers*, I didn't have to stress out. I just looked up the list of State and National

Standards for first and second grade, and compared them to my local school district's notebook of Science Standards. There were lots of topics to choose from to include as potential topics in the book of 25 Science plays. Then, after the proposal was accepted and the contract signed, Sherri and I got to work brainstorming and writing adorable and kid-appealing plays that fit each topic we had listed.

If you thought teaching reading was just about language arts, think again. Teachers are always looking for material that is "cross-curricular" or that "teaches across the curriculum." This means that if they can read a beginning reader story to their students that also ties in with the math lesson or science concept they're teaching, they can meet two requirements for standards at one time. For writers, when we write a cross-curricular beginning reader or story that teaches across the curriculum by incorporating another subject within its text, it increases our sales. Not only will language arts teachers purchase our story, but so will math teachers or science teachers. Sales will increase because we're giving teachers material they can use to meet the Standards.

If the Common Core State Standards, State, and National Standards seem very complicated, I want to encourage you. When I first started looking at them, they seemed very confusing, too. The standards for Math seemed the trickiest of all! But once a local writer friend who is very prolific in the educational market shared with me that she was terrible at math when she was in school. Yet she has written math books for teachers to use! I asked her what her secret was. She shared that she had learned how to become a temporary expert at anything for six weeks so that she could write a book about it—even junior high math!

To learn how you, too, can become a "temporary expert" and write about a variety of topics publishers in this market are looking for, read the next section. We'll discuss even more tools you can use to help you succeed as a writer of leveled readers.

Beginner's Tip

Don't try to understand or read all the Standards at once. Just choose one subject, one grade level, and one key concept kids are expected to learn. Explore that one concept until you feel you understand what teachers are teaching in the classroom to help students learn that concept.

Professional Track

Before you go on your next school author visit, prepare a short read-aloud play for students to perform together during your presentation. Use the *Children's Writer's Word Book* to gear the play's vocabulary words and sentence length for the grade level you are visiting.

Strengthen Your Writing Muscles

Look at the State and National Standards as well as the Common Core State Standards listed at www.educationworld.com/standards/. Choose a subject such as math or science. Find a topic for a specific grade level. Then write a story about it.

For instance, if you choose science as your subject and first grade as your grade level, as a topic you can select an animal that lives in a den such as a bear or fox. Look up this animal in an encyclopedia. Use your research to write a nonfiction story about how this animal builds its den and how it uses its den for a home. Next, rewrite the story as fiction. Give the animal a fun name, create a problem about the animal's den, and then have the animal solve its problem with a satisfying ending. With carefully chosen vocabulary words and controlled sentence length, try to gear both your nonfiction and fiction stories for a child in first or second grade because this is the level that students are expected to learn about animals and their homes.

3.3 Build Your Personal Research Library

Master carpenters each have their own set of tools they use to build beautiful furniture. If they don't have any tools, it's impossible for them to build anything at all. Professional chefs each have their own set of cooking utensils they use to prepare delicious meals. If they don't have any, it's impossible for them to cook anything at all. As children's writers for the beginning readers and chapter books market, we each need our own set of tools to craft manuscripts that will be published in today's market. You can acquire these tools so that you will have what you need to write successfully in this market.

Start building your own personal research library of tools that will help you navigate successfully within the world of beginning readers and chapter books. Without these tools at your fingertips, the journey will be much more difficult. You'll waste an entire morning running to the library or to the school district to get a book you suddenly need when you could have reached instantly for that book, found what you needed, and spent the rest of the morning writing.

It's possible to build a personal research library on a low budget. In fact, until you start earning income from your writing, I encourage you to keep purchases at a minimum. Fortunately, there are a number of ways you can build a personal research library for the beginning readers and chapter books market that are very cost effective.

For starters, a nice resource to add to your personal research library are the collections of beginning readers such as the two volumes complied by Joanna Cole and Stephanie Calmenson, *The Beginning Reader's Treasury: Ready...Set...Read!* as well as *A Funny Treasury for Beginning Readers: Ready...Set...Read—and Laugh!* Volumes such as these provide a nice selection of some of the earlier beginning readers for you to evaluate and use as examples to improve your own writing skills for this genre.

Readability Level References

I've already mentioned the importance of purchasing your own copy of the *Children's Writer's Word Book* by Alijandra Mogliner. This should be the number one priority on your list. If you can't find a used copy at a reasonable price, ask for it as a birthday gift or save up and buy it. As you develop solid footing writing for this market, consider purchasing other reference books such as the ones I listed in *Section 3.1 Reading Levels and Readability Lists*.

School Textbooks

I refer often to my own personal sets of school textbooks I've collected over the years while writing beginning readers. School textbooks can be quite costly, but a bonus for us as writers is that schools adopt new sets of textbooks regularly even in tough economic times. Many school districts recycle their old textbooks and donate them or sell them at a large discount. Some even throw theirs away. Get connected with someone in your local school district. Explain that you are a children's writer. Ask if they are planning on adopting new textbooks. If so, ask if they would be willing to give you a complimentary set.

I have acquired the teacher's edition set of four math textbooks from kindergarten through third grade as well as student math textbooks from fourth through seventh grade. I have acquired science textbooks, history textbooks, and language arts textbooks. All have been given to me for free. When a school is getting rid of hundreds of textbooks at once, they are usually very happy to donate one copy of each grade level to someone who will use them for such an important task as writing new material to help children learn to read.

If your local school district turns up a dead end, network with people in other nearby districts. You won't acquire all your books at once because a district usually only upgrades one textbook at a time. But when they do adopt a new textbook, it usually covers quite a few grade levels. Learn to be on the lookout for these events, and ask for at least one copy of their old textbook at each grade level. Better yet, try to acquire both the teacher edition and the student textbook for each grade level. The teacher edition can be filled with all sorts of teaching strategies and important information that you'll not find in the student edition. And of course, you can always look for cheap deals on textbooks online.

Why is it so important to acquire your own personal set of outdated textbooks? Even though the teaching techniques might vary, the lesson concepts are still very similar. You'll have material that will help you write cross-curricular beginning readers that can be used to teach language arts as well as another subject. And even if you are writing for the trade picture book market and not the educational market which thrives on producing products that can be used across the curriculum to teach a variety of subjects, it helps to know what students are learning at each grade level.

For instance, if you want to write a beginning reader with a story about a first grade girl who overcomes shyness in school, you can look at your textbooks to brainstorm ideas for the story plot. If you look at your first grade science book, you'll be reminded that students learn about the life cycle of a butterfly in first grade. You could choose a science project for your main character where she becomes so enrapt with watching her caterpillar change into a beautiful butterfly that she forgets all about her shyness in her eagerness to share the miracle with her classmates.

Just before I started writing this book, *Yes! You Can Learn How to Write Beginning Readers and Chapter Books*, I had a book deadline to write a set of Readers Theatre plays with controlled vocabulary and sentence length for a middle grade readability level. Even though this was a leveled reading book, it was also a math book. Now, I hadn't studied junior high math since, well, junior high! But just as my friend said she had learned how to be a temporary expert at anything while she was writing about it, I became a temporary expert at junior high math. How did I do it? With the help of my own set of math textbooks. When I wrote the proposal for the book, I included a table of contents based on the topics taught in my set of math textbooks. After I landed the contract to write the book, each day when I sat down to work on a reader's theatre play, I first spent time reading over that topic in my math textbooks. Because textbooks are put together in such a way to *teach* key concepts, I had the tools I needed to write about math in my leveled reader even though I hadn't studied these math concepts for many, many years.

Building your own personal research library that includes sets of textbooks at various grade levels and in various subjects will help you during your brainstorming sessions. Reading through the textbooks will give you an amazing amount of potential ideas. Having your own sets of textbooks will make it easier to write proposals. You can see at a glance which concepts students need to learn in the manuscript you plan to write. Having your own sets of textbooks will help you become a temporary expert on your topic during the writing process. You can refer to these textbooks frequently to double check that you're creating a realistic world of fiction or presenting information accurately. Make it your goal to gather sets of textbooks on different subjects and at different grade levels over the years ahead.

Sample Books

Another key resource to add to your personal research library includes sample books from the trade book market. It's fairly easy to start acquiring a nice collection of beginning readers and chapter books on a low budget. Just visit your local library used bookstore or local thrift stores. Look for leveled readers in the trade picture book market such as *Hello Reader!*® books by Scholastic, *Ready-to-Read* books by Simon & Schuster, and *Step into Reading* ™ books by Random House. Often these books can be found for just a quarter or even a dime each. Try to gather a wide variety of different publishers' books at all different levels.

Since these are intended for research, maximize your use of them. Mark them up. Write notes along the margins. Memorize favorite passages of text. Post sticky notes on pages for easy reference.

Count the words and write down the total number of words on each line, the total number of words on each page along with the total number of lines per page, and the total number of words in the entire book. Actually write these numbers on the page itself.

Compare the font size of the printed text from one level to the next. Note the size of artwork and its style according to the various levels. Compare the size of the margins or white space on each page from one level of reader to the next. Compare the theme, setting, and plot to concepts taught in school textbooks. Note how these support the State and National Standards as well as the Common Core State Standards.

Once you have begun building your basic research library of beginning readers and chapter books, you can continue to add to your collection by gathering sample books from publishers you target.

When I want to earn income as a children's writer, I target a specific publisher with the hopes of landing a contract to write a book. (To learn more about earning a steady income as a children's writer, targeting a publisher, and landing a contract before you write the book, read my first book in this series, *Yes! You Can Learn How To Write Children's Books, Get Them Published, and Build a Successful Writing Career.*) First I study a publisher's catalog which is usually found online at their Website. I look for a series of books they write that I could pitch an idea to fit into.

At this point, unless I have already found inexpensive copies of their books, I usually don't purchase a sample of their books. I order their books in at my local library. I look online at Amazon and also at their own Website to find out as much as I can about their specific books that I'm targeting. I then send a query letter, or letter pitching my ideas, to the editor and ask her if she'd be interested in receiving a proposal for a book based on one of my ideas. If I eventually land a contract to write a book, I usually ask the editor to send me complimentary sample books that I can use as reference.

Most editors are happy to send authors sample books. In fact, some publishers send out sample books as part of the standard author's packet they send to authors under contract to write a book.

Whenever I sign a contract to write a book for the beginning readers or chapter books market, I usually allocate a small budget for acquiring several more samples of my target publisher's books. By collecting several samples from my publisher as well as purchasing several more samples of my publisher's books, my personal library of research books continues to grow at a steady rate without much strain on my budget. These sample books become the cornerstone of my research as I write my next book under contract and aim it to fit my target publisher's line of beginning readers like a glove.

Beginner's Tip

Make it a long-term goal to build up your personal research library for the beginning readers and chapter books market. Just start with one book. Then add another. Have fun watching your library grow.

Professional Track

Build your personal research library by swapping your published books with books by your published author friends. (Especially if they write beginning readers!) Whenever you sign your book contracts, there is usually a clause that states the publisher will send you a certain number of free author's copies. Before you sign your next contracts, e-mail your editor and ask if you can request 5 or 10 more copies than they offer. Even small publishers are usually flexible to give up that small of a quantity for free. They'll instruct you to cross off the typed amount on the contract, write in the new amount above it, and print your initials next to it. After you get your extra free copies, swap them with your friends.

Strengthen Your Writing Muscles

Students in fourth through sixth grade learn about shapes in math. Write a silly beginning reader story with a sixth grade readability level about outer space. (Use the *Children's Writer's Word Book* as a guide.) In your story, make each planet a different shape such as a cube, a cone, or a sphere. When finished, you'll have a beginning reader that also reinforces key math skills—a cross-curricular success!

3.4 Creating Beginning Readers and Chapter Books Logs

Along with gathering key books to use to improve your craft, you can also create your very own set of tools that will help you achieve success in the beginning readers and chapter books market. The two main tools I recommend you add to your writer's toolbox are a Beginning Readers Log and a Chapter Books Log. Not only are these logs essential to help your career grow, but spending time working on them adds an ingredient of fun and sparkles of creativity to your writing day.

Even though they have many similarities strong enough to put them together in this book, beginning readers are vastly different in content and format from chapter books. That is why I recommend making a separate log for each. Also, make a mental note that for our purposes in this book, we will be focusing on titles commonly referred to as "First Chapter Books." Chapter books for older readers include middle grade and young adult novels, which this book doesn't cover.

First chapter books are beginning readers at the top end of the leveled-reading spectrum. They include the first books that advanced readers can read on their own that also have chapters. Often, the entire word count for a first chapter book is about as long as one single chapter in a novel. You can learn more about first chapter books in *Chapter 12: First Chapter Books.*

Creating a Beginning Readers Log as well as a separate Chapter Books Log will help increase your awareness of the books that are already published in this market. The first books you can include in your log are the titles you check out from the library. You have the option to create a spreadsheet, write in a blank journal, or type everything into a Word document. A spreadsheet can be revised, reorganized, and printed out. A blank journal can be tucked into a purse or pocket and carried to the library or bookstore to take notes. A Word document can be typed up at any time in a user-friendly format that best suits your style.

Whichever method you choose, include the following items in your log (each term will be explained more fully below):

Rating of the book
Title of the book
Name of author
Name of illustrator
Name of publisher
Copyright
Reading level
Short book review

One-sentence plot summary
Sample of text
Date you read the book

In your log, include the author's and illustrator's names in case you want to search for more books by either one. The publisher's name is important to note because most publishers in this market produce series, and you might want to read more books in this publisher's series.

Be sure to write a short book review of the content. Evaluate the content both as a *reader* and as a *children's writer*. Note what you liked and didn't like. Examine specific fiction techniques such as use of dialogue, character development, setting, and plot. Take time to write a one-sentence plot summary. If it's nonfiction, note the structure, the voice, and the clarity of the presentation of information to a child. As you read more and more beginning readers or chapter books and add them to your logs, this review will help you discern titles that stood out above the others and jog your memory to remember why.

Jot down a brief sample of text for each book. Be on the lookout especially for well-written portions that you can collect here in your log as handy references to help you improve your writing skills.

Note the reading level. Each publisher usually has its own system that is often printed on the front and spine of the book's cover and explained either in the front or the back of the book's text. Some publishers hire a reading specialist to oversee their beginning readers and chapter books. Often these publishers include a portion in the front or back of the book where the reading specialist offers tips or explanations about using their series to help children acquire essential reading skills. Make a note in your log that explains what this particular publisher's reading level means.

Include the copyright date as a reference for which year the book was written. Because this market can change from year to year, it's important to track which year each title was published. What was popular in a past year might not be popular in today's current market for many different reasons. Tracking the name of the copyright holder also tells you at a glance the type of contract this publisher probably offers for its beginning readers or chapter books. If the copyright is under the name of the publisher, the contract was probably work-for-hire and the author probably received one flat fee for the book. If the copyright is under the name of the author, the contract was probably royalty-based and pays the author a percentage of each book that is sold.

Take time to rate each title that you read. At the top of the page, give it a rating of one to five stars with five being the best. As you're writing your own beginning readers or chapter books, refer often to the titles you rate the highest. Purchase some of the best of the best to build your own research library of beginning readers and chapter books. Dig deeper to discover what made those particular books sing for you personally. Try to incorporate those very same ingredients in your own manuscripts to help make your story shine.

Beginner's Tip

Enjoy the world of writing for children! Don't hurry past suggested exercises here in this book, but take the time to do each one so that you progress forward steadily to realize your dreams. Always remember that writing for children is fun! Do whatever it takes to make each step in your journey a scrump-dilly-icious treat. Try to view the Beginning Readers Log and Chapter Books Log as an adventure, not a chore. Add wacky designs, sweet pictures, or cool graphics on the pages. Award your favorite titles with goofy trophies. Treasure each moment and enjoy the journey!

Professional Track

Join or create a community of professional published writers that focuses on beginning readers and chapter books. From a Yahoo listserve to an online critique group to a local writing group, make this a place to discuss unique issues pertaining to this market, share current marketing news, and swap tips of the trade.

Strengthen Your Writing Muscles

Write a list of animal pairs who could be best friends in a beginning reader or chapter book. They can be pals because of their similarities or they can be totally opposite. Include several pairs that actually live in each of these unique environments: Australia, India, Africa, Arctic Circle, Antarctica, rainforest, desert, pond, prairie, and mountains. Keep your list in an idea file to spark creative juices during future brainstorming sessions.

PART II

Exploring the Markets

for

Beginning Readers

and

Chapter Books

Chapter 4

TRADE BOOK MARKETS

4.1 Exploring the Market

What an exciting world the trade book market is for beginning readers and chapter books. Full-color illustrations draw young readers into these first beginning readers books that they can read by themselves. Attention-grabbing first chapter books with adorable black and white illustrations feature favorite characters kids are eager to read more about. Humorous incidents, memorable characters, and interesting plots are hallmarks of these fiction series. Nonfiction titles present fascinating facts. These trade books are the eye-catching books arrayed in prominent racks at the bookstores. No wonder they've tugged at your heartstrings and captured your interest as a children's book writer. You want to write for this delightful market, and in this chapter you can learn strategies and secrets of the trade.

For starters, let's explore this world. As we discussed in *Section 2.2 Beginning Readers are Born!* this world burst into existence in 1957 with the publication of Dr. Seuss's beloved classic *The Cat in the Hat.*

Since that time, many different publishers have published their own line of trade beginning readers and chapter books. These publishers are basically divided into two camps: those who require agents and those who don't. On both sides of that division, some publishers offer work-for-hire contracts and some offer royalty-based contracts. Some keep the copyright in the publisher's name. Others register the copyright in the name of the author.

Copyright and types of contract may even vary within the same publisher's line or series of beginning readers and chapter books, often depending on whether the idea for the book or series originated with the publisher or with the author. If a publisher generates an idea and hires an author to write the series, that publisher will probably register the copyright in its name. However, if an author approaches a publisher with an original idea for a beginning reader or chapter book in the trade book market, the publisher might register the copyright in the author's name.

Even though new series can appear on the market at any time, here is a smorgasbord (though by no means a comprehensive or complete list) of some of the publishing houses and their beginning readers series that have established their presence in this market over the years. Included here are the levels as described by the publishers themselves either on the back cover of the book or inside in a separate section such as the Introduction. Note that sometimes publishers sell their beginning readers series to another publisher to distribute, or they redesign the criteria for their reading levels. Therefore, you may have a series with a different publisher's name than the one listed here or may have a different description of this same publisher's reading levels. Look for the most current listings of publishers and their reading levels to know which criteria various publishers are using today.

Aladdin Paperbacks (Simon & Schuster)

Ready-to-Read

Pre-level 1: Recognizing Words: word repetition, familiar words and phrases, simple sentences

Level 1: Starting to Read: simple stories, increased vocabulary, longer sentences

Level 2: Reading Independently: more-complex stories, varied sentence structure, paragraphs and short chapters

Level 3: Reading Proficiently: rich vocabulary, more-challenging stories, longer chapters

Ready-for-Chapters Books

Bantam Doubleday Dell Books for Young Readers

Bank Street Ready-to-Read™

Level 1: Getting Ready to Read—read-alouds for children who are taking their first steps toward reading

Level 2: Reading Together—for children who are just beginning to read by themselves but may need a little help

Level 3: I Can Read It Myself—for children who can read independently

DK Publishing

Eyewitness Readers

Level 1: Beginning to read: Preschool – Grade 1: Word repetition, limited vocabulary and simple sentences, picture dictionary boxes

Level 2: Beginning to read alone: Grades 1-3: Longer sentences and increased vocabulary, information boxes full of extra fun facts

Level 3: Reading alone: Grades 2 and 3: More complex sentence structure, information boxes and pronunciation guide

Level 4: Proficient readers, Grades 2-4: Rich vocabulary and challenging sentence structure, additional information and alphabetical glossary

Grosset & Dunlap

Read with Dick and Jane

All Aboard Reading ™

All Aboard Math Readers™

All Aboard Science Readers™

Picture Readers: super-simple texts, rebus pictures, and flash cards

Station Stop 1: Beginning to Read: simple words, big type, picture clues, word repetition

Station Stop 2: Reading with Help: short sentences, simple plots, simple dialogue

Station Stop 3: Reading Alone: longer text, harder words, more complex stories

HarperCollins Publishers

I Can Read Books

My First: Shared Reading: Basic language, word repetition, and whimsical illustrations, ideal for sharing with your emergent reader

1: Beginning Reading: Short sentences, familiar words, and simple concepts for children eager to read on their own

2: Reading with Help: Engaging stories, longer sentences, and language play for developing readers

3: Reading Alone: Complex plots, challenging vocabulary, and high-interest topics for the independent reader

4: Advance Reading: Short paragraphs, chapters, and exciting themes for the perfect bridge to chapter books

Kids Can Press

Kids Can Read

Level 1: Kids Can Start to Read: Short stories, simple sentences, easy vocabulary, lots of repetition and visual clues for kids beginning to read.

Level 2: Kids Can Read with Help: Longer stories, varied sentences, increased vocabulary, some repetition and visual clues for kids who have some reading skills, but may need a little help

Level 3: Kids Can Read Alone: More challenging topics, more complex sentences, advanced vocabulary, language play, minimal repetition and visual clues for kids who are reading by themselves

Random House

Step into Reading™

Step 1 Books: very large type and extremely simple vocabulary for the very youngest readers, Preschool through Grade 1

Step 2 Books: longer and slightly more difficult than Step 1, Grades 1 through 3

Step 3 Books: for mid-second-grade reading levels for children with even greater reading skills, Grades 2 and 3

Step 4 Books: exciting nonfiction for the increasingly proficient readers, Grades 2 through 4

Scholastic

Hello Reader! ®

Hello Reader! Science ™

Hello Reader! Math Books! ™

My First Hello Reader! With Flash Cards

Level 1: Preschool-Grade 1, Ages 3-6

Level 2: Kindergarten-Grade 2, Ages 5-7

Level 3: Grades 1 & 2, Ages 6-8

Level 4: Grades 2 & 3, Ages 7-9

As you explore the large variety of stand-alone beginning readers, or individual beginning readers books, you may discover titles that *look* like they are part of the trade book market, but in actuality they are published by educational publishers for the educational market. For instance, the series of beginning readers *True Stories in the News* by Sandra Heyer are actually targeted for the English as a Second Language, or ESL, market. They are published by Pearson Longman, a division of Pearson Education. To learn more about educational publishers, the ESL market, and how to write for these types of leveled readers, see *Chapter 5: Educational Markets* as well as *Chapter 6: Magazines and Other Markets.*

Whether you want to write a beginning reader and then send it on its rounds of submissions to publishers, or want to try to land a contract before you write a beginning reader so that you earn income while you write, read the next section. You'll learn all about how to contact editors and break into the world of beginning readers in the trade book market.

Beginner's Tip

As you're exploring this market, look in the front of the book for the copyright date. Try to find beginning readers that have been published in the last two or three years. Use these as a guide for the types of beginning readers publishers are currently looking to acquire.

Professional Track

Host contests for beginning reader manuscripts on your blog. Set up rules and offer prizes. Give away free prizes such as a free manuscript critique or give away items such as a totebag or how-to-write book. By evaluating and judging groups of beginning reader manuscripts, you'll quickly learn what makes a winner stand out from the crowd. You can use these observations to help improve your own writing skills.

Strengthen Your Writing Muscles

Brainstorm and write down a list of first experiences children might have in first grade such as first pet, first plane ride, first loose tooth, first soccer game, and first best friend. Write a second list of "firsts" already published by one publisher of beginning readers for children in first grade. Compare the two lists. Try to add one or two fresh, new topics to *your* list that this publisher hasn't yet published. These can be potential topics for you to write about.

4.2 Landing the Contract

At first, the business side of writing, especially contracts, may seem overwhelming. You've probably been attracted to the simplicity and fun of delightful beginning readers in the trade book markets. The complexity and legalese of the world of book contracts could be the last thing you want to deal with at this point. You just want to enjoy writing cute stories that bubble over with kid-appeal. I totally understand! I feel that way, too! However, by learning more about the world of contracts at this point, you'll be better equipped. And having the tools you need when you begin your journey will help so that you can experience success each step along the way.

In the trade book market, publishers offer either work-for-hire contracts or royalty-based contracts, depending on a number of factors. (A work-for-hire contract is when a publisher usually pays a flat fee and registers the copyright in the publisher's name because the publisher owns all rights to the book. A royalty-based contract is when the publisher pays the author a percentage from the sale of each book and usually registers the copyright in the author's name.) Some publishers prefer to offer contracts to first time authors after a completed manuscript has been submitted and accepted. Others accept proposals and are open to offering a contract to write the book. By studying publishers' Websites and following their submission guidelines, you can gain a firmer grasp of how each different publisher operates.

In order to break into the trade book market for beginning readers, you will need an agent to represent you if you want to write for houses that only accept agented material. If you do not currently have an agent and want to write for these publishing houses, search the Internet for authors who write for this market and see if you can find which agents represent whom. Instead of connecting with a publishing house, you will need to target these agents.

Most agents expect to receive a complete manuscript submission before they will consider representing you. If they feel they can sell your manuscript, they will offer you a contract to represent either your individual manuscript or your career. Once you sign that contract, the agent will submit your manuscript to publishers in the beginning readers and chapter books market.

If you are targeting trade book publishing houses which do not require an agent, think about whether you want to target them for the goal of personal fulfillment or whether you want to target them for the goal of earning income. If you are writing for personal fulfillment, write your beginning reader or chapter book manuscript first and then try to find a publisher to accept it. If you are writing for the goal of earning income, contact a publisher by pitching a query for several ideas that would fit into their product line and try to land a contract to write the book. (I offer an in-depth explanation of the different strategies I use to meet each different goal in *Chapter 5: The Triple Crown of Success* in my first book of this series, *Yes! You Can Learn How to Write Children's Books, Get Them Published, and Build a Successful Writing Career*.)

Some beginning readers and chapter books publishers in the trade book market prefer receiving a completed manuscript from authors they have not yet worked with. This helps them better determine if they think your writing will be a good match with their product line or not. If this is the case, you might want to consider including a cover letter along with your manuscript that pitches three to five potential ideas. For instance, I have landed contracts with various publishers by including the following wording in a cover letter of a proposal or completed manuscript I submit:

If you can't use this proposed manuscript at this time, would you be interested in receiving a proposal on any of these ideas?

_____ first idea

_____ second idea

_____ third idea

_____ fourth idea

_____ fifth idea

I then list three to five ideas for manuscripts that I have not written but think would fit specifically into this publisher's product line. (If I am trying to break into a new publisher, I resist the urge to list manuscripts I've already written. I save those for submission *after* I break into a new publisher and land my first contract to write a book.) I have landed contracts this way several times even though the publisher rejects my original manuscript.

Rather than simply rejecting your manuscript because they don't have a current need for the topic, they can easily request a proposal on another topic if they like your writing, but just can't use your submitted manuscript. Here is a sample of actual wording you might use in your cover letter to pitch ideas along with your completed manuscript.

If you can't use my manuscript at this time, would you be interested in receiving a proposal for a beginning reader on any of these ideas?

_____ child adopts kitten from animal shelter

_____ second grade girl is first girl on boy's ice hockey team

_____ little bee can't buzz but finally learns how

_____ child helps naturalist parents rehabilitate injured owl

_____ Nonfiction: bear found in hot tub so relocated to local zoo

The Query

If you are trying to break into a publisher you have never worked with before, send them a query if they accept queries. If their submission guidelines state they require a completed manuscript, send them your completed manuscript along with the cover letter as I explained in the previous section. However, if they accept queries, send a query and try to land a contract to write the book.

If they accept e-mail, always use e-mail. Many publishers respond faster and have a two-week window for answering e-mail queries. If they require snail mail submissions, or queries submitted via the postal service, send your query in the mail, along with an SASE or self-addressed, stamped envelope. A standard wait is three months to hear a response through the mail. If you have not heard back from them in three months, you can assume that your query was rejected.

To save time, I've developed a query template I like to use. You can use it, too! Here's a sample e-mail query. Just fill in the blanks on this template and you're ready to send it on its way:

Dear _____ (first name of editor)

I have studied your line of beginning readers on your Website. I see that you publish _____ (list titles or series that are similar to the one you want to write). Would you be interested in receiving a proposal about _____ (list three to five ideas for manuscripts that you haven't yet written that would fit well into the titles you listed earlier)?

Sincerely,

_____ (your name)
_____ (your contact information)

If you don't have many published credits yet, don't worry about it. (To learn more about how to build up your line of published credits by writing for the no-pay/low-pay market, look in my book, *Yes! You Can Learn How to Write Children's Books, Get Them Published, and Build a Successful Writing Career*.) If you do have published credits, however, be sure to list them briefly in your query. Here is an example of a finished query that you could e-mail as your initial contact with an educational publisher:

Dear Mark,

I have studied your line of beginning readers on your Website. I see that you publish titles for your beginning readers Science series. Would you be interested in receiving a proposal about Animal Homes, Planets, the life-cycle of a Butterfly, Seeds, or Deserts?

Sincerely,
Hannah Writer
Author of 7 books and numerous magazine articles
1234 Alphabet Way
Learnville, PA 98765
987-654-3210
www.hannahwriter.com

When I landed the contract to write a series of beginning readers for Concordia, I had already written a number of work-for-hire books for this publisher. I wanted to start landing royalty-based contracts so I contacted my editor and asked if she'd like me to send her a proposal for a beginning readers series.

If you already have a relationship with a publisher, learn to pitch ideas to your editor at a very basic level so that you can start landing contracts to write more books. Writing books under contract helps guarantee you're earning income while you're writing. This is an essential ingredient of establishing a successful writing career and helps you earn a steady income. Start pitching general ideas to your editor in short query letters. Learn to ask simple, short questions such as, "Would you be interested in a beginning reader series?" or "I see that you just published a beginning reader about going to the dentist. Would you be interested in a beginning reader about going to the doctor, getting a haircut, or visiting the library?"

The Proposal

Because I already had a relationship with Concordia, I pitched a very generalized idea in a brief query. I didn't even have a topic or idea in mind at the time. I simply asked my editor if she'd be interested in a new series of beginning readers. My editor was interested, so I began working on my proposal. I searched for a kid-appealing character, readability level, and theme for the potential series. I studied existing beginning readers and landed on the *Nate the Great* series by Marjorie Weinman Sharmat as the level of readability I wanted my series to be. I discussed this with my editor and she said she'd be interested in publishing a new series for this reading level. It was important for us both to be on the same page at this point.

Next, I brainstormed a list of themes and characters that were already being published. First I wrote these down on a list. *Nate the Great* was about a boy detective. *Amelia Bedelia* was a housekeeper. *Cam Jansen* was always solving mysteries.

Then I made a second list of kid-appealing themes and characters that hadn't *recently* been published in a beginning readers series such as firefighters, cowboys, and park rangers. I chose the theme of a cowboy who solves mysteries as my personal favorite because both my boys loved *Nate the Great,* and they liked to ride our rocking horse, Blacky, and wear cowboy hats and cowboy boots. Because Concordia publishes books for the Christian market, I knew that each beginning reader just couldn't be about a cowboy solving a mystery—this publisher wanted their children's books to have spiritual take-away value. So I made a list of key values various Christian books and magazine stories featured in their fiction stories such as honesty, sharing, and godliness.

My next goal was to brainstorm something unique about my series that could make it stand out on the shelf. Once again, I examined successful beginning readers series on the market. I saw that some had a craft at the end. I decided to include a craft at the end of each of my books, too.

Finally, I was ready to submit the proposal for the *Marshal Matt Series: Mysteries with a Value.* The editor liked the proposal and offered me a contract. The exciting adventure began and I eventually wrote five books in the *Marshal Matt* series! Here is how the beginning reader level was presented on the back cover of the first book, *Marshal Matt and the Slippery Snacks Mystery*:

Four- to seven-year-olds love reading to solve puzzling mysteries with Marshal Matt. This humorous mystery series uses beginning reader vocabulary and short sentences to help kids develop reading skills and learn Christian values.

If you catch an editor's eye with a query, and that editor requests a proposal, take time to celebrate. No matter what happens after this, you have reached an important milestone! You actually pitched your idea and the editor caught it. Hip hip hooray for you!

Now, you need to write a proposal. Sometimes an editor will request one completed manuscript along with a proposal for a series based on that first book. Other times, as with my *Marshal Matt Series*, an editor won't require a completed manuscript but simply wants a proposal explaining your idea for a beginning reader or chapter book and perhaps a series. An editor may want sample text, or may not need it. This might be especially true if you've already published a variety of books and have a track record.

A typical proposal for a beginning reader in the trade book market includes a cover letter and a synopsis of the proposed book or series. As I mentioned before, some editors also want to see a completed manuscript or at least several pages of sample text from your proposed book. A market analysis is also helpful.

If you're working with a work-for-hire project in the trade book market, the editor may send you guidelines to follow as you prepare your proposal. Follow these guidelines carefully, rather than information or advice you may read here or elsewhere. If you have questions about the guidelines, it's okay to contact the editor briefly for clarification.

In the cover letter that you prepare, mention that this proposal was requested if the editor asked for it. Give a brief synopsis of your manuscript. Include a short synopsis of three to five other titles if you are proposing a series. These can be short. A working title for each book plus a one or two sentence summary of each is fine for proposing a beginning readers series. If you're proposing a series, it's okay for your cover letter to be longer than the standard one page.

Explain how your potential manuscript would fit into the publisher's product line. Either mention it as part of an existing series, as a complementary series, or as a title that would complement two or three of the publisher's titles that you list here.

State the target age, the target audience, the estimated word count or page number, and the reading level of your projected manuscript. If your publisher already has pre-set reading levels, state in which level your book or series would fit. To determine the estimated word count, just find out the word count or number of pages in a similar book by this publisher.

List your published credits. If you don't have many, don't worry. Everyone starts at the beginning. If you have a few published credits, list them in one paragraph on your cover letter. If you have a lot of published credits, create a separate page resumé or curriculum vitae to include with your proposal.

It also gives your proposal a boost when your cover letter includes a market analysis. This can be one paragraph on your cover letter or a separate page in length. In the market analysis, list three to five titles of books published in the last five years that are similar to your projected manuscript. This shows the editor that there is a current market for this type of book. For each of these titles, however, clarify how your book will be unique or set apart from them and fill a specific need in this market.

If you have any questions about the proposal you are preparing, it is acceptable to many editors for you to contact them briefly. Don't badger them, but do step out to ask key questions that will help you prepare the specific type of proposal they'd like to see. Or course, if they give very detailed instructions in their submission guidelines about how to prepare a proposal, always follow their instructions over the advice I give here.

If your editor requires sample text, follow the guidelines in Chapters 7 through 13 to write for the level you're targeting. Use published books specifically from your target publisher's catalog as examples to follow.

When your proposal is prepared, submit it to the publisher. If the publisher invites you to submit via e-mail, always use e-mail. It's fast and it's free. If not, submit your proposal via the postal service. Be sure to include an SASE, or self-addressed, stamped envelope. Personally, I prefer enclosing a business-sized envelope with one stamp on it. This provides enough postage for them to send me either a letter of acceptance or a rejection letter. They can then recycle my proposal. The standard wait time to hear back from a publisher is three months. If you have not heard back from them by that time, you can assume that your proposal was rejected.

If the editor responds and offers you a book contract, give a great big shout! Go outside in your backyard and play a game of fetch with your favorite poochie pal and tell him how great a writer you are. You landed a book contract for a beginning reader! Now it's time to sign the contract and start working with an editor. Read the following section to find out what comes next.

Beginner's Tip

Do you feel overwhelmed when you look at a market guide because it seems like publishers only accept submissions from authors who have an agent? Don't despair! Make your very own "Million Dollar Market Guide." Explore JacketFlap at www.JacketFlap.com and other market guides. Just look for publishers of beginning readers in the trade book market who accept unsolicited submissions or do not require an agent. Print out a one-page information sheet about each publisher that includes the publisher's name and Website as well as any other information you want handy. (Or photocopy the page with each publisher's listing from your market guide.) Collect all these pages in a 3-ring binder. Now, when you're ready to search for a publisher to target, you'll just be looking through lists of publishers who *do* accept unsolicited submissions. You'll enjoy the process so much more!

Professional Track

Ask one of your book editors if he would be interested in a brand new series of beginning readers you develop. Pitch a short query with three to five ideas, and see if he's interested in hearing more. To give you the confidence to pitch an entire series, rely on your published track record and know you can fill in the gaps with research.

Strengthen Your Writing Muscles

Gather one or more writing friends and hold a "pitching" session. First, have everyone write down this template:

I see you publish books about _____. Would you be interested in a proposal for one of these ideas that fits into your series? 1_____ 2_____ 3_____.

Next, play a game of "catch" with your writing buddies. Pitch ideas back and forth for these imaginary publishers:

Say there's a publisher with a series on ocean animals. They already have books on sharks, whales, and starfish. Use the template and pitch them an idea for 1-3 more titles that could fit into their series.

Say there's a publisher with a series on extreme sports. They already have books on skateboards, mountain bikes, and snowboards. Use the template and pitch them an idea for 1-3 more titles that could fit into their series.

Say there's a publisher with a series on puzzles. They already have puzzles on school days, holidays, and sports. Use the template and pitch them an idea for 1-3 more titles that could fit into their series.

4.3 Working with Editors

People come in a wide variety of shapes, sizes, personalities, and temperaments. Some of us are well-organized. Others slog through swamps of random paper piles. Some of us prefer e-mail. Others work best over the phone or with stamps and envelopes. Some of us are approachable. Others keep our distance. Some of us are prompt. Others lag further and further behind at attending to a constantly growing to-do list. As writers, we bring our own personalities and quirks to the table. So do editors. That's because we're all people. Learning what to expect while working with an editor in the trade book market will hopefully make your relationship smoother so that you can maneuver successfully from contract to published book, no matter how unique you and your editor are.

If you submitted a completed beginning readers manuscript and landed a contract, there is a typical production schedule most publishers follow to publish your book. During this process you'll be working with your editor. This could be one single editor or you could work with different editors to accomplish different tasks.

If you submitted a query or a proposal and landed a contract to actually write the book after the contract is signed, now it's time to roll up your sleeves and sit down to write the manuscript. When I landed the contract to write the *Marshal Matt: Mysteries with a Value* series, most of the interaction with my editor took place before I landed the contract. After I signed the contract, I was pretty much left on my own to write the book. After I wrote the first title in the series and submitted it, my manuscript followed the typical production schedule most publishers follow to publish a book.

Some publishers, for a variety of reasons, are more involved with the writing process than others. These publishers might be creating a work-for-hire series of beginning readers in the trade book market. They might be planning on releasing a number of titles by different authors all at the same time. Sometimes publishers want to see your manuscript at certain phases to keep track of everyone's progress. There might be short, tight deadlines that occur frequently before the final submission deadline.

If you're already a detail-oriented and well-organized type of writer, these skills will help you tremendously in this type of situation as you work with an editor who is very involved with the writing process. If keeping track of details and organization skills aren't necessarily your strength, make it a point to develop a system that will help you stay on top of things. Organize your e-mail into separate folders so that every e-mail from this editor lands in its own folder. This will help you keep track of your editor's correspondence and not lose it in a mass of e-mails from list-servs, friends, or other editors. Each time you chat with the editor on the phone, write down notes, mark the date and time of the phone call, and store your notes in a file labeled for this purpose.

In your Word documents, make a separate folder on your computer containing files just for this project. Store papers in clearly labeled file folders that you keep all in one pocket folder so that every paper is in one spot. Create a separate place in your office or home exclusively set apart for this project. Keep your research books here, your files here, and everything here that relates to this project alone. This space can be as simple as one shelf on a bookcase. You can set up a card table or take over an entire desk for this project. Whatever it takes, create its own separate space so you can enjoy this fast-paced and often intense journey.

Production Schedule

Once an editor receives a completed manuscript and a contract has been signed, that manuscript undergoes a typical revision process. A beginning reader is carefully examined to make sure it meets all the readability requirements for its reading level as well as has an engaging story. You'll either work with your Acquisitions Editor (the editor who acquired your manuscript) or you'll be assigned a separate Project Editor (the editor who actually works with you during the revision and production process). Many times these are one and the same person, but there are also many times they're two or more different people.

It's typical for a manuscript to undergo a series of revisions. There might be several back and forth sessions between you and your editor where you are asked to revise chunks of text or tweak certain sentences. Don't feel as if you are a poor writer when your editor requests revisions. This is all part of the work it takes to shape a manuscript into the best possible book it can be.

Once the text is nearly finalized, an illustrator will be brought on board. Because beginning readers in the trade book market are fully illustrated, this process can be very similar to the process of illustrating a picture book. However, there is one key difference. In beginning readers, the illustrations must provide a literal interpretation of the text on each page. This is because children who are beginning to decode words, or figure out how to read words by themselves, rely on pictures to give them clues. Unlike general picture books where the illustrator often elaborates and adds his own interpretation through the illustrations, the illustrations in a beginning reader trade picture book must be very literal and exact.

Authors are therefore sometimes sent art specs, or illustration samples, at varying stages of development, to double check that the art is a literal interpretation of the text. Most editors will give you detailed instructions on how they want you to mark any corrections. Read these carefully. Every publisher has their own unique way of having the author check art specs. Plus, sometimes editors have their own unique system they use themselves. Try to pay close attention to what they want you to do, even if it's different from another editor you've worked with before.

When publishers send these art specs to the author, there is usually a very tight turn-around such as three days to two weeks for the author to approve the art. I've even had some art specs sent by courier that required an overnight return. That is because by this time, everyone is working on a super tight schedule with the projected publication date looming closer and closer.

I've learned to drop everything when art specs suddenly arrive either in my e-mail or on my doorstep. Sometimes editors give fair warning, but many times they don't. It just gets so hectic for editors who are juggling different manuscripts at different stages of production. They don't mean to be inconsiderate regarding anyone else's schedule. They're swamped. So I've learned to keep an ear out for when art specs might arrive unannounced.

It's the same with proofs. Once the art is finalized and the final layout of the book has been designed, the proofs arrive for one last, final check for accuracy. By now, the date to send the book to the printer is often just days away. Everyone has been rushing to keep this book on schedule.

Sometimes, just before the proofs are sent my way, I've gotten an urgent call from my editor. By this point, it's a last minute issue such as when the graphics person or designer enlarged the text to be the final font size for the layout of the actual book, one line had too many characters (letters, spaces between sentences, and punctuation) to fit on the page. Since each line of text is very critical, especially in the earliest levels of beginning readers, a last minute scramble takes place to change the text to fit on that line without having to change any of the illustrations. It's especially tricky if the text is written in rhyme.

When the proofs arrive, once again I drop everything and sit down to examine the pages. Sometimes the cover arrives separately. Other times it arrives as part of the final proofs. Even if it disrupts my other work, however, it's so exciting to see the printer-ready pages. I'm eager to stop in my tracks and focus on my new book. This is the last opportunity to catch any typos or errors, so I want to look over everything as carefully as I can.

All of this back and forth with your editor, often with express delivery by private couriers, can get to be very expensive. Some publishers provide a code for you to use so that they pay the postage bill. Other times, they don't. If your publisher doesn't provide a code for them to pay for the return shipment, always ask politely if they might give you one. Some publishers have given me their code after I've asked. Others haven't, so I've had to pay out of my own pocket. It never hurts to ask in case they might agree to pay for it themselves.

Sometimes an editor does not involve the author at any point during the production schedule. The finished, published book arrives in the mail, and it's the first time the author sees it since submitting the completed manuscript. Other times, the editor might involve the author during one phase of production but not another. Each publisher, and sometimes even each editor within that publishing company, has its own unique way of working with its authors.

Now that you know a little bit more about working with editors in the trade book market, let's talk more specifically about writing beginning readers for the trade book market. In the next section, we'll explore the writing process together.

Beginner's Tip

Make it your goal to treat everyone politely and professionally in this industry and relationships with all editors will go smoother, even over bumpy roads that are bound to come.

Professional Track

Make it a practice to start e-mails to editors with a one-sentence personal note before you tackle the business at hand. For instance, if your editor works in Michigan and you heard there was a huge snowstorm, ask if the weather is affecting her day. Also be sure to thank editors frequently for the hard work they are doing to help make your manuscript shine. Kind and thoughtful words make everyone's workday a little bit easier.

Strengthen Your Writing Muscles

Interview an editor on your blog. Check out how other blogs feature editor interviews and write your own short list of questions to ask. Learn more about working with editors from an editor herself. Interview an editor you know, or e-mail one who provides her e-mail address in a market guide. If possible, interview an editor of beginning readers!

4.4 Writing for the Trade Market

As children's writers, our hearts delight in children's picture books. We love to hold these beautiful, sometimes quirky, full-color books in our hands. We love to open these books and explore the treasures inside their pages. Because beginning readers are actually a type of picture book, most with full-color illustrations, we get the same thrill of delightful anticipation when we pick up a beginning reader in our hands as we do when we read a hardback picture book. We want to write stories like the ones we read. We want to see our names on the front of our own beginning readers. We want to catch some child unawares who has picked up a beginning reader we wrote and is giggling with delight, lost within its pages. This is my dream, and it's probably yours as well. Even though each of our journeys will be different, I want to encourage you. You *can* chase after your dreams—these aren't impossible pie-in-the-sky fantasies! Many writers have experienced success in this market. Come along! I invite you to join in the journey!

My neighboring community of Chino Hills recently opened a brand new facility for their library. What a joy it is to walk past the beautiful stone wall that is a fountain with the peaceful sound of gently cascading water inviting all to enter and explore. I always head straight to the children's room, a vast area with cozy seating arrangements, silhouettes of jungle animals climbing the walls, and stars sparkling on the ceiling. A "tree" grows from floor to ceiling as a central hub where even the tiniest tots sport headphones and sit next to parents keenly engaged in reading e-books together on the computers.

Everywhere I look, I see young children perched on benches or snuggled up on comfy couches, each with a beginning reader in hand. Here, in this wonderful literary world designed just for them, children are naturally overcome with the desire to read one of these delightful treasures all by themselves. They instinctively head to the low shelves stocked with beginning readers books they can try to read on their own without any help from an adult.

This is the world of beginning readers and chapter books in the trade book market. You're instinctively drawn to it, just as these young library visitors are. It's a world of wonder and delight. It's a world of growing up. It's a world of exploration, imagination, knowledge, and empowerment. It's the world of learning how to read, a journey that takes flight and promises a lifetime of uncharted and exciting adventures. This is the world you want to write for.

So what practical steps can you take to start making your dreams come true? Some of the best advice I've seen for learning how to write great beginning readers is found in the General Guidelines for Zonderkidz' I Can Read Books®, "The key to creating great I Can Read Books is to combine good writing with engaging stories. The best way to understand the nature and rhythms of these books is to look at examples of successful I Can Read Books."

Read examples of the best of the best. That's what this publisher suggests, and I agree wholeheartedly with their advice.

For general tips about writing beginning readers, refer to *Chapter 7: Writing Strategies for Beginning Readers and Chapter Books*. In Chapters 8 through 13, find specific guidelines for topics such as sentence structure, vocabulary, plot, and character development for each reading level.

As you're learning how to write beginning readers for the trade book market however, be sure to include significant portions of focused reading time in your day. Don't just read randomly; read with purpose. Read and take notes in your Beginning Readers Log. (For more information, see *Section 3.4 Creating Beginning Readers and Chapter Books Logs*.) Read the giants of beginning readers, written by authors that would be listed in the Beginning Readers Hall of Fame if one ever exists. Look for books by Crosby Bonsall, Russell Hoban, Syd Hoff, Arnold Lobel, Else Minarik, Peggy Parish, Cynthia Rylant, and of course, Dr. Seuss. However, because today's market for beginning readers is different from the early years, be sure you add to your literary cuisine a full diet of current titles such as ones by the newest beginning reader giant, Mo Willems.

Engage in pre-writing exercises that train your brain to write beginning readers well. Begin with reading successful examples. Move forward to brainstorming ideas for your own new story. Don't just stare into blank space, however. Armed with these piles of beginning readers, list titles that are your favorite. Write down a list of themes these beginning readers use. Make a list of favorite characters and list each one's quirky and unique traits. Write down a list of one-sentence plot summaries for various beginning readers. (Refer to your Beginning Readers Log for information about titles you have already recorded there.)

Use these lists you've created to brainstorm three to five potential themes for your new story. Brainstorm a list of characters for your own story and list each one's quirky and unique traits. Write down three to five potential one-sentence plot summaries for your own book based on the ones you've already listed from other books.

When I was brainstorming for my *Marshal Matt: Mysteries with a Value* series, I chose the theme of a cowboy who solves mysteries. My cast of characters was based on my brother, his wife, their two children, and my nieces and nephews. My brother's son, Matt, was the main character. My brother's daughter, Janie, was Matt's best friend. Matt had a horse, Mister E, who always helped Matt when he was stumped. Janie had a pet parrot named Blinky.

Each one had unique personality traits. Matt liked to wear a cowboy hat. He always pinned a badge to his shirt when he discovered a mystery and announced, "I, Marshal Matt, will help solve this mystery." After he solved a mystery, Marshal Matt always liked to eat pizza.

Matt's horse, Mister E, loved to eat carrots. Mister E communicated with Marshal Matt by stamping his foot to count. He also wiggled his right ear to answer *yes* and wiggled his left ear to answer *no*.

Janie was usually the one who had a problem and needed help solving a mystery. Her parrot, Blinky, added humor to the stories. Blinky talked and often spoke by repeating one word. If he thought he saw the thief, he squawked, "Thief! Thief!" even though usually he was wrong. Other times, Blinky said things in rhyme such as "Hi, Fly!" when he saw Janie's little brother, Fred.

Fred, as well as the other minor characters in the series, each had their own unique and quirky traits, too. I developed these during brainstorming sessions. Take time to develop your own cast of characters with a big dose of kid-appeal during brainstorming sessions of your own. You can even write down each character's unique voice, or samples of dialogue, that effectively reflect their personality by the words they speak.

After brainstorming for theme, character, and plot ideas, I like to move forward to brainstorm the story arc, or structure of the plot. The best reference I have ever seen for this stage of writing is Eve Heidi Bine-Stock's landmark book, *How to Write a Children's Picture Book, Volume 1: Structure.* I sit down with this book during my pre-writing sessions, and develop a "map" for the structure of my story. Following Bine-Stock's charts as a guide, I plug in events at key points to add crucial elements of foreshadowing, plot twists, and turning points to the progression of my plot. By learning to structure my story *before* I start to write it, my stories end up much stronger and are more engaging.

When I'm ready for my actual writing session, I like to start fresh in a comfortable place, often away from the computer. My pets would often come running to sit down near me and take a nap during these sessions. During the winter months, however, when the days are much too chilly even in southern California it seems, one of my cats named Humphrey liked to take his nap all curled up on my lap. Weighing in at a hefty 26 pounds or so, this added new dimension to my writing sessions, one that I'm sure you can relate to if you have furry writing buddies of your own.

I begin each writing session by first reading one to five favorite beginning readers books by the same publisher I'm targeting and at the exact same reading level my book is geared for. Then I pick up my pen and a pile of scrap paper, readjust my position so my legs don't fall asleep under my current furry pal, and start to write.

I "allow" myself to write. I "invite" myself to write. I "encourage" myself to write. First I write one word, and then another, and I'm constantly reminding myself that this is a first draft. I try to envision a baby taking her first step. A baby's first steps will be wobbly, and so are my first attempts to write my new beginning reader. A baby will fall down and go bump, and so do I as I make my first attempts to write my new story.

By this point, I let go of all those lists and rules and book maps that I spent time making during my brainstorming sessions. I use them as a guide, but I don't let them stifle the story from being told. I try to relax and enjoy the process of writing as something very primary, a journey that I can enjoy for the experience itself rather than rushing to reach the end.

I want to enjoy the writing process just as much as I'll enjoy holding the published book in my hands. So I think of things like a baby learning to walk, an eaglet learning to fly, and a young child learning to read. These are visuals that tell me it's okay not to be perfect as I'm writing my first draft. These are pictures in my mind that give my writer's soul the permission to experiment with words and not fear failure of someone else's criticism (or even my own).

The art of telling a story may come naturally to some people. Don't worry if you're not one of those people. I'm not. It takes time to develop the skills needed to write engaging and captivating stories. But the more we practice, the better we'll become. I'm learning how to be a better storyteller. I've made it one of my lifetime goals. I'll always be learning. I invite you to join me in the journey! You can learn how to be a master storyteller, too.

As I continue my writing session, I sometimes hit a roadblock. If I get stuck at a point, I put my writing down and take a 15-minute break. During this short break, I grab scrap paper and pen to jot down any random thoughts that pop into my mind. Then I plunge myself into a vigorous, mindless task such as ironing my husband Jeff's shirts, washing the dishes, or planting strawberries in a hanging basket in the spring so we'll have ripe red berries all summer. As I complete my short task, I focus on my writing roadblock and brainstorm ideas to push ahead. I jot these ideas down while I'm working at my task—I don't want to lose a single fleeting gem. Sometimes I hardly get started on a sink full of dishes when I stop to write down ideas instead. Armed with these new ideas, I return to my writing session and continue to work on my first draft. Once again, I remind myself that a first draft does not have to be perfect. It just has to have a beginning, a middle, and an end. I can hone it to perfection during the upcoming self-editing phase.

When my first draft eventually comes to its end, either through one writing session or several, I'm ready to self-edit my beginning reader. I refer often to Eve Heidi Bine-Stock's other two essential books for children's writers. *How to Write a Children's Picture Book, Volume II: Word, Sentence, Scene, Story* helps me examine each word and sentence in my story. *How to Write a Children's Picture Book, Volume III: Figures of Speech* helps me take my story from mundane to delightful.

I use Jan Venolia's two books, *Write Right!* And *Rewrite Right!* to help me polish my punctuation and grammar. I go over my story until it's the best I know how to make it.

Another valuable process for helping a beginning reader shine is to take it to a critique group. Not just any critique group will do, however. It's important to share your beginning reader with other writers who are also writing beginning readers. Otherwise they may unknowingly offer feedback that will damage your story, not help it. If you do not belong to a beginning readers critique group, form your own. Even having one more pair of eyes from someone who is focusing on the same market as you are will benefit your manuscript in countless ways. It is also a valuable experience to have under your belt before you submit your beginning reader to the scrutiny of an editor's eyes.

Beginner's Tip

Write new beginning readers stories frequently. The more you do, the easier it will get, and the better you'll become.

Professional Track

Teach a class on how to write beginning readers. Host a writer's mini-retreat or volunteer to teach a workshop at your local writer's group. Use this book as a guide to prepare. By teaching key concepts to others, even though you're not yet an expert, you'll make steps in the right direction for your own career as a writer of beginning readers.

Strengthen Your Writing Muscles

Rewrite a fairy tale, tall tale, myth, or legend as a beginning reader. The characters are already created and the plot is already in place. Work on your storytelling skills within the framework of a beginning reader by rewriting a story that's already been told.

Chapter 5

EDUCATIONAL MARKETS

5.1 Exploring the Market

The beginning readers and chapter books market is geared for teachers, so naturally, educational publishers work hard to help provide classroom material for beginning or struggling readers to gain reading fluency. More and more educational publishers are jumping on the bandwagon to create leveled reading material not only for elementary grades, but on up through middle grades and even high school. This means there is an ever-expanding need for new material, and you can learn how to help provide it.

Most people think of beginning readers and chapter books as being part of the popular trade book series found in local bookstores or huge bookstore chains. They're right. (Think of the *Frog and Toad* series and the *Magic Tree House®* Series.) For the purposes of this book, however, I am including leveled readers in all markets and lumping them together as part of the beginning readers and chapter books market. This is because a variety of publishers outside of the trade book market acquire new leveled reading manuscripts and will continue to offer contracts for new leveled reading manuscripts even when the economy drops and the trade book market slows down production as a result. As I mentioned, teachers constantly need new material for their classrooms even during slower economic times, and educational publishers keep busy attempting to fill this need.

Who are these educational publishers? They exist in a world not usually discovered by many children's authors. I refer to educational publishers as one of the world of "hidden" publishers because you can't find them listed in some market guides, and they rarely send editors to speak at children's writer's conferences. Why aren't they advertising their publishing needs to children's authors? It's because they're not looking for people who want to get their picture book published or who dream of being a famous writer for young adults. They're looking for writers, hopefully educators, who are eager to write the material that the publisher needs.

In the educational market, the focus is not on what an author wants to write. The focus is on what the publisher wants to publish. Therefore, when I write for the educational market, I always try to land a contract or an assignment before I write the manuscript. I try to find out what a publisher wants—exactly what they want—before I spend months writing a manuscript. A benefit of doing this guarantees that I'm earning income while I'm writing—a definite bonus when trying to earn a decent income from writing. (To learn more about how to land a contract or an assignment before you write the manuscript, read my first book in this series, *Yes! You Can Learn How to Write Children's Books, Get Them Published, and Build a Successful Writing Career.*)

If you want to write leveled readers for the educational market, explore the various educational publishers. You'll find some under the list of Education/Resource Material in the Category Index of *Book Markets for Children's Writers* (Writer's Institute Publications™). *Writer's Market®* (Writer's Digest Books) includes a list of educational publishers for both the adult and children's market in the Nonfiction section under Education in its Book Publisher Subject Index. Educator and prolific writer (and dear friend) Evelyn B. Christensen maintains a highly-recommended site of Educational Markets for Children's Writers at www.evelynchristensen.com.

You can also visit your local teacher's supply store and browse through their teacher's books for names of educational publishers. A visit to your local school district will help you find the names of textbook publishers or publishers of standardized test material that you might want to contact. You can also search for key terms such as "elementary textbooks" or "teacher resources" at online bookstores such as Amazon.com or online stores such as Discount School Supply at www.discountschoolsupply.com, the online site CM School Supply® at www.cmschoolsupply.com, and the online website for Lakeshore® stores at www.lakeshorelearning.com.

Explore the various educational publishers, study their Websites, read their catalogs, and look for ones who are producing leveled readers in their product line. Look until you find products where you can say, "I think I can try to write that." Then contact them with your ideas. To learn how to do this effectively, continue reading.

Beginner's Tip

Browsing through publishers' catalogs can feel overwhelming. Don't worry about all the titles you think you could never write. Just keep looking for something similar to what you think you *can* try to write.

Professional Track

Learn to network. If you have a writer friend who already writes for the educational market, ask if he might introduce you to his editor. Offer to exchange the favor with one of your own editors.

Strengthen Your Writing Muscles

Find a copy of a student workbook such as one of the *Little Critter Workbooks*. Create a sample student worksheet similar to the ones in the workbook. Write the instructions on the worksheet for the student to follow based on the readability level for that grade. Even though this type of book isn't classified as a typical beginning reader, the author does have to follow guidelines to produce material geared for the target reading level. If you discover you enjoyed creating a sample worksheet, add publishers to your list to explore who publish student workbooks.

5.2 Landing the Contract

If at all possible, I like to make initial contact with a publisher I've never worked with by sending a short pitch, or query, to the editor of the department that interests me. I did this as a writer before I had much experience in the beginning readers and chapter books market, and I still like to do this today. Whether you're a beginning writer or experienced published author, you can learn how to pitch ideas to an educational publisher and try to land a contract before you write the manuscript.

When you choose an educational publisher you'd like to target, search for their author's submission guidelines. These can usually be found on a publisher's Website, but it is often hidden because most design their Websites to attract educators to purchase their products, not to invite authors to write for them. Search for terms such as "Writers Guide," "Submissions," or "Submission Guidelines." Look under the links for "Contact Us" or "About Us." If you can't find any guidelines anywhere, call or e-mail a general department and ask for Editorial. Explain that you are a freelance author interested in writing for the publisher. They might connect you with an editor or an editorial assistant. Be brief, but clear. Introduce yourself as a freelance author, even if you do not yet have published credits. Explain that you are interested in the potential of writing for this publisher and that you are looking for submission guidelines.

Some educational publishers have very clearly defined submission guidelines for you to follow. They explain which departments are open to new freelance authors and what educational background, if any, is desired. Others might not be as specific.

Study the publisher's product line. Look for a series you think you could fit into. Brainstorm three to five ideas for leveled readers that could fit into their existing product line. If you're an educator or literacy specialist without much writing experience, you can brainstorm ideas to fit into products that require more teaching resources and fewer leveled reading materials. If you have more writing experience and aren't an educator, you can brainstorm ideas to fit into products that feature more leveled reader content and a minimal amount of teaching resources. (Another option is to pair up with a co-author who is a teacher, or a children's author, depending on the expertise you lack. I have co-authored several books for the educational market with my husband, Jeff, who has taught elementary school for over 25 years.)

I am not a teacher. I'm a children's writer. So when I made initial contact with Scholastic Teaching Resources, I pitched ideas to write books with beginning reader mini-plays and mini-books. These were mostly reproducible beginning readers with only a minimum of teaching instruction.

When I first contacted Libraries Unlimited, I did the same. I pitched ideas to the editor to write a book of Readers Theatre plays to fit into their line of Readers Theatre books for middle grades. The only teaching tips I needed to write were limited to the Introduction and suggested classroom activities after each play. (To learn more about writing material for teachers, see *Section 5.5 Teacher Activities and Classroom Resources*.)

The Query

The advent of e-mail has made the art of query-writing so much easier. E-mails can be short and to the point. When I make initial contact with a brand new publisher I've never worked with before, I often like to send off a short, quick e-mail query pitching three to five potential ideas that could fit well into their product line. Because my goal is to try to land a contract and earn income while I write, I don't want to spend a lot of my time preparing lengthy tomes for a manuscript someone isn't even interested in, regardless of how well it might be written. So I send off a short query, by e-mail if at all possible.

Sometimes it can be confusing about the difference between a query and a cover letter. Sometimes people, even editors, mistakenly switch the two terms around, so this can add to the confusion. A query is basically a letter that you send to an editor all by itself. On the other hand, a cover letter is the letter that you send along with a proposal or a manuscript. When I send a query, I like to use e-mail. E-mail is quick and e-mail is free. Unless a publisher specifically states on their Website that they do not accept e-mails, I always look for an e-mail address to use to submit a query.

I've written hundreds of queries. At first, it was agonizing to try to write the "perfect" pitch. Now, however, I don't stress. Why not? I've contacted enough editors whom I've never communicated with before and discovered that most are ordinary, regular people. They're busy and appreciate things that don't drain their time or sap their energy. If I send them a quick query over e-mail that's short and to the point, they'll often send me a quick reply back.

Please note that I'm not talking here about cover letters that accompany a proposal. I'll discuss that next. I'm talking about the initial contact you make with an educational publisher to see if there's a nibble for any of your ideas that might fit into their product line.

I'm also not talking about contacting an educational publisher regarding a manuscript you've already written. Save that for *after* you land your first contract with a new publisher.

I'm talking about getting your foot in the door with an educational publisher you have never worked with before. I'm talking about focusing your efforts on landing a contract to write a brand new leveled reading manuscript for an educational publisher. The strategy I've tried that gives me the most success usually starts with a quick, short query. To save time, I've developed a template I like to use. You can use it, too! Here's a sample e-mail query. Just fill in the blanks on this template and you're ready to send it on its way:

Dear _____ (first name of editor)

I have studied your line of educational products on your Website. I see that you publish _____ (list titles or series that are similar to the one you want to write). Would you be interested in receiving a proposal about _____
(list three to five ideas for manuscripts that you haven't yet written that would fit well into the titles you listed earlier)?

Sincerely,
_____ (your name)
_____ (your contact information)

Here is an example of a finished query that you could e-mail:

Dear Sarah,

I have studied your line of educational products on your Website. I see that you publish Readers Theatre plays for classroom use. Would you be interested in receiving a proposal about Readers Theatre Science, Readers Theatre Nursery Rhymes, or Readers Theatre Math?

Sincerely,
Hannah Writer
Author of 7 books and numerous magazine articles
1234 Alphabet Way
Learnville, PA 98765
987-654-3210
www.hannahwriter.com

If you don't have published credits yet, don't worry about it. (To learn more about how to build up your line of published credits by writing for the no-pay/low-pay market, look in my book, *Yes! You Can Learn How to Write Children's Books, Get Them Published, and Build a Successful Writing Career.*) If you do have published credits, however, be sure to list them briefly in your query.

If your target publisher does not accept e-mail queries, simply format it like a business letter. Include an SASE, or self-addressed, stamped envelope. Then put it in your mailbox and send it off.

One thing to note is that this type of query is not for simultaneous submissions. Unlike a manuscript submission, this is just an idea pitch to a very specific target. This isn't something you could send to a lot of publishers because this is a list of one-of-a-kind ideas uniquely suited to fit into one publisher's product line. If you contact a different publisher, you'd have to create a new query tailored with ideas suited to their unique product line. Just send out a query like this one at a time.

As soon as your query is on its way, start looking for another educational publisher to target. Don't worry that the first one might reply and offer you a contract immediately. These things usually take time. If two publishers contact you at the same time and both offer you contracts to write different books, just schedule one deadline first and the other deadline several months later. Publishers are used to working with busy authors' schedules. For instance, one time I was offered a book contract by an educational publisher for a series of books written by various authors that all needed to be submitted by December 30. The problem was that I was currently working on a deadline for another book that was due the same date. There was no way I could write both books at the same time. I explained this to them, and they allowed me to change the contract for a February 15 deadline for my book. The reason? They said they could be editing all the other books in the series while I worked on mine.

If you e-mailed the publisher and don't hear back from them within two weeks, simply send them another e-mail that says that you are just double checking that they actually received your e-mail. Paste your original e-mail at the bottom for reference. If you mailed your query via the post office, a typical waiting period is three months.

If you don't hear back from the publisher either by e-mail or postal mail for a full three months, that usually means they are not interested in your ideas. Many publishers simply do not respond these days or send out a rejection letter. This practice has developed due to the tremendous amount of submissions they receive in this electronic age where one manuscript can be submitted to 50 publishers at once, all with the click of one button.

If the editor responds and says that yes, she would like to receive a proposal for one or more of the ideas you sent to her, contact her right back. Use e-mail if she e-mailed you. If she sent you a letter in the mail and included her e-mail on that letter, again it's best to use e-mail since it's fast and it's free. If, however, she sent you a letter and did not include her e-mail in the letterhead, send her back a letter right away. Thank her for her interest and tell her that you will prepare a proposal to send to her within about one month. That is a standard time that an editor waits to receive a proposal in this industry.

Before you roll up your sleeves to start working on your proposal, however, take time to celebrate! You got a nibble! You caught an editor's eye. No matter what happens down the road, you actually thought of an idea that sounded like a winner. Hip hip hooray! E-mail all your writer friends and share the news.

The Proposal

Now that an editor is interested in your idea, you do want to take time to prepare a professional proposal. A proposal for an educational publisher typically includes a cover letter, an outline or table of contents for the entire book, and sample text.

In the cover letter, be sure to mention that this proposal was requested. Explain your idea once again because with the busy schedule most editors have, they probably don't have your original query handy. Besides, editors often share cover letters and proposals with other editors or committees and it helps to have all your information here in one place.

List your published credits if you have any. Describe your educational background if you are an educator. If you don't have any published credits or an educational background, don't include them. If you have a lot, prepare a separate page to include in your proposal such as a resumé or curriculum vitae. This page would immediately follow the cover letter.

Explain how your potential manuscript would fit into the publisher's product line. Either mention it as part of an existing series, as a complementary series, or as a title that would complement two or three of the publisher's titles that you list here.

State the target age, the target audience, the estimated work count or page number, and the reading level of your projected manuscript. For instance, the target age (who would actually read the book) could be for Grades 1 and 2. The target audience (who would actually buy the book) could be first and second grade teachers and home-schooling parents. To determine the estimated word count, just find out the word count or number of pages in a similar book by this publisher. The reading level should always complement the target age unless it is a hi-lo book.

It also gives your proposal a boost when your cover letter includes a market analysis. This can be one paragraph on your cover letter or a separate page in length. In the market analysis, list three to five titles of books published in the last five years that are similar to your projected manuscript. This shows the editor that there is a current market for this type of book. For each of these titles, however, clarify how your book will be unique or set apart from them and fill a specific need in this market.

If you have any questions about the proposal you are preparing, it is acceptable to many editors for you to contact them briefly. Don't badger them, but do step out to ask key questions that will help you prepare the specific type of proposal they'd like to see. Of course, if they give very detailed instructions in their submission guidelines about how to prepare a proposal, always follow their instructions over the advice you read here or elsewhere.

Include a short synopsis, or summary, of your book in the cover letter. If you are proposing a series of leveled readers, include a short synopsis of the series along with three to five suggested titles and a brief blurb describing each. If this is lengthy, you can opt to make a separate page describing the series that follows the cover letter.

Since an editor requested your proposal, your cover letter may be longer than just one page. Try not to be too wordy, but be sure to include all the information an editor will need to see in order to make an informed decision.

Prepare an outline or table of contents for the entire book. Sometimes educational publishers refer to this as a "scope and sequence." Unless the educational publisher has a line of stand-alone beginning readers, they usually publish a collection of beginning readers that a teacher can use in the classroom. For instance, there might be 15 Readers Theatre plays, 25 reproducible beginning reader mini-books, or 50 student worksheets. List a working title for each one.

An outline or table of contents is necessary for the editor to understand the entire scope of your project. Since this is an educational publisher, they usually want to have the skill or standard listed that each item in your outline supports. For instance, here is a sample outline for you to view that's from the actual proposal I submitted for my book, *Hello Hi-Lo: Readers Theatre Math* (Libraries Unlimited):

Hello Hi-Lo: Readers Theatre Math
Scope and Sequence

This book will have 15 plays. Each play will have extended activities for the teacher to incorporate the math concept into the classroom. It can cover 15 math concepts, or it can cover 12 math concepts and 3 plays about the history of math. Here is an outline for 12 math concepts and 3 plays about the history of math.

Outline of Math concepts for 12 plays:
Order of operations
Area of solid figures, i.e. prism, cylinder, pyramid, cone (Sample Play Included)
Fractions
Equations
Inequalities
Rounding
Positive and Negative Numbers
Points, Lines, and Planes
Angles
Percentages
Probability
Graphing on coordinate plane

3 plays on the history of math:
Euclid, the Greek Mathematician
Gauss Adds to 100
Isaac Newton: The Mathematician of Light

Note that this is just a sample outline. My editor did not require a detailed outline, but perhaps yours will. Prepare your outline as it seems best suited to your projected manuscript. Also note that the outline in your proposal is not written in stone. Most editors understand that as you work on writing your book, things might change. As long as your book stays close in overall content to your proposal, it's perfectly fine to change certain parts as you're actually writing the book. For instance, if you look in my published book, you will see that I have several completely different topics than were mentioned in this original outline.

Another key ingredient of your proposal is a sample of your text. This sample can vary with each different type of project, but ten pages of sample text or one completed part of the book is usually sufficient. For instance, in my proposal for *Hello Hi-Lo: Readers Theatre Math*, I included one sample play that I wrote specifically for this project.

If you have published samples of work that are similar to your proposed manuscript, you may also want to include this with your proposal. However, do not include published samples that are not similar. Once I did this and it was for a different target age than the project I was proposing. The editor was concerned that I wouldn't be able to write for a different target age if I was already successful in writing for another.

After you have prepared your cover letter, outline, and sample text, submit it to the editor you are working with. Many editors accept e-mail submissions. If they do not, submit it through the postal mail with an SASE. After you submit your proposal, start immediately on another project. The standard wait to hear back from a publisher is three months. If you have not heard back from them at this time, assume that it was rejected.

Many times, an editor will respond to your proposal and ask you to revise it to better suit the publisher's needs. By working with an editor at this stage to revise the outline and sample text, it will save a lot of revision after the finished manuscript is submitted. Do the revisions the editor requests and submit the proposal again.

If the editor contacts you and offers you a contract, it's time to celebrate! Do a happy dance. Dance all around your living room while listening to your favorite CD. All your hard work has paid off. Now it's time to sign the contract and start working with the editor as you write the manuscript. The next section will help you on your way.

Beginner's Tip

Search on the Internet or in writer's market guides such as *Writer's Market*® for examples of bad queries and poorly written cover letters. This will help you to not make the same mistakes as others have done.

Professional Track

Ask one or more of your editors if they could share a winning cover letter or proposal with you that really caught their eye. Analyze it and refer to it to help make yours shine.

Strengthen Your Writing Muscles

Pretend that you're at a writer's conference and step into an elevator, only to discover you're alone with the editor of your target publisher. You have one minute to pitch your manuscript before you reach the next floor. What will you say in that minute? Practice writing a one-minute elevator pitch. Then use it as a launching point to help pitch ideas to an editor in a query.

5.3 Working with Editors

Some editors work very closely with authors during the process of writing a book. Because many educational publishers are used to working with their authors to write the book after the contract is signed, this can be the case for your manuscript. This can actually build your confidence as a writer because it helps you stay on the right track. You can follow an editor's guidance to hit your target right on the bull's eye.

Many educational publishers have an Author's Packet. This is sometimes referred to by other names such as an Author's Guide or Planner. Some publishers send these to you by postal mail, some by e-mail, and some will give you an access code to retrieve it on an online site. Because the Author's Packet is the guide that you'll follow closely while you write your manuscript, always print out the entire thing if they don't send you a hard copy. You'll refer to it frequently and most likely highlight key sections and mark it up with notes along the way. Keep it in a prominent place. I like to prepare a pocket folder for the manuscript I'm writing, and I place the Author's Packet in its own separate file folder in the pocket folder.

When I first receive an Author's Packet, I always feel overwhelmed. Some Author's Packets can be much longer than my projected manuscript! I like to schedule myself a mini-retreat after I receive it. I set aside a three to five hour chunk or spread chunks out over several days where I can sit down and really connect with it. Before I read it, I like to set a relaxing atmosphere so I can go over it with a positive attitude rather than panic. Sometimes I put on soft piano music, light a candle, get a favorite treat to eat, and sit by the fireplace cuddled up in a warm blanket.

Every publisher prepares its own unique Author's Packet, but there are usually key guidelines each one includes. Because an Author's Packet is often handed out to all of their authors regardless of which manuscript they're writing, many of the sections usually do not pertain to my particular project. I lightly draw a big X over these sections so I don't waste time reading over them again.

In an Author's Packet, there is usually a Style Guide. This tells you how to format your text, name your saved files, which spellings or abbreviations are preferred for certain words, and how to prepare a bibliography or index.

There might be guidelines on how to prepare images, diagrams, or art if your contract requires you to submit these. There might be instructions on how to prepare an introduction, the table of contents, or the back cover text of the book. Sometimes, there is a calendar of key dates the publisher expects to see certain portions of the manuscript completed by. Often a final checklist is included to make sure you submit everything that's expected.

For beginning readers, some educational publishers include actual word lists in their Author's Packet. These word lists have been carefully prepared by reading specialists. Usually, detailed instructions on how to use these word lists will accompany them. For instance, one small publisher I worked with provided me with two word lists. One list contained words I could use freely within my stories for the reading level I was writing for. The second word list included new vocabulary words the students at this grade level needed to learn. I had to use 15-20 new vocabulary words in each story. I was not allowed to use a word in any of my stories that wasn't on either of those two lists.

There might be a Layout Planner or Thumbnail Sketch included in the Author's Packet. This is also sometimes referred to as a Book Map. This provides specific instructions on how to organize each page of your manuscript so that it fits into the finished book. (A thumbnail sketch is usually a series of two or three-inch squares or boxes representing each page of the finished book with a word or words on each page denoting which portion of your manuscript goes where.)

One of my favorite ingredients in an Author's Packet is when the publisher includes samples of winning manuscripts or refers actual published titles for their authors to examine. This really helps to know exactly what they prefer to see in a final manuscript.

Some Author's Packets include instructions on how the publisher expects authors to help market the book after it is published. There might be a marketing person or a publicist whose contact information is provided in the packet because she will work with you on certain tasks as explained in this guide.

Usually, there is a questionnaire to complete that will help market your book. You might need to provide names of professional contacts or organizations who could endorse your book, venues that might be interested in selling your book, or media contacts who could review the book. All this information will be used by the marketing person or publicist to help sell your book.

Along with an Author's Packet that is distributed to all their authors, many educational publishers will also provide you with detailed instructions on preparing your specific manuscript. This is especially true if you are working on a project that is a work-for-hire project or is a series which various authors are all working on simultaneously. If you are working on a project that is uniquely yours, there will probably be fewer instructions like this for you to follow.

Sometimes educational publishers work on a tight schedule that involves an entire chain of people from editors to authors to copy editors who edit the submitted manuscript for typos and grammatical errors, to printers to sales reps, or representatives who help sell the book. If I'm late, it will cause a domino effect and knock everyone else off schedule. I like to have a separate calendar to keep track of key deadlines within my final book deadline to help keep me organized in situations such as these.

Some editors like to go over an Author's Packet with the author. If so, I schedule my mini-retreat before a phone conference and list any questions I have. If I have a lot of questions about the Author's Packet but no phone conference is offered, I'll ask my editor to schedule one so we can go over everything before I start.

For scheduling a phone conference with an editor, it helps to have a hands-free phone set so you can write notes, look things up on the Internet or the publisher's Website if you need to as you chat, and look through your Author's Packet quickly together.

Even though we get the impression at writer's conferences that we need to keep our distance from editors, once we have signed a contract to write a manuscript not yet written, the editor will expect to work with us to some degree. Don't be afraid to ask questions that only your editor can answer. Of course, if your questions are general in nature, ask your critique group or writer's list-serv first. (A list-serv is an online e-mail group with one focus.) It's important not to badger an editor or drain her precious time or energy with questions or issues that we can solve on our own.

Because each editor is an individual, I've found that each one has her own preferences for communication. Some are phone people. Others prefer e-mail. Still others like to read your question in an e-mail but then talk about it on the phone. Some even like Skype, a service where you can both speak into your computer and see your face on the computers at the same time. Some editors like to work on one small issue at a time. Others prefer one long list of questions or issues all in the same e-mail to tackle all at once. As I'm working with a new editor, I try to figure out which kind of communicator she is. Learning this and responding accordingly helps keep both of our frustration levels at a minimum.

Some editors wear a variety of hats. Especially at smaller publishing houses, some of the editors I work with are actually the publisher. In essence, the publisher is in charge of everything that goes on at the publishing house. An editor, however, usually oversees manuscripts without being involved in the running of the publishing house. In smaller publishing houses, however, the publisher and editor can be one and the same. These editors/publishers work closely with the author at every single stage of the journey from acquiring a manuscript to editing it and getting it ready to send to the printer.

At some publishing houses, I've worked with several editors during the process of writing the manuscript. My first contact was with the Acquisitions Editor, whose job it is to acquire new manuscripts or land new book contracts for the company. Then I was assigned a Project Editor who worked with me during the entire process of writing the manuscript. Then I was assigned a second Project Editor who worked with me through the revisions stage. At times there has been an Author Relations Coordinator who helped work on certain aspects of the book such as answering questions about the contract or keeping an author on schedule.

Working with editors, whether it's just one editor or an entire editorial team, can be a very exciting and rewarding experience. Writing your book and making it the best it can be becomes a team effort. It's thrilling to know there are others who have caught the vision for your book and are working hard to help you bring it to life while you are focused on writing the manuscript. To learn more about the process of actually writing a leveled reader for the educational market, read the next section.

Beginner's Tip

Join a critique group or start your own. A critique group is a writers group where members bring their own manuscripts to read and share. Start sharing your manuscripts on a regular basis for critique by peers. Receiving constructive feedback will help prepare you for an editor's revisions requests.

Professional Track

Put on an editor's hat to help you understand what it's like on the other side of the fence. Contact one of your publishers and ask if they have an opening for an acquisitions editor or a proofreading editor. By looking critically at other publishable manuscripts on a regular basis, you'll learn how to improve your own.

Strengthen Your Writing Muscles

Interview three to five junior high students. Find out how they like to communicate. Do they text each other? E-mail? Or...? Armed with this knowledge, write a humorous hi-lo Readers Theatre play about ways friends communicate in junior high. Make your story "high-interest" in that the topic appeals to students in seventh or eighth grade, but make it a "low reading level" for a fifth to sixth grade reader.

5.4 Writing Leveled Readers

In the educational market, leveled readers are often presented in a format targeting teachers. This means that most likely, educators choose these books or materials first and then distribute them or use them with their students. Understanding how leveled readers are "packaged" for teachers will give you the tools you need so that you can write with confidence for this market.

Sometimes leveled readers geared for classroom use are made into individual small books that can be grouped together in a box as a classroom set. If this is the case, most likely these books will closely resemble the beginning readers in the trade picture book market. If your contract is for this type of leveled readers, refer to *Chapter 4: Trade Book Markets* for more information on how to write them. Also, refer to Chapters 7 through 13 for specific guidance on writing for each different readability level.

Often leveled readers geared for classroom use are a collection of reproducible mini-books or plays or stories all in one supplemental book such as a reproducible student workbook. These books measure 8 ½ x 11-inches so that the pages can be photocopied and distributed easily to students. There often is a notice on the copyright page that states the publisher gives teachers permission to photocopy certain portions of the book for classroom use. Some of these books even have perforated pages so that teachers can tear out the pages and easily place them on the photocopy machine. Some have lines depicting where the teacher or students should cut apart the pages in order to assemble them into mini-books or scripts for plays.

Standard page count in these books can be 64 pages, 96 pages, 128 pages, or longer. As you're planning the content of your book, keep the page count in mind so that there are the corresponding numbers of leveled reading stories along with teaching materials in the front or back matter, or sections, to match your total page count. Some educational publishers such as Scholastic Teaching Resources provide authors with a thumbnail sketch, or book map. Scholastic's book map has 162 numbered blank squares on this 11 x 17-inch page to help authors plan the layout of the entire book. Some publishers request authors to submit a completed book map with the final manuscript submission.

Because these teachers' books contain leveled stories that students will actually be reading themselves, the same guidelines for writing any leveled reader are still best to follow as you actually write your manuscript. Refer to *Chapter 7: Writing Strategies for Beginning Readers and Chapter Books* for general tips about writing beginning readers that shine. In Chapters 8 through 13, find specific guidelines for topics such as sentence structure, vocabulary, plot, and character development for each reading level.

As you're writing leveled readers for your educational publisher, surround yourself with the best of the best. First find one or more similar books to the one you're writing that your publisher has already published. Study the format of these stories and make it your goal to fit into their line of readers as closely as possible. Make a list of strengths from various stories that you want to implement into your stories. Use these as examples to follow as you write your own leveled readers. Once again, *Chapter 7: Writing Strategies for Beginning Readers and Chapter Books* will help you determine which examples are the best for you to mirror in your own writing.

When I have written beginning readers in a reproducible mini-book format, I have been required to also submit sample mock-ups of each mini-book. These can be prepared on a publishing program or drawn by hand. I am not an artist, but an educational publisher does not mind. The reason they require a mock-up of each mini-book is to see the suggested placement of text and also the exact placement of suggested art. Because the text in these mini-books is very, very basic, as the author I need to give art examples to the illustrator to follow. Simple stick figures are absolutely fine. The position of these stick figures on the page of the mock-up is what is important. I need to include detailed art directions in the actual manuscript as well as mock-ups. The illustrator will use my detailed instructions along with the actual drawing samples I send along with the completed manuscript.

A lot of times, when writing beginning readers, it is expected that the author will include detailed art instructions within the body of the manuscript text for the illustrator to follow. Most publishers expect to see these art instructions within [brackets]. (This is different from when you are writing a picture book where no illustration suggestions are needed except if absolutely necessary because of very limited text.) Any text written inside brackets means that it's for the eyes of the editor or illustrator and is not part of the final text of the beginning reader story. When you are writing a manuscript like this, just keep your font standard sized and double-spaced throughout. Usually, Times New Roman 12 is a standard font to use when preparing any manuscript. There is no need for fancy font or a variance in spacing between lines on the actual manuscript itself. Educational publishers don't want to see any frills or unusual manuscripts unless they specifically state this in their Author's Packet.

For instance, here is an example of the text for my book of beginning reader mini-books for Scholastic Teaching Resources called *Cut & Paste Mini-Books: Science* (used by permission of Scholastic Inc.). "Matt's Pictures" is the name of one of the 15 mini-books that can be reproduced and distributed to students in kindergarten and first grade. The text inside the brackets includes the art instructions for the illustrator. The text without brackets is the actual text the student will read in the reproducible mini-book. I also submitted an accompanying sample mock-up along with this text to show the illustrator exactly what I meant in the art instructions I wrote.

[Pages of the Mini-Book]
Cover:
Matt's Pictures
[Art: Show an outdoor scene. Matt is holding a camera.]

Page 2:
One day Matt saw
a tiny egg on a leaf.
He took a picture.
Click!
[Art: Show a boy taking a picture with a camera.]

Page 3:
[Art: Show a snapshot of a leaf hanging from a branch.]

Page 4:
Soon Matt saw
a very small caterpillar.
He took a picture.
Click!
[Art: Show Matt taking a picture.]

The key to remember if you are preparing art samples to submit along with your manuscript is the term *exact placement.* For instance, in the mock-up I submitted, I didn't just cut out little pages and make a dummy of the mini-book, "Matt's Pictures." That would have been appropriate for a stand-alone title in the trade picture book market, but not here in the educational market. Because the finished pages of the teachers' book I was writing would be in an 8 ½-inch x 11-inch book, I drew four of these small pages on one sheet of typing paper: two on the front and two on the back. I double-checked on a photocopy machine so that when the teacher photocopied that page front and back, each of the pages of the mini-book would be in the *exact placement* it was supposed to be. As a guide, I referred to other similar books by my publisher and followed their layouts of the mini-book pages.

The publisher and illustrator needed to see the *exact placement* of how each page of the mini-books would appear in the final book. On each of these small pages, I drew stick figures or simple images and pasted a copy of the text in the correct finished font size and in the *exact placement* each of these elements would appear in the final book. (I double-checked with my editor first to determine the finished font size of the mini-books because beginning readers are often printed in larger fonts for young readers than the standard Times New Roman 12 font size of a typed manuscript.) In other words, I prepared my art samples to appear exactly in the place they should appear in the finished book. I also included about a 1-inch margin of white space around the entire edge of each page in my samples to allow for a "bleed" zone during printing when sometimes pages shift slightly while on the printing press. To look at concrete examples of these books, look at my titles with Scholastic Teaching Resources that are listed under my name at www.Amazon.com. Many feature a "look inside the book" option so that you can better visualize how this process is done.

As with most books published in the educational market, my book of reproducible beginning readers included suggested teacher activities and classroom resources. Chances are, if you are writing a reproducible book of a collection of beginning readers or leveled readers for the educational market, you will need to include suggested teacher activities, too. Read the next section to learn more about writing these resources.

Beginner's Tip

Make your own notebook of your favorite beginning readers in the educational market. Type out each one on its own page. Note the author and the title of the book it's from if it is in a collection of leveled readers. Print these out and create a personal notebook of the best of the best. Each time you sit down to write a beginning reader, spend 15 minutes reading these first. By typing and then reading these outstanding examples, it trains your brain to create new material that is of the same caliber.

Professional Track

Host a blog chain of published writers for the educational market. Invite five to ten published authors of beginning readers for the educational market to join in the fun. (More than that makes a blog chain cumbersome to follow.) During the one-week event, ask each writer in the blog chain to post tips and strategies on their blog giving an insiders-peek about writing leveled readers for the educational market. (If you're not yet published in this genre, on your own blog, post observations of a newbie's perspective of breaking into this market.) For a blog chain, each person includes a link on their own blog each day for their readers to go to the next person's blog in the chain. Not only will this give you great tips and advice, but it will expose more followers to each of your blogs.

Strengthen Your Writing Muscles

Practice how to type a manuscript and prepare an art sample for the educational market. Find one reproducible mini-book in a teacher's book of leveled readers such as my mini-book, "Little Boy Blue Has a Job to Do" in *15 Easy-to-Read Nursery Rhyme Mini-Book Plays*. Type out the text and art instructions as if you were writing it in a manuscript. Remember to use brackets for the illustration or art instructions. Then use a publishing program or draw by hand a sample mock-up of the page layout, text, and illustration design for each page of that mini-book so that each element has the *exact placement* in your mock-up as it appears in the finished book.

5.5 Teacher Activities and Classroom Resources

Many teachers' books containing leveled readers also feature activities and classroom resources for teachers to use. Whether or not you are an educator, you can learn to write solid resources for this market. There is a wealth of published material to draw from as well as numerous opportunities available in your own community to help you along your journey to experience success as a writer of resource material for teachers.

If you have never set foot inside a classroom or worked with a group of children before, it is to your advantage to gain experience first. While my own two sons were in elementary school, I volunteered to help with holiday parties, help their teachers, and teach art lessons. I didn't just jump in head first, though! I'm not a teacher, so I started gradually. I assisted the Room Moms before I volunteered as a Room Mom myself. I attended volunteer training sessions held at their school to learn how to teach parent-led art lessons in their classrooms. I helped their teachers with simple tasks such as running the photocopy machine before I stepped forward to help work with groups of students by myself.

If you're not already a teacher, volunteer at your local elementary school with the goal of gaining hands-on experience working with students in the classroom. If your local school really isn't an option for some reason, there are also other volunteer opportunities to work with kids such as with your local Girl Scouts, at your church, at the public library, or at various community events.

Gain experience working with small groups of kids as well as groups of up to 30 or 40 children. This will better equip you to create teacher activities and write classroom resources for a teacher to use with an entire class at once or use with small groups within a standard-sized classroom. Along the way, you'll learn many valuable lessons such as the importance of using inexpensive and easy-to-find materials. You'll also observe how long it takes for a large group to complete a teacher-guided activity in comparison to a small group. Things like this are best learned from experience itself.

If you already are an educator, you know first-hand what type of activities work best in the classroom and which ones don't. You have a wealth of material to choose from! You're already well on your way to writing top-quality classroom resource material.

As I gather ideas for teacher activities and classroom resources, I have kept folders to organize my favorites. I love to read through magazines and periodicals and online sites that feature activities for kids. I print out my favorites or photocopy them and add to my folders. Over the years, I have subscribed to teachers' creative ideas magazines such as *The Mailbox®*. Crafts stores have a wide selection of magazines with fantastic crafts for kids, many of which can be adapted for classroom use. I keep these magazines in my personal research library as handy resources for brainstorming ideas.

Try to be very careful not to infringe on someone else's copyright. To help avoid this complication, I always try to change the craft I've seen in some significant way. For instance, if I saw a craft for making pink foam tulips for a Mother's Day gift, I'll change it to making paper flowers to decorate a holder for Valentine's cards.

As you're collecting your own idea files, look for activities that will work well when displayed on the wall. This is a huge plus for some teachers! Look for activities that might do well as teacher-led large group activities, as homework assignments, as small group parent helper-led activities, as center activities, or as activities for students to complete during free time. Be on a search to find creative bulletin board ideas. List safe Internet sites designed for teacher or student use. Also try to look for activities and classroom resources that generate an excitement and thrill for learning versus ones that are perceived by students as a dreaded task to complete.

Collect ideas for games. Look for common, childhood games that most children know and most teachers are familiar with. For instance, good games to use include Bingo, Go Fish, and Simon Says. As you adapt these games as extension activities to use with your beginning readers, try to keep the rules for playing the games fairly close to the original. Change the manipulatives or other key ingredient to correspond with your beginning readers. For instance, suggest that teachers create Bingo cards using words from the same word family or using vocabulary words from your beginning reader in the squares instead of typical Bingo numbers.

Each teacher activity or classroom resource you provide should be educational in scope and should correlate with the State and National Standards or Common Core State Standards. For instance, an activity could help build vocabulary, practice writing skills, or develop critical thinking or logic skills. Activities can be cross-curricular and involve subjects other than language arts.

To format your teacher activities and classroom resources, follow the format in similar books your publisher publishes. Some prefer this section to come at the front of the book. Others prefer it to be at the back. Some prefer that each leveled reader be accompanied by its own section of teacher activities or classroom resources.

To see an example of one format to use, here is a sample of the teacher activities and classroom resources I included with the mini-book, "Matt's Pictures," in my book for teachers, *Cut & Paste Mini-Books: Science* (used by permission of Scholastic Inc.).

Matt's Pictures: Teacher Activities
Getting Started
Work with children to list facts they already know about butterflies. Write each fact on a separate construction-paper butterfly cutout. Display the facts on a bulletin board…

Taking It Further
Ask children to color, cut out, and glue a copy of each of the five patterns (page 14) to a separate index card. Have them glue the cards to craft sticks to make puppets…

Teacher activities and classroom resources are common ingredients in a book of reproducible beginning readers in the educational market. By familiarizing yourself with the format and types of resources your publisher already publishes, it will help you write these for your own manuscript. Even if you lack an educational background, you can use research to help fill in the gaps.

Beginner's Tip

If you really want to write beginning readers for the educational market but feel overwhelmed with the thought of writing the teacher resource material, pair up with a teacher as your co-author. You can write the leveled readers and she can write the corresponding teacher extension activities.

Professional Track

Look for ways to include your other published books as part of the teacher activities and classroom resources. As long as you present these options in a professional way, most publishers are open to having published authors feature their other books as suggested resources.

Strengthen Your Writing Muscles

Write step-by-step instructions to make a simple child's craft. Pretend you are writing instructions for a child to read and follow. Format it to look like a recipe with a list of materials followed by numbered steps to make the craft. When finished, rewrite those same instructions in paragraph form telling a teacher how to have students make that same craft. For added fun, you can even submit this to a magazine for teachers, parents, or children.

Chapter 6

MAGAZINES AND OTHER MARKETS

6.1 Writing for Magazines

Young children love to receive magazines in the mail, especially if the subscription is in their name. They feel like the stories inside the glossy pages were especially written just for them! Many magazines feature some form of beginning reader story occasionally, and some children's magazines feature a beginning reader in each issue. By exploring the children's magazine market and searching for ones that welcome beginning readers, you can start submitting manuscripts or pitching ideas for beginning readers you want to write.

In general, the magazine market is not as concerned about writing for the State and National Standards or the Common Core State Standards as the book market is. True, some children's magazines are published by the educational market or are geared for teachers to use in their classrooms, and those magazines will clarify in their guidelines if manuscript submissions must support the standards. No matter what their purpose or who their target audience is, however, many children's magazines like to stay current with the times and will incorporate standard-related articles or beginning readers features such as phonics-based content or a rebus. This gives parents tools to reinforce concepts they observe their children learning at school, even if the parents themselves don't know about the standards.

For instance, Focus on the Family's *Clubhouse Jr.* magazine at one time featured phonics-based stories. They highlighted a certain beginning sound or other phonics element. My feature fiction story in their 2003 Christmas issue, *Away In a Manger*, had every beginning *sh* letter combination highlighted in red.

Read through current issues of children's magazines. See if you can spot feature stories or fillers such as puzzles or activity pages that are either a beginning reader in their own right or contain some element of leveled reading. When you find this, target these magazines as potential markets where you can write beginning readers.

Even if your search does not turn up magazines where you find beginning readers, you can go ahead and pitch ideas to the editor for stories with a beginning reader focus. For instance, explain to the editor that your submission can be similar to a feature title they recently published, or your submission can be formatted as a beginning reader.

To experience breakthrough in the magazine market, a significant number of magazines require submissions of a completed manuscript. Learn to include a cover letter with your manuscript submission that includes a pitch with three to five potential ideas for other manuscripts. Since you're interested in writing beginning readers, go ahead and pitch ideas for beginning readers fiction stories, nonfiction articles, puzzles or activities—even if you haven't yet seen a beginning reader in their pages.

Once you experience breakthrough and get an article accepted with a children's magazine, contact your editor and pitch three to five more ideas for other potential manuscripts you have not yet written. Try to land assignments to write future articles.

Pitching ideas to magazines is slightly different than to books. Why? Book publishers are working within the lengthy time frame it takes to publish a book. You can study their catalog and look for series to plug into. The magazine market works in a totally different time frame. They're changing all the time. They're working months in advance. Pitching ideas to magazine publishers is an essential way to get your foot in the door because you may spend several months writing an article for them and polishing it to perfection only to send it in and they have changed their format slightly and aren't even featuring pieces like that any more. Your writing might be fine, but they changed.

I have known writers who submit and submit completed manuscripts to a magazine publisher and always get rejected. But when they start pitching ideas, the editor is interested and asks for more. Learn to pitch ideas to magazine editors, too. If an idea catches her eye, the editor will automatically feel an investment now. Even if your eventual submitted manuscript is not up to the quality they want, the editor will probably work with you to bring it up to her standards.

There are different kinds of pitches I like to make for magazines. I call one the Title Pitch. You can just list three to five different titles that go along with titles they've recently published. You don't need anything more than that because they know what your article idea is just from the title.

Another pitch I like to make for magazines is what I call the One Sentence Pitch. This works well if the title of your projected manuscript fits into a series but the editor might not know what the topic is about. In this case, list the title and include a one-sentence description of what the topic will be about.

The other pitch I like to make for magazines is one I call the Paragraph Pitch. Sometimes you need to flesh out your idea a little bit so the editor can grasp your concept. Include a short paragraph description of each of your potential ideas.

Some magazines often offer an "on spec" assignment if they like one or more of the ideas you pitched to them. This is okay. This means that if they don't like your completed manuscript, they don't have to offer you a contract. I've found, though, that because magazine editors have an investment in your idea at this point, they'll usually work with you to revise the manuscript until it's what they want. I often have to revise my magazine stories and articles after I submit them to fine-tune them even more closely to the editor's needs. It's just part of the process. This is still much better than just getting an automatic rejection letter because you didn't first pitch your idea to an editor.

Don't be afraid to pitch ideas to magazine editors for features with a unique angle such as a beginning reader element. I get comments from magazine editors who say they appreciate my fresh, new ideas. These editors are the same editors who contact me and ask me to generate ideas for brand new features when they want to update their magazine and revitalize its format with fresh, new kid-appeal.

One of the most common beginning readers format many children's magazines feature is the much-loved rebus. To learn how to write a rebus, continue on to the next section.

Beginner's Tip

Aim high and aim low—both at the same time—to see if you can score a hit. Write a beginning reader for a high-paying, highly competitive magazine and also write a different one for a small magazine that only pays in copies. (Find these listed in writer's market guides.) Submit to both and see if you get one—or both!—accepted.

Professional Track

Target magazines whose readership would be interested in your published book. Even if they're small and can't pay cash for your beginning reader story or filler, even small magazines usually have a readership numbering 10,000 subscriptions or more. This is great exposure and publicity for your book. Be sure to include in your byline, or tag after your story, "-written by (your name), author of (title of your book)."

Strengthen Your Writing Muscles

Find a story, article, or filler in the magazine you are targeting. Rewrite the published story as a beginning reader. Use the *Children's Writer's Word Book* as a guide. Even if you are reworking a puzzle, you can rewrite it with grade-level vocabulary words and instructions written so that it's geared for that specific readability level.

6.2 Writing a Rebus

Did you ever read a rebus when you were a child? If you did, you remember how much fun it was! The little word pictures inserted in place of text throughout the story added interest and excitement. The repetition built up the anticipation for the surprise ending. And when the end did come, you felt very, very satisfied. That's what a rebus is designed to accomplish, and you can experience the thrill of writing your own.

A rebus is a story that substitutes pictures for some of the words. It is written with the same goal of every beginning reader—to build confidence in reading fluency. Tiny illustrations are scattered throughout the text, most replacing concrete nouns such as *flower, car,* and *dog*. These picture words help young readers decode the rest of the text by offering clues for what the story is all about.

A rebus contains one single focus and has a punch line at the end. A retold folk tale, fairy tale, or nursery rhyme can work well as a rebus. If a rebus is a story, it has one simple plot with a beginning, middle, and end. If it's a poem, it can list ingredients all tied together under one topic and then feature a satisfying conclusion. If it's nonfiction, it can list step-by-step instructions for how to make something.

The ending is key in a rebus. It's a surprise. It's a twist. It's the solution to the mystery. It's a finished craft. It's a conclusion to the events leading up to it. And it's always very, very satisfying.

Word counts vary for a rebus. If you're writing a rebus for the magazine market, many magazines prefer between 75-125 words with some open to a longer rebus of up to 200 words. Online publishers of rebus stories may have their standard word counts as well. If you're writing a rebus for a stand-alone beginning reader book or a collection of reproducible rebus stories in a teacher's book for the educational market, there might be more flexibility regarding word count. If a publisher's submission guidelines clarify their preferred word count for a rebus, keep yours within that limit. In general, however, a rebus is short.

Words that can easily be illustrated with a picture form the backbone of a rebus. Concrete nouns such as *ear*, *house,* and *pencil* work best. Some publishers put just the picture in the final rebus, but some put the picture and the word next to it.

When I type my rebus manuscript, I usually put these picture words in [brackets] because anything inside [brackets] designates that it is art or is for the editor's eyes and is not part of the final text itself. Some publishers may state in their guidelines that authors should highlight or underline these picture words, but when there are no directions given, I prefer typing these words in [brackets] to conform to standard editing marks used by most editors regarding art directions. Here is a sample of the manuscript for a rebus I wrote. It was published in the March 2003 issue of *Clubhouse Jr.* Note how I typed the picture words inside [brackets].

It's Almost Here!

[Duck] counted three [eggs] in her nest. "It's almost here!" [Duck] said with a quack.

[Bird] saw the new [leaves] on the trees. "It's almost here!" [Bird] said with a tweet.

[Dog] lay in the hot yellow [sun]. "It's almost here!" [Dog] said with a ruff.

[Cow] smelled the pretty pink [tulips]. "It's almost here!" [Cow] said with a moo.

[Pig] lay down in the warm [mud]. "It's almost here!" [Pig] said with an oink.

[Sheep] munched on tasty green [grass]. "It's almost here!" [Sheep] said with a baa.

[Cat] snuggled down close to her four new [kittens]. "It's almost here!"

[Cat] said with a purr.

[Hannah] went to the [barn]. She counted three [eggs] in the nest. She looked at the new [leaves] on the trees. She felt the warm [sun] on her back. She smelled the pretty pink [tulips]. [Hannah] walked by the [mud] and skipped over the green [grass]. She knelt down and stroked the four new [kittens]. "It's here!" [Hannah] said with a grin. "Spring has arrived!"

To gather ideas for a rebus, I created a file folder to collect samples of published rebus stories. I went to the library, grabbed stacks of magazines, and photocopied as many rebus stories as I could find. (A note about photocopying is that when I checked at my local university library they informed me that their patrons are permitted to photocopy any item in their entire collection, as long as it is for research purposes and not for sale.) Then I read through those sample rebus stories again and again, especially noting my favorites and examining the format and pizzazz factor of the ones I chose as the best of the bunch.

Different publishers prefer different types of rebus stories. For instance, some prefer stories while others are open to poems or nonfiction such as instructions on how to make a simple craft. Some prefer repetition of the picture words several times within the story, while others do not require this as long as the picture words are used effectively to tell the story. Here is an example of a rebus I wrote incorporating repetition. It is based on the folk tale of the *Little Red Hen.*

The Farmer and the Corn
"Who will help me plant this [corn]?" asked the [farmer].
"Not I!" quacked Mama [Duck] sitting on her [eggs].

"Not I!" clucked Mama [Hen] sitting on her [eggs].

"Who will help me hoe this [corn]?" asked the [farmer].

"Not I!" quacked Mama [Duck] sitting on her [eggs].

"Not I!" clucked Mama [Hen] sitting on her [eggs].

"Who will help me pick this [corn]?" asked the [farmer].

"Not I!" quacked Mama [Duck] sitting on her [eggs].

"Not I!" clucked Mama [Hen] sitting on her [eggs].

"Who will help me eat this [corn]?" asked the [farmer].

"We will!" quacked the baby [ducklings] and Mama [Duck].

"We will!" clucked the baby [chicks] and Mama [Hen].

So they all ate the [corn] together. Yum!

Before you begin writing a rebus, first choose a publisher to target. Read their guidelines for submitting rebus stories. This will help you determine the exact parameters they want to see. Then study rebus stories your target publisher already published to grasp a familiarity of the style, voice, and overall presentation they prefer.

Here is an example of a poem I wrote that was published in the November 2005 issue of *Clubhouse Jr.* Even though this format may not have caught the eye of an editor in a different magazine, it was a perfect fit for this one. *Clubhouse Jr.* sometimes features poems and sometimes features rebus stories. This one turned out to be a combination of both. Each picture word appears only once.

Thank You, God

[One] yellow [sun] to start out my days.

[Two] happy [lips] to sing out your praise.

[Three] leaves on a [clover], just like Your name:

Father, Son, Spirit—One and the same.

[Four] wheels on our [car] to turn left and turn right.

[Five] shiny points on each [star] late at night.

[Six] legs on a [ladybug] tickling my [nose]

when I bend down to smell a pretty pink [rose].

[Seven] days in the week for You and for me.

[Eight] arms on an [octopus] swimming at sea.

[Nine] [planets] that orbit the sun out in space.

You put every one in its very own place.

[Ten] fingers folded while on bended knees.

I thank You, God, for all of these!

As with beginning readers written for the earliest reading levels, you do not need to describe the setting, develop complex characters, or write complicated plots when you are writing a rebus. You do not even need to include an introduction in a rebus. A well-crafted rebus story starts right in the middle of the problem, involves action, and heads straight to the punch line at the end.

Most rebus stories target beginning readers ages four to seven, or pre-kindergarten through second grade. Unlike a beginning reader that has limited vocabulary, however, a rebus can use select vocabulary words from a much more advanced level if they can be illustrated with simple pictures. For instance, a rebus can contain the words *binoculars, mattress,* and *medal,* which are listed as sixth grade words in the *Children's Writer's Word Book.* This is because these are concrete nouns that can easily and clearly be shown in a picture instead of the word.

Rebus stories are delightful reading adventures for the very young. They're also great exercises for us to practice learning how to write beginning readers. On top of this, they're lots of fun to write. To learn how to write another form of beginning reader, continue on to the next section about writing plays for Readers Theatre.

Beginner's Tip

If you submit a rebus and it gets rejected, don't give up. Getting one rejection doesn't mean you weren't meant to write rebus stories. Have fun writing these sparkling gems in the world of beginning readers. Recycle published ones or post unpublished ones on your blog as free downloads for kids and teachers. Grab free clipart, plug cute graphics in place, enlarge the font size, save as easily-downloadable portable document files (PDF files), and post to your blog.

Professional Track

There are limited resources for learning how to write a rebus. After you have a few published rebus stories to your credit, create a how-to-write resource based on your own tips, strategies, and writing samples. Post this on your site to generate traffic to your blog or Website from writers who are searching online for information about writing a rebus.

Strengthen Your Writing Muscles

Look up children's jokes in online collections or in a children's book. Rewrite a favorite children's joke as a rebus. Because jokes are short and have a punch line at the end, they make great possibilities for using to practice writing rebus stories. Be sure to choose a joke that has a number of concrete nouns to designate as the picture words.

6.3 Readers Theatre

Beginning readers come to life when children perform them as read-aloud scripts. Teachers, students, parents, and kids can all experience the thrill of the stage with beginning readers written as Readers Theatre plays. As a writer of Readers Theatre plays, you can experience this same thrill from the ground up, creating a cast of memorable characters and scripting exciting dialogue that sparks energy like lightning bolts through the hearts of cast and audience alike. Readers Theatre is an exciting world. You can be a part of it!

I've written a number of Readers Theatre plays for leveled readers in kindergarten on up through eighth grade. Most of these are in books of reproducible mini-plays with Scholastic Teaching Resources and Readers Theatre books for Libraries Unlimited, but a few can be found tucked in by themselves between the pages of other books I've written.

What exactly is Readers Theatre? First of all, you'll see it spelled a variety of ways: *Readers Theatre* or *Reader's Theater* or any combination of the two. Each publisher chooses its own spelling. Personally, I prefer the spelling my publisher, Libraries Unlimited, uses with no apostrophe (it's easier to spell), and I feel that *–re* in Theatre adds a hint of British English and thus Shakespearean feel to the term.

In essence, Readers Theatre is a tool to help children develop strong oral reading skills and build confidence in reading fluency, or the speed and ease at which they read. The emphasis is not on "theatre" as much as it is on "readers." In other words, the goal of a Readers Theatre play is not to memorize the script and act out the play. Instead, the goal is to keep students reading the script from practice to performance so that they build stronger reading skills. In general, Readers Theatre plays are intended for the educational market because teachers are the main target audience who purchase and use Readers Theatre plays.

Characters are important and how you assign the parts, as a writer, is key. There is a purpose to the number of characters in each play. Some plays have few parts with only five or six characters. Teachers can assign these plays to small groups. Or, they can divide their large class into five groups and have each group read one part in unison.

Some plays have more characters with up to 15 or 20 roles. Teachers with a small class can assign one child several parts so he has the opportunity to read at various points throughout the play. Or, teachers with a large class can use plays with lots of characters and involve the entire group of students at once.

In most plays, a balance of speaking parts is helpful with most characters having about the same amount of lines. However, there can be major characters in a play with each of these characters reading longer portions of text than the minor characters. In general, though, I try not to create passages that are too lengthy for any single character. If I find that one of my characters has too much to say, I try to split that part into two characters such as two announcers or two narrators.

I like to include in most of the plays I write at least one open-ended group of characters. For instance, I'll include a group of sailors, children, or newspaper reporters in a play. This gives teachers the option of having one child read that part or assigning that part to a large group. They can therefore use these plays with a small group or with their entire class, no matter how many students they have. As an example, here is a portion of text from the play, "Detective Smart, Private Eye." It includes an open-ended group of characters (penguins) and it's from the book my husband Jeff and I wrote together for Libraries Unlimited for fourth through eight grade students, *Hello Hi-Lo: Readers Theatre Math.*

Detective:

I'm hard on the trail of the thief. I'm here at the South Pole looking for Max the Penguin. He's no ordinary thief. He's known for hanging out with a rough crowd down here at the bottom of the world. His favorite place is in the Valley of the Penguins. It's 3,516 feet below sea level.

Penguins:

Who are you? And what are you doing down here? Nobody travels to this place unless they have some negative business.

Detective:

I'm Detective Smart, Private Eye. Here's my card.

Penguins:

So we see your card. What's your business? You better have a valid excuse for being here.

Detective:

I'm on the lookout for Max. Have you seen him?

Penguins:

Max hasn't been in these parts for months. They say he got in a bad deal with a seal. Or maybe it was a walrus. You get the picture. They ran him out of town.

Detective:

You're positive he hasn't been here where the temperatures are as negative as 94 degrees below zero? It's worth 10 grand to anyone who can give me a clue of absolute value.

Penguins:
Keep your money. We haven't seen him. Now get lost before we make you get lost.

There are different kinds of Readers Theatre plays. Some are nonfiction. Some are fiction. Some are humorous and silly. Basically, any genre can work as a Readers Theatre play as long as you can format the text into a read-aloud script. When Jeff and I wrote our two books of Readers Theatre plays for middle grade students, we tried to include a variety of genre to give teachers as much opportunity as possible to utilize these plays throughout the school year and in a variety of settings.

For nonfiction, sometimes it's nice to create a more informational script with a more formal tone. This can appeal to older students who need to strengthen reading skills but don't want to feel babyish. As an example, here is a portion of text from a play in the book Jeff and I wrote together for Libraries Unlimited, *Readers Theatre for African American History*. This script is basically paraphrasing an important document in history, the Preamble and Articles of the Free African Society, founded in 1787 by Richard Allen and Absalom Jones. In essence, we created a cast of the eight founding members of the society and had the characters read through this important document in a conversational tone as if they were talking with each other instead of actually reading the document. A narrator introduced the background and setting of the script. Here's the excerpt from "Richard Allen and the Free African Society."

Richard Allen:
This is our first general meeting. Let's have a discussion about the rules and guidelines for our society. We, the free Africans and our families, of the City

of Philadelphia, in the State of Pennsylvania, or elsewhere, should all agree on these guidelines.

Samuel Baston:
Without money to support our efforts, we will not be able to accomplish much good. It is reasonable for each one of us to agree to pay one shilling in silver Pennsylvania currency each month.

For variety in that same book, *Readers Theatre for African American History*, we created an entirely fictional cast of characters who experienced an event in history, the emancipation of African Americans in Texas after the Civil War was over, now celebrated as the holiday Juneteenth. For plays of historical fiction and fiction in general, it helps to incorporate the same techniques found in all fiction: memorable characters and a strong story arc with a clearly defined beginning, middle, and end. The difference between fiction in a beginning reader story and writing fiction for a Readers Theatre play, however, is that the setting is explained by the narrator as part of the script or even sometimes within the characters' own lines. And, as with all Readers Theatre, each character's dialogue *becomes* the story. In the following example, the narrator had already explained to the audience that the scene opens with a group of slaves working in the fields near Galveston, Texas. Here is the excerpt from "Juneteenth: A Historic Day."

Felix:
The soldiers! They're coming!

Prince:
What soldiers?

Felix:

The Union soldiers of the United States of America. They're riding into Galveston.

Cesar:

What difference does that make? Us folks don't have anything to do with soldiers.

Felix:

These soldiers are different. Talk in Galveston says that these soldiers bring freedom.

As you're preparing to write Readers Theatre plays of your own, it helps to consider which vehicle will work best to convey the information you want to present. This is true both for fiction and nonfiction. In other words, learn to ask yourself, "What format and which characters and what voice or theme will work best to present this story or concept to students in the most effective way?"

For example, in my K-2 book (kindergarten through second grade) *15 Easy-to-Read Nursery Rhyme Mini-Book Plays* with Scholastic Teaching Resources, I chose the theme and plot of a racecar racing around the clock to be based on the nursery rhyme, Hickory Dickory Dock. In my Readers Theatre play, "Race Around the Clock With Hickory Dickory Dock," there is an announcer who announces the Mouse Town Car Races and a crowd of mice to cheer Hickory, the mouse driving the racecar, on her race. Even the clock becomes a character when it strikes one and says, "Bong!" This allows the kids who are at the lowest reading level to have an important part in their classroom play. Here is a portion of the text (used by permission of Scholastic Inc.).

Announcer:
She's off!

Hickory:
Zoom! Zoom! Zoom!

Announcer:
There she goes
Up the clock!
Look at that speed!

Hickory:
Zoom! Zoom! Zoom!

Clock:
BONG!

Your writing will benefit if you look for opportunities for fresh and new formats to use with Readers Theatre plays. For instance, as I was considering which voice and format and cast of characters to use to explain a historic event in the middle ages in Jeff's and my book *Readers Theatre for African American History*, I decided to create a cast of three griots, or storytellers, to share the story with an audience of children. I chose this vehicle because in actuality, oral history passed on to new generations by griots is a rich part of African culture. In other words, the method I chose to present the play actually enhanced the story experience as well as the topic itself. Here is a portion of the text from "Abubakari and the Empire of Mali."

Griot 1:

Come everyone! Gather around us today.

Come hear our stories. We have much to say.

Griot 2:

Our fathers' words, we believe are true.

We want to tell their words to you.

Griot 3:

Our history is a glorious one!

Of scholars, riches, and battles won.

Children:

Tell us what happened so long ago.

Tell us, wise ones, for we want to know.

As with all beginning readers, the best way to learn more about the preferences each publisher has for the Readers Theatre plays they publish is to study their product line. Familiarize yourself with your target publisher's product line as well as samples of their Readers Theatre text.

Some publishers provide detailed guidelines on how to type a manuscript for submission, but if they don't, use the samples I provided in this section as a guide. Type the character's name and follow it by a colon. Go to the next line and start typing the dialogue. Double space your text throughout and use a standard font such as Times New Roman 12. There is no need for bold or all caps in most manuscript submissions. Those details are added by the publisher.

Since Readers Theatre plays are mostly published for the educational market, many books include a section for teachers on activities or suggestions for incorporating Readers Theatre effectively into the classroom. If you have never worked with students in this capacity, fill in the gap by researching other Readers Theatre books to discover strategies and tips you can offer in your own book. This will probably include suggestions for staging and acting, using costumes or props, and effective reading strategies to help struggling readers build reading fluency while using the Readers Theatre scripts.

Writing Readers Theatre plays is a rich opportunity to get published in the leveled readers market. To learn about writing for English Language Learners as part of the leveled readers market as well, read the next section.

Beginner's Tip

Perform a Readers Theatre script with your writers group or your own kids to see how the logistics work. Note issues such as the timing, the staging, and the actual performance. Use this experience to help you write.

Professional Track

Develop one scene from your published book into a Readers Theatre script. Keep this short and use it as a blurb to e-mail schools, teachers, and librarians as a "teaser" to promote your current book.

Strengthen Your Writing Muscles

Adapt a beginning reader book from the trade picture book market into a Readers Theatre play. Using the samples in this section from my books as a guide, type it out as a Readers Theatre script. Omit dialog tags such as *she said* or *he exclaimed*, incorporate setting into the dialogue, and omit unnecessary narrative. Perform the play with writer friends or family when finished.

6.4 English Language Learners

If you like the idea of writing for the beginning readers and chapter books market, consider writing material for students who are learning English. This is commonly known as the ELL Market (English Language Learners) and ESL Market (English as a Second Language) and ELD Market (English Language Development) and EFL Market (English as a Foreign language). This market uses leveled reading materials from elementary age up to and including adults. Private companies as well as international publishing houses publish instructional material for students and teachers to use. By exploring the different possibilities available, you can better determine if you have the qualifications, skills, and interest to write for this market.

If you already work as a teacher with ELL students, you know which leveled reading materials you like to use the most. Search online for the publishers' Websites of these materials and dig around until you find their author's guidelines. Sometimes these are hidden under "Contact us" or "About us." If you can't find submission guidelines on their Website, look for an e-mail address and send them an e-mail asking how someone can write and submit material for their product line.

If you don't know a lot about this market, start by exploring several of the main publishers' Websites. Teachers of English to Speakers of Other Languages, Inc., or TESOL, is a major publisher of material in this market.

Its Website is www.tesol.org. TESOL actively seeks new material and posts calls for manuscript submissions as the need arises. Explore their site, read their links to information for authors, and check in frequently to see what their current manuscript needs are.

The *ESL Magazine* is devoted to staying current with the latest information about teaching methods, educational materials, and international news concerning the English as a Second Language market. This is a rich resource to have if you want to write for this market. Its Website is www.eslmag.com.

The *ELT Journal* is another publication targeting educators who teach English as a second or foreign language. It covers the span from kindergarten to twelfth grade and includes college and adult students. Within the pages of this publication, you'll find many solid tips and strategies to use as a writer for this market, as well. Its Website is at http://eltj.oxfordjournals.org/.

Writing for the ELL market can be very similar to writing beginning readers for the educational market, especially for materials used with elementary-age students. However, in material geared to high school, college, and adult students, the writing experience is more similar to writing for Hi-Lo readers. (For more information on writing for this target audience, see *Chapter 13: Hi-Lo Readers*.) In other words, the level of information presented should be geared *high* and appeal to an older audience. It should cover topics such as current world news, history, or work-related issues. Genre can include adult-level mysteries, romance, science fiction, and nonfiction. However, the language skills and readability skills must target a *low* level because many of these older students and adults are starting from square one to learn English as a brand new language.

There are also different topics and skills leveled reading materials focus on for the ELL market. For instance, materials for reading and understanding idioms, figures of speech, and cultural nuances are needed at various reading levels. An understanding of the culture who will be using the material is also a huge plus when writing for this market.

Similar to the educational market, some ELL publishers want authors to provide teacher's tips or supplemental activities along with leveled reading material. An excellent resource of 97 classroom-tested tips can be found in Dorit Sasson's e-book, *Yes! You Can Teach K-12 English Language Learners Successfully*. To order the e-book, visit Sasson's Website at www.newteacherresourcecenter.com.

As you're exploring the potential of writing for the ELL market, you might want to search for other opportunities to write leveled reading material. Read the next section to explore even more.

Beginner's Tip

Do you have a friend whose second language is English? Ask him what his favorite genre is to read as an adult. Then ask him what he struggled with the most as he was learning to read English. Next pitch an idea to a publisher in the ELL and ESL market for a leveled reader story or article that addresses the language skills your friend mentioned within the format of his favorite genre.

Professional Track

Volunteer to help with the ESL or ELL programs at your community center or local library. Rewrite portions of your published articles and books as leveled readers to use for teaching or supplementary material. This gives you practical experience working with this market as well a great exposure.

Strengthen Your Writing Muscles

Write an article about a current world news topic at a third grade readability level for adults to read. Keep in mind that you are writing for an adult audience and not a child who is in third grade.

6.5 Other Opportunities

Beginning readers can be found everywhere, it seems. The world is rich with opportunity for writers to produce leveled reading material, especially when you learn how to look for it. Each generation has its own unique challenges for teaching children how to read. New material is constantly being created to help meet this need for parents or teachers with children in public or private schools, for special education, and for home schooling families. You can explore and tap into this vast and wide-open market, building up published credits and gaining valuable experience as you go.

There are numerous online resources that offer leveled reading material. Some sites offer printable books such as Enchanted Learning at www.enchantedlearning.com. Other sites offer interactive games and e-books for children to use online such as Starfall at www.Starfall.com whose motto announces, "Where children have fun learning to read!" The Website, Reading A-Z at www.readinga-z.com/ offers leveled reading books that parents and teachers can download for a membership fee. Search for sites such as these by typing key words into the search engine such as: phonics, beginning readers, reading practice, and learning to read.

When you find an online site that features leveled reading material, search for information on the site about author's or writer's guidelines. Because a significant number of these sites aren't maintained by traditional publishers, you may not find specific, clear guidelines about submitting potential material to them. Don't be discouraged. If a site catches your eye, look for an e-mail or a phone number to initiate contact (usually under the

"Contact Us" tab). Contact them and explain that you are a freelance writer and like the materials they offer on their site. Ask if they might be interested in having you write new material for them to use.

Sometimes private schools such as Christian schools decide to publish their own line of beginning readers and leveled reader curriculum. For instance, some of my writer friends and critique group buddies have written hundreds of beginning reader stories for a curriculum published by a local Christian school. One of my friends first heard about this opportunity when they advertised in a local Christian newspaper, and she spread the news that the school was looking for writers. The school hired a reading specialist who provided word lists for each level. We were assigned themes, word counts, and specific instructions regarding how to format each story for publication in books as well as oral reading classroom exercises. We had a simple contract to sign that gave all rights to the school and explained how we would be paid.

Teacher supply stores and other stores occasionally publish their own product line of beginning readers. Sometimes venues such as these advertise or put out a call for needed writers at online job listings. To tap into freelance opportunities such as these, subscribe to free e-mail job-posting services and read them regularly. You can find these services by searching for key words such as: freelance writers wanted, hiring freelance writers, writers needed, or children's writers needed. Because this type of material is usually based on a store's own product lines and their in-house ideas, these projects are often work-for-hire but may also pay very well. Work-for-hire usually means that they are paying a flat fee or one-time payment and keep the rights to all the material that is written.

Many local newspapers, community magazines, and church newsletters have a children's page. If you want to write beginning readers for one of these opportunities, contact them and introduce yourself as a freelance writer. Ask if they would be interested in having you write beginning readers for their children's page. If they are unfamiliar with what a beginning reader is or don't know which reading level your manuscript should target, ask them what age their children's page targets. Then suggest writing stories, puzzles, or activities written at that target age's reading level so the children themselves can read that portion of the page without needing a parent to read it to them.

Because a significant number of these venues have not worked with a freelance writer before, be sure to have some sort of contract drawn up and signed by both parties that specifies the rights regarding the material you're writing and also if there is any payment involved. Typically, because the writer is producing material to fit into a product line developed by the venue and did not create the initial ideas, the rights to all material belong to the venue, especially if there is payment involved. However, some no-pay venues such as a church newsletter or community newspaper usually allow the rights to remain with the writer and might not even have a contract to sign.

I have written for no-pay and low-pay opportunities such as these for many years all throughout my career. Often, my manuscripts become the property of the place I'm working for. Because I'm writing for this market to gain actual writing experience and build up my published credits, I am fine with this arrangement and thankful for the experience I gain working frequently with editors and regularly seeing my work accepted for publication. I save other writing projects for the goals of earning income and writing for personal fulfillment.

Beginner's Tip

Writing for no-pay/low pay opportunities can be like taking a college course…for free! Editors are more open to working with beginning writers and will often provide detailed instruction and personal feedback.

Professional Track

Contact a local private school and introduce yourself as a published author. Ask if they would like you to help develop the school's very own curriculum for beginning readers. Private schools, especially those affiliated with a specific organization, are ripe opportunities for developing an entire leveled reading program that teaches their unique values to their students. There are also Christian schools that choose curriculum from publishers such as A Beka Book and BJU Press who are also sometimes interested in developing their own readers.

Strengthen Your Writing Muscles

Find an interactive e-book or online game for early elementary children such as the ones available on www.Starfall.com. Without worrying about the "interactive computerized" element, write text for a brand new interactive game or e-book.

PART III

Writing

Beginning Readers

and

Chapter Books

Chapter 7

WRITING STRATEGIES FOR BEGINNING READERS AND CHAPTER BOOKS

7.1 Fresh and Original

We all have our favorite stories. They're the ones that tug on our heartstrings. They bring a smile to our face. These are the books we cherish as some of our dearest friends. Whether it is the thrill of excitement, a tickle of delight, the joy of discovery, or the security of an imaginary world, there is a special something about each of these stories. They stand head and shoulders above the rest. These are the types of stories you want to learn how to write. These are the kinds of manuscripts you want to write in the beginning readers and chapter books market. You can make it your goal to learn how as you work toward making your dreams come true.

The first step is to create stories that are fresh and original. As with all children's books, magazine stories, and for most writing in general, editors love manuscripts that are "fresh and original." If you've attended writers' conferences, you've probably heard this phrase before, yet you might wonder just exactly what does it mean?

To give a concrete example of what it means to write something that is fresh and original, Suzanne Lieurance, successful children's author and writing coach for Working Writer's Club (www.workingwritersclub.com) shared an experience. When the publisher of the Rookie Readers series held an open call for submissions, Suzanne submitted a manuscript that caught the editor's eye. The editor said that one of the reasons they selected Suzanne's manuscript out of over 900 submissions received was because she had chosen a topic they didn't see in any of the other manuscripts—learning to tie your shoes. They had dozens of submissions about loose teeth and losing a tooth, but none about shoelaces. It was a fresh and original idea, yet very appropriate for children who are just beginning to read. Suzanne's book *Shoelaces* was published as a Rookie Readers book for the beginning readers market.

One way to write a fresh and original manuscript is to select an age-appropriate universal childhood theme and present it in such a way that has not yet been published in many children's books or periodicals. To help brainstorm ideas that are fresh and original, I like to start by creating a list of universal childhood themes or experiences. I keep this list handy in my own personal reference book that I've created called *A Zillion Zany Zingers: Nancy's Dictionary of Wow Words, Fun Phrases, and Tips to Tickle Young Readers!* This is a 3-ring notebook that I fill with all sorts of fun lists to use, especially during brainstorming sessions and for a quick reference of ideas when I'm stuck writing a certain passage.

In this notebook I include a section of potential words that work great as part of a title to grab young readers and hook them so they will pick up my book. This list includes words such as *spy, frozen*, and *search*. I have a list of fun words I've made up or seen such as *daycation, staycation,* and *awaycation*. There's a list of cute sayings such as "itsy bitsy" and "yippee skippy" and "going off like a frog in a sock" which in Australia means something's really going crazy. I include a dictionary of fun words in my notebook such as *blah, e-e-ek,* and *ooze*. I write down a list of great action phrases such as *tore down the hall* and *dropped down on all fours*. I also have a list of universal childhood themes.

I like to add new things to my notebook, *A Zillion Zany Zingers*, and use it to help brainstorm fresh and original ideas. You can make your very own personal reference notebook, too. It's fun! To get you started, here is a list of universal childhood themes just right for a beginning readers audience of children in early elementary school. You can add to this list by observing children, or by searching through series of picture books, beginning readers, or chapter books with characters such as Frog and Toad by Arnold Lobel; Arthur by Marc Brown; Franklin the turtle by Paulette Bourgeois; and the Berenstain Bears by Stan, Jan, and Mike Berenstain. Just write down many of these book titles in your notebook and you'll have a list of universal childhood themes.

List of Universal Childhood Themes

Making a new friend

Having a bad day

Experiencing a thunderstorm

Being messy

Holidays

Going to the hospital

Fear of the dark

Being too bossy

Bullies

First day of school

Family

A new baby sister or brother

Learning to ride a bike

Skating

Saying "I love you"

Loosing a tooth

Playing in a sport

Finding something

Losing something

Keeping something in a pocket

Learning to whistle

Playing with bubbles

Learning to play an instrument

Neighborhood and community

Being slow

Pets

Keeping a diary

Secrets
Organizing a club
Playing games
Bedtime
School days
Grandparents
Going on a trip

As you look over your list of universal childhood themes, compare it to the book catalog of your target publisher or past issues of your target magazine. If your target publisher does not have a story about losing a tooth, they will probably want a manuscript on this topic for their own product list or magazine. However, they will want it to be a fresh and original idea.

Or as in Suzanne Lieurance's case with *Shoelaces*, a publisher might want an idea that hasn't been published very much in children's books before. To see if the universal theme you'd like to write about has been overused in children's books, go to Amazon.com and type the key word or phrase in the search field. Compare the results of several different key words or phrases. For instance, compare the number of children's books listed about "new baby" to the number of books listed about "shoelaces." Quite a difference isn't there?

To help brainstorm a fresh and original idea, first choose one of the universal childhood themes you have on your list. Then list three to five potential ideas for each of the following situations:

1. Tell a story about this universal childhood theme that takes place in an exotic setting.
2. Tell a story about this universal childhood theme that features a fun cast

of unique characters.

3. Tell a story about this universal childhood theme that takes place in a unique era of history.

4. Tell a story about this universal childhood theme that is based on an historical event or person.

5. Tell a story about this universal childhood theme as a retelling of a folktale, fairy tale, or nursery rhyme.

As an example, let's take a universal childhood theme of returning a book on time to the library and plug it into each of these five situations:

1. Exotic setting:
Idea A: A boy in Alaska grabs his library book, rides his dogsled through the snow, gets chased by a bear, and makes it to the library just as it's closing time!

Idea B: A girl who lives on Mars is flying in her space ship to return her 3-D interactive talking book to the library on Saturn, but is chased by an alien and has to take a detour around Jupiter to escape.

2. Fun cast of unique characters:
Idea A: A dog is going to obedience school and has to fetch his library book and bring it back to the library on time.

Idea B: A school of fish visit an under-the-sea library but can't return their library books because a shark is swimming nearby.

3. Unique era of history:
Idea A: A young knight must return the ancient manuscript he borrowed from the shelves of his tutor before the tutor finds out or the knight will not

be allowed to be in the next jousting tournament.

Idea B: A girl borrows a library book but then has to leave with her parents in a wagon train to head west on the Oregon Trail. She realizes on the journey that she still has the book, so starts a library in her new town and donates it as the first book.

4. Historical event or person:

Idea A: A girl borrows a book from a neighbor's personal library and on her way back to return it walks past Independence Hall when the Declaration of Independence is being read aloud for the very first time.

Idea B: Young Abe Lincoln borrowed a law book and has to walk ten miles barefoot to return it.

5. Folk tale, fairy tale, or nursery rhyme:

Idea A: Goldilocks finds an overdue library book in the three bears' house and falls asleep reading it in bed. Little Bear comes back and finds her so she promises to return it for him if she can come visit again.

Idea B: Jack takes a book from the Giant's castle, but when he gets home he realizes it's a library book so he has to climb back up the beanstalk and find the library to return it on time.

Do you see how taking a universal childhood theme and brainstorming ideas about that topic for these five different situations can help you think of fresh and original ideas? When I wrote beginning readers for a local Christian school curriculum, I was given assignments to write over 100 stories, each with a different theme. As I brainstormed fresh and original ideas for each story and reviewed my word lists of selected vocabulary words for each reading level, I made lists of potential stories for each of those five situations we just discussed. Next I'd choose which idea I liked the best from my brainstorming list. Then I wrote the story.

You can brainstorm fresh and original ideas for beginning readers by brainstorming in this way. If you think of other situations to include with these five, add them to your list. Your stories will stand head and shoulders above the rest and you'll start hearing feedback from editors that they like your fresh and original approach to presenting universal childhood themes, or your unique way of handling an age-old topic.

Another step to take in order to learn how to write winning beginning readers and chapter books is to learn how to create characters with kid-appeal. Read more about creating winning characters in the following section.

Beginner's Tip

To discover how a certain universal childhood theme is handled when writing for children, read three to five children's books on that topic. Make it a practice to regularly gather and read books on the theme you're writing about. Each time you sit down to work on your manuscript, start your writing session by rereading several of these books. This will help your brain get in gear to write successfully about this same theme.

Professional Track

Have you written about universal childhood themes before and experienced published success? Consider specializing as a writer for one of these themes. Brainstorm fresh and original ideas for one universal childhood theme, and try to land contracts for several of your ideas. For instance, you can write a bedtime book with a cast of under-the-sea characters, a different one with a cast of African animals, and a completely different one with a cast of Arctic animals. Be sure not to write books that *compete* with each other, but write beginning readers stories that *complement* each other. You may have to reword a competing book clause in your contract that clarifies this. (I've done this several times on various contracts with different publishers and most are open to this.) The benefit of specializing is that when a customer purchases one of your books on a certain theme, they might end up buying your other books on the same theme, too! Publishers like this as well, if they can see an advantage for increased sales.

Strengthen Your Writing Muscles

Choose one beginning reader that is about a favorite universal childhood theme. Rewrite the story using the same characters, the same plot, and the exact same words. Just change the setting and place the story in an exotic location. Change only the words that need to be changed to make the story fit in its new setting. When finished, note how fresh and original the story feels just by incorporating one of these five brainstorming techniques described in this section.

7.2 Characters with Kid-Appeal

What makes the *Frog and Toad* chapter books so appealing to kids and adults alike? The characters themselves! Frog is an incurable optimist while Toad worries his way into our hearts. What made *The Cat in the Hat* an instant and successful classic? That zany character, the Cat in the Hat, himself. Characters with kid-appeal romp through the pages of our favorite beginning readers, tickle our funny bone, and bring a smile to our face. Using various techniques of the trade, you can learn how to create winning characters who star in the imaginary worlds you're creating in your own beginning readers manuscripts.

Usually, there is one main character in a beginning reader or chapter book. Sometimes two main characters interact, but the rest are in the background. If there is a group setting such as a classroom, a group of friends, or a family, focus on one character or at the most two. Young children like to identify with one strong main character, and introducing an entire cast of key characters in books children are struggling to read on their own can be too confusing.

It's important to note that characters in beginning readers aren't usually *described*. This is because most levels of beginning readers simply don't use much descriptive language to develop the setting, characters, or plot. Beginning readers incorporate lots of dialogue and high-interest action verbs even on up through the higher readability levels. Because of this, characters in beginning readers are seen and heard through the things they do and the words they say. The concrete and usually full-color illustrations accompanying the text give all the description a child needs in order to see what the characters look like.

Dialogue is a key ingredient in beginning readers and chapter books. Because it's easy for kids to get confused about who is saying what, dialogue tags are essential. *He said* or *she said* are simple dialogue tags, but serve their purpose effectively to help children learning to read and identify which character is speaking.

Because dialogue is such an important element of beginning readers, the *voice* of a character is the essential vehicle for developing his personality. His actions and reactions to everything and everyone in his world should always work together to support the dialogue he wants to say.

How can you determine your character's unique voice and one-of-a-kind personality? Start by creating a Top Secret Detective File about your main character. This keeps all your notes and information handy in one convenient spot while you're working on your manuscript.

To create the file, staple two manila file folders together so that the back of the first folder is stapled to the front of the second folder. Label the tab on the first file folder with your character's name. Label the tab on the second file folder with your character's name and "Notes."

Since we write for kids, we get to have lots of fun, so have some fun decorating the front of your folders. You can write *Top Secret* in big black letters to look like an official detective file. Or, you can glue on a picture that relates to your story.

On the inside top left of the first folder, glue a picture of your main character. Search the Internet, take a photograph of a niece or nephew, draw a picture, or cut out a portrait from a magazine. Taking the time to find a picture of what you envision your character to look like will help this character come alive to you. This is an important step in the process of creating a character kids will really, really want to read about. Just remember, however, that this picture is only for your own use during the writing process. The artist will create his own illustration of your character. However, sometimes, such as in the case of my Marshal Matt series of beginning readers, I have submitted a picture of the main character as a *suggestion*. Since Marshal Matt was based on my nephew, Matthew Hershberger, I sent in a picture of Matthew when I submitted the completed manuscript. Of course, I did *not* say that this was what I expected the main character to look like, but I did explain that I based him on my nephew. The illustrator, Larry Nolte, ended up drawing Marshal Matt to resemble my nephew, so that was a lot of fun.

On the inside left side of the first file folder, underneath the picture of your main character, create a Word Wall, or list of words, that relate to your main character. A Word Wall is a list of words, often posted on a bulletin board or wall, that teachers create in their classrooms. If a teacher is teaching about farm animals for instance, her Word Wall might have the words *sheep, cow, calf, pig, chicken*, and *horse* on it. Students use a Word Wall to help brainstorm ideas or look for theme-related words to use in the stories they write about that topic. As writers, we can use a Word Wall to help us brainstorm ideas as well as develop a character's voice.

Write down on your Word Wall a list of words or phrases that relate to your character. For instance, Dr. Seuss's Word Wall for *The Cat in the Hat* might have included words such as *zany, outrageous, hilarious, daring, silly, fun,* and *cleans up his messes.* There is no right or wrong regarding creating a Word Wall. Just write down any words or phrases that come to mind about your character as he is forming in your mind. Continue to add words to your Word Wall as you're working on the manuscript and other words or phrases pop into your head. Refer to this list often as you're writing the manuscript to brainstorm ideas and develop your character's unique voice.

On the right side of the inside of the first folder, staple a one-page interview that you use to ask questions to your character to discover more about him. Again, a lot of these details might not ever make it into your manuscript. But interviewing your character will help you create a unique personality with a strong voice that will come to life in your manuscript for beginning readers. Here is a sample interview you can use, but feel free to create your own:

INTERVIEW
Name:
Address:
Date/place of birth:
Family background:

Physical description

Hair Color:

Eyes:

Height:

Weight:

Favorites

Food:

Hobby:

Book:

Toy:

Best friend:

Quirks

Bad habits:

Personality flaws:

Enemy:

Unique traits:

Strengths:

In the second file folder of the Top Secret Detective File, store any notes, extra pictures, or other papers that you have collected about your character. It's nice to keep these for future reference if you ever need more ideas.

When I'm developing a character, I love to sit down and read my favorite beginning readers. As I read, I ask myself, "What appeals most to the child within me about each of these characters?" As I read, I make a list of the characteristics and personality traits that I like the best about each one.

If there are obvious traits that I really don't like, I list these as well, to avoid incorporating those traits unknowingly into my own character.

Armed with this fresh knowledge and these lists, I then create a Top Secret Detective File and try to develop my character's personality for my own beginning reader with a huge dose of kid appeal.

Creating and using Top Secret Detective Files will help you develop your own characters that young readers will love. Because each level of beginning readers and chapter books is aimed for a very specific target audience, however, there are subtle differences between the kinds of characters each level tends to feature. To learn more about specific character development for each different level of beginning readers and chapter books, refer to Chapters 8 through 13.

Creating great characters will really take your beginning readers and chapter books to the next level. Also, plot and setting are handled differently in this market than in other manuscripts such as picture books or middle grade novels. To learn more, read the following section.

Beginner's Tip

Create a Top Secret Detective File for one of your favorite characters in a beginning reader or chapter book. Use this as an example to help create files for your own characters.

Professional Track

Invite your editor or agent to brainstorm with you as you create a brand new character. I've found that sometimes editors or agents love to be part of this brainstorming process and really feel an investment in the character you're developing. Of course, you'd only want to do this with an editor or agent you have already established a great relationship with and who knows you'll respect her time constraints during the process.

Strengthen Your Writing Muscles

Write down answers to imaginary interviews of three kids you knew when you were a child. These can be schoolmates, relatives, or friends you used to have. Next, take the best, the funniest, the most unique, and the worst traits from each of these interviews and combine them into one brand new character. Write a beginning reader based on an actual childhood experience using this brand new character as the star.

7.3 Plot and Setting

Storytellers create a wonderful world tickling our senses and sparking our imagination. The art of telling a story seems to be born in some people and in others it's not. Whether you're a natural-born storyteller or not, you can incorporate simple techniques and strategies to help create stories with plots and settings that come alive to young readers in your beginning readers and chapter books.

First and foremost, a story with a plot has a beginning, a middle, and an end. This is referred to as the story arc, or arch, and can be visualized by thinking of the St. Louis Gateway Arch. The Arch starts at ground level, then rises up to the sky. At the top it curves back down toward the ground where it ends at ground level again. The plot of a story arc is very similar structure. The beginning of the plot is where the conflict begins. The middle of the plot is where there are attempts to solve the conflict. The end of the plot and thus the end of the story is where the conflict is resolved. The main difference between the St. Louis Gateway Arch and a story arc is that the top of the arc isn't in the middle. It's right before the end of the story where the tension has built up the most. Crafting a story with a structured plot and strong story arc is a very effective technique used by storytellers that you can use when you write for this market to produce a vibrant sense of story that will make your young readers feel very satisfied.

Beginning readers and chapter books use simple and very basic plot structures. Because these books are books children are attempting to read on their own, complex plot structures will be too confusing for them to figure out when most of their mental energies are being used to figure out how to read the words of the story.

Here are samples of simple plots you can use when you write beginning readers or chapter books. Note that each of these plots has a clearly defined beginning with a goal or conflict, a middle where an attempt is being made to reach the goal or solve the conflict, and a satisfying end with a resolution to the problem presented at the beginning:

Main character wants to sail across a lake for a picnic, rides in boat through unexpected storm and past rocks, and makes it to the other side of the lake for the picnic.

Main character wants to buy a new toy to give to new baby brother, looks through the toy store, and finds a special toy.

Main character decides to mail a letter to his friend, waits with friend for the mail to arrive, and then reads the letter together with his friend.

Main character is going to birthday party but lost the address, walks through the neighborhood but can't find the right house, then arrives at the right house in time for the birthday party.

Main character makes a mess helping to prepare for a holiday, makes even more messes helping to fix it, but then fixes mess so all looks nice when grandparents arrive.

As an example of a basic plot, here is an entire beginning reader story that I wrote as part of a series of reproducible mini-books for teachers to use in the PreK-1, or pre-kindergarten through first grade classroom. This is from the mini-book, "The Penguin" in my book with Scholastic Teaching Resources, *26 Read & Write Mini-Books: Beginning Sounds From A to Z* (used by permission of Scholastic Inc.):

The penguin took the path to a party at the pool.

To demonstrate the plot in this very simple one-sentence beginning reader story, here's a breakdown of the pages of the mini-book:

Cover: The Penguin

Page 1: The penguin took the path… (This is the story's *beginning.* The art on page 2 shows a penguin walking along a path. The simple "conflict" begins with the readers wondering why the penguin is walking along this path.)

Page 3: The penguin took the path to a party… (This is the story's *middle.* The art on page 4 shows several penguins walking along the path and the other penguins are wearing party hats. There is a sense that something is about to happen. The readers instinctively know that soon they will find out more about this party and then the conflict will be resolved.)

Page 5: The penguin took the path to a party at the pool. (This is the story's *end.* The art on page 6 show a group of penguins swimming in a pool with balloons and party hats. The readers feel satisfied because now the conflict is over. The penguin made it to the party and is having fun in the pool with his friends.)

As you can understand from this page-by-page breakdown, there was a lot going on in the art that was not expressed in the simple text. Both the plot and the setting were portrayed through the art and not through the words of the story. This is often the case with beginning readers for the youngest levels.

Plots are very simple in the earliest levels of beginning readers. As you advance up to higher reading levels such as books for advanced readers, however, you can create stories that have more complex plot structures. Because beginning readers are in essence a type of picture book (in the trade market, they are fully illustrated just like picture books) there are two main references I recommend that you explore as you're learning to create more complex plot structures in the more advanced levels of the beginning readers and chapter books market.

Eve Heidi Bine-Stock's book, *How to Write a Children's Picture Book, Volume I: Structure,* explains the plot structure classic picture books incorporate for young readers. Bine-Stock includes diagrams that map out the structure of favorite children's picture books. These are outstanding resources to help you develop your own plot structure in the manuscripts you write.

Anastasia Suen's book, *Picture Writing: A New Approach to Writing for Kids and Teens* contains storyboard visuals as well as instructions for creating your own plot structure for your children's books. Suen draws on the classic "tradition of threes" to develop plot. Exposition is identified as the introduction of the main character, the main problem, and the setting.

Problems are developed in three distinct parts as the story unfolds. Each of these parts has its own problem that the main character attempts to solve, but just makes worse. After these three sets of three smaller problems, the main character is forced to make a decision to solve the main problem introduced in the exposition and finally, the main problem is resolved.

Because beginning readers in the earliest levels don't usually describe setting in the text itself, it is a standard in the industry for writers to include very detailed art instructions in [brackets] in these manuscripts. When I wrote my manuscript for "The Penguin," not only did I include detailed art instructions inside brackets for the illustrator, but I also submitted a mock-up of the actual mini-book with stick figures and exact placement on each page of crucial elements of the story's setting. Both mock-ups, or dummies, of the setting as well as detailed art instructions within the manuscript are beneficial and often expected from authors who write for this market, especially in the lowest reading levels such as PreK-1 where text is at a bare minimum and context clues are provided through the art to help young readers decode the words on their own.

Even though as a writer you will not usually write text to describe the setting, the setting is still very crucial to the success of the beginning reader story. Don't ignore the ingredient of setting simply because you won't write about it in the text. Take time to create a real sense of place as you're developing the story by imagining the setting and fleshing out the details in your own mind. Jot down notes about key elements in the setting you think will add to the story. Even if you are not an artist, enjoy taking time to sketch the setting for your story so that it becomes real for you. Make black and white drawings or have fun using colored pencils or crayons. Add elements with kid-appeal to the setting such as the balloons and party hats I included in my art instructions for my very simple story, "The Penguin."

Along with the plot and the setting, the format and sentence structure incorporated into beginning readers and chapter books are often different from writing for other markets. Let's explore this together in the next section.

Beginner's Tip

A story arc that includes an element of surprise at the end adds special charm to beginning readers and chapter books. Young children—and editors!—love a surprise ending.

Professional Track

Reevaluate one of your beginning reader manuscripts that has been rejected and never found a home. Strengthen its story arc to give it a more clearly defined beginning, middle, and end. Add more elements to the setting that score big on kid-appeal (mostly through art instructions). Try submitting it again.

Strengthen Your Writing Muscles

Read ten beginning readers. Write down each manuscript's story arc: its beginning, middle, and end. Be sure to identify the problem, how the main character works through the problem, and how the problem is solved. Choose one of these story arcs and use it as the plot structure to write your own story with a new setting and a new cast of characters.

7.4 Format and Sentence Structure

Sentences are the building blocks of every story. In beginning readers and chapter books, careful attention is paid to the structure of sentences because young children are learning how to read the sentences on their own.

Different levels of beginning readers structure sentences differently, according to the ability of their target age. This variety of sentence structure affects the format of beginning readers and chapter books, especially in the earlier levels. By understanding the parameters publishers and educators expect to see in the various levels of beginning readers, as a writer you can better know how to craft your stories. This understanding will also give you the ability to experience a higher degree of success working in this market.

For starters, the appearance of the text and the methods used to present sentences to young readers on the written page are taken into account. The earliest beginning readers use larger font sizes and a lot of white space or empty space on each page. This affects the number of lines of text that can fit on each page. This in turn affects the number of characters—or letters, spaces, and punctuation marks—that can fit on each line. All of this is taken into consideration with the goal of making the appearance of the text, or format, in a beginning reader not feel overwhelming to a young child.

If younger children open a book and find small print covering whole pages of text, they will quickly put the book down and think it's too hard for them to read. Even if all the sentences are very short and the words are all simple grade-level vocabulary words, they will feel intimidated from the first glance at the book. Therefore, publishers make it their goal to produce books for the youngest readers that appear to be easy to read simply due to their format, or appearance of large font and lots of white space on each page. As the target age increases for each level of beginning reader, the text gets smaller, the sentence structure becomes more complex, and more text is printed on each page. To learn more about each level of beginning reader's parameters regarding sentence structure and format, read Chapters 8 through 13.

The easiest way to understand the overall differences in format and sentence structure is to look at several beginning reader books from the same series but from different levels within that series. Notice how the earliest levels such as Levels 1 and 2 use larger font than the more advanced levels such as Levels 3 and 4. Also note how the earlier levels use wider margins on both sides of the text than the more advanced levels do. There is also more space between each line of text in the earlier levels. This gives more white space which makes it "feel" easier for younger kids to tackle reading on their own.

Unlike middle grade novels for older readers, beginning readers usually do not indent the first line of paragraphs or dialogue. In other words, beginning readers often do not use proper paragraph formatting. In earlier levels and even on up to some more advanced levels, each short sentence can be on its own line. Also, incomplete sentences are usually avoided because beginning readers are all about teaching children how to read sentences and form complete thoughts. Here is an example of the difference in the format between a middle grade novel versus a beginning reader format:

Middle grade novel format:
    "Come with me to find the treasure!" I said.
    Jeff came with me. Dan came, too. Even Ben came along. But Sue did not come. We went to find the treasure.

Beginning reader format:
"Come with me to find the treasure!" I said.
Jeff came with me.
Dan came, too.
Even Ben came along.
But Sue did not come.
We went to find the treasure.

The format of the text is also different between picture books and beginning readers. Unlike a picture book, which features running text of the sentences from left to right on the page, text in the earliest beginning readers can be broken up into chunks on different lines. In other words, instead of having entire sentences run horizontally from left to right, beginning readers especially in the lower levels, divide sentences into vertical chunks so that one sentence might cover four lines of text. This is done to help younger children gain confidence reading the words in a sentence, one chunk at a time.

Here is an example to illustrate how the sentences might appear on the actual page format or layout in a picture book versus a beginning reader:

Picture book format:
It is Monday, and the party is today. Tim brings balloons. Tina brings a gift and a card.

Beginning reader format:
It is Monday,
and the party is today.
Tim brings balloons.
Tina brings a gift
and a card.

How do these variances in format affect you as a writer? For one thing, as you write the actual beginning reader manuscript, it is permissible and sometimes even required for the author not to use paragraph formatting and to break sentences into chunks on the actual manuscript itself like these examples show. Also, some beginning readers publishers state in their submission guidelines that there is a maximum number of characters you can type on each line of text. This is because they are using a larger font and also wider margins than a typical picture book, so more characters simply will not fit on the layout of the page when it goes to the printer.

What are "characters" and how do you count them? *Characters* include every letter, space, and punctuation mark you type. For instance, let's look at the previous example. The sentence, *It is Monday.* has ten alphabet letters, two spaces between the words, and one punctuation mark. This adds up to a total of 13 characters in the first line of text. The sentence, *The party is today.* has 15 alphabet letters, three spaces between words, and one punctuation mark. This adds up to a total of 19 characters in the second line of text.

Chunks of text aren't divided randomly, however. Natural pauses in speaking signal an appropriate place to divide a sentence into chunks. Phrases and clauses, either separated by commas or not, are also good places to divide a sentence into chunks. For instance, let's examine the sentence: *Tina brings a gift and a card.*

Example A:
Tina brings
a gift and a card.

Example B:
Tina brings a
gift and a card.

Example C:
Tina brings a gift
and a card.

Example D:
Tina brings a gift and
a card.

Example E:
Tina brings a gift and a
card.

Let's discuss why Example C is the best way to divide this sentence into two chunks. In Example A, the first chunk, "Tina brings" is an incomplete thought. Tina brings what? Young children learning to read complete sentences cannot form the words together to make much sense because they don't know what Tina brings. Learning to read is all about learning to put words together to make sense, and so far this doesn't make much sense. It's the same with Example B.

However, in Example C, "Tina brings a gift," a complete thought is formed. There is a subject, a verb, and a direct object. It is a natural break to divide the sentence into this first chunk. The second part of the sentence in this example, "and a card" is a group of words that describes another direct object. Therefore, Example C is also the best way to divide this sentence into two chunks because the second part of the sentence also forms a distinct group of words. Dividing up that final grouping as is shown in Examples D and E seems more awkward.

To gain a better sense of where and how to break up sentences into chunks, read a variety of beginning readers, noting especially how individual sentences are divided among different lines of text. The more you take time to observe these details, the more natural it will feel to break your own sentences into small chunks just right for young readers. If you simply can't figure out the best way to divide your sentences, however, don't stress out. Just do the best that you can and your editor will help with the rest. Some publishers do not even require you to break up the text but do this part themselves.

As you write your very own beginning readers and chapter books, format and sentence structure are essential for helping young children learn to read. Plugging in the pizzazz factor to your stories will help draw your readers in and will instill a love for reading at a very young age. Read the next section for ideas on how you can add lots of punch and kid-appeal to your beginning readers and chapter books manuscripts.

Beginner's Tip

Brush up on grammar skills and parts of speech to help you know the best places to divide sentences into chunks. Learn to identify phrases such as prepositional phrases and participial phrases. Become more familiar with groups of words and clauses such as independent clauses and dependent (or subordinate) clauses. *The EveryDay English Handbook* by Leonard Rosen is a user-friendly grammar book I have on my writer's bookshelves.

Professional Track

Volunteer to teach a workshop to your local writers group on sentence structure and format for beginning readers. Taking time to develop your speech and then trying to answer questions from writers less experienced than you are will help your own writing skills grow stronger.

Strengthen Your Writing Muscles

Type out at least two complete books from the same beginning readers series but which are on different reading levels. As you type, copy the format in each book exactly as it appears. Make your manuscript look exactly like the text in the published book, line for line. When finished, compare and contrast the different formats used at each different level.

Chapter 7.5 The Pizzazz Factor

What's your favorite children's book? Why does even the thought of it bring a smile to your heart? What elements in that book tugged at your heartstrings when you were a child and still bring a sense of wonder and delight to you today? By learning to evaluate the pizzazz factor and kid appeal in other books, you can learn how to strengthen your own beginning readers and chapter books in similar ways.

As I've written numerous reproducible beginning readers for Scholastic's teacher's market, my editor would occasionally remind me to check for the three R's: rhyme, rhythm, and repetition. Okay, I admit it. I'd heard of those words before, but what exactly do they mean? And how are writers supposed to know if our own beginning reader manuscripts utilize these three essential ingredients in the most effective way? Along my journey writing beginning readers, I've made it my goal to explore the three R's and work to learn how to weave them into my stories. I invite you to join me in my journey, too!

Rhyme

For starters, let's explore the concept of rhyme. Sure, I knew I could write beginning readers as poems that rhyme at the end of each line. Yet somehow I sensed there was more to writing in rhyme than what we learned in elementary school by reciting *Twinkle Twinkle Little Star*. For instance, how can we use rhyme in a beginning reader that's written in prose, or narrative, and not as a poem? The answer? Learn to incorporate *elements* of poetry into your beginning reader manuscripts—whether writing in rhyme or not.

Poetry utilizes key devices such as alliteration, internal rhyme, onomatopoeia, metaphors, similes, and wordplay based on homonyms, synonyms, and the use of puns. To polish your poetry skills in order to use these devices and strengthen your beginning reader manuscripts, embark on your own journey to explore each of these topics as well as other related topics you might encounter along the way, beginning with the examples I provide for you in the following sections.

If you haven't made one yet, create your own notebook like mine, *A Zillion Zany Zingers! Nancy's Dictionary of Wow Words, Fun Phrases, and Tips to Tickle Young Readers.* (For more information about making your own notebook, read *Section 7.1 Fresh and Original.*) Add a separate page in your notebook for each of these poetic devices. Write down the definition of each one, using an encyclopedia and dictionary as a guide. Explore poetry books or Websites to look for examples of each poetic device and list these examples on the corresponding pages in your notebook. Be on the lookout for beginning readers that incorporate these devices within their books and also write down examples of these in your notebook. During your own writing sessions, you can then refer to the notes you've gathered with the intent of incorporating elements of poetry into your beginning reader manuscripts.

If you are writing beginning manuscripts in rhyme, learn to know the difference between *perfect rhyme* and *imperfect rhyme*. Imperfect rhyme is sometimes referred to by other terms such as *near rhyme* or *off rhyme*. An example of perfect rhyme are the two words *ate* and *bait*. An example of imperfect rhyme are the two words *school* and *gold*. Even though both words have "-ol" they are not perfect matches. Many children's editors and agents insist on using perfect rhyme and consider it a sign of amateur writing if a manuscript's lines do not end with perfect rhymes. However, there are some editors who like the fun, punchy, off-the-wall feel of occasional imperfect rhyme.

If you're a writer who likes to use imperfect rhyme, use it effectively for editors who also like this technique. (You can learn an editor's tastes by reading the books they published most recently in their catalogs.) Don't just resort to imperfect rhyme because it's too hard to find two words that have a perfect match, however. If that's the case, rearrange your text and work to find words that do rhyme perfectly. Rhyming dictionaries or online sites with rhyming dictionaries can help tremendously.

Rhythm

If you're writing in rhyme, be sure to choose a rhythm or meter that works as an effective vehicle to transport your story into the hearts of your readers. In other words, match the rhythm with the theme of your story so they complement each other. A story about a ballerina can use a lilting meter that feels like she's dancing across the pages of the book. A story about a train can use a strong, steady beat that automatically makes your readers feel they are chug, chug, chugging along on the tracks. A sweet story about the love between a mother and child can use a soft, soothing rhythm that feels like a blanket wrapping around your readers with a hug.

If you're not writing a poem, you can still search for ways to include rhythm in your beginning reader manuscript. For instance, if you're writing a story in prose, not poetry, about a girl who builds a doghouse, you can incorporate a rhythmic sense into the scene where the girl is nailing the boards together so that the reader feels the rhythm of the pounding of the nails into the wood. Here is an example:

Tami started building the doghouse.
Pound, pound, pound went her hammer.
Down, down, down went the nails.

Soon the doghouse was done.

Repetition

When writing for middle grade and young adult readers, repetition is something you want to avoid. If you use the same word twice in a paragraph, editors will ask you to change one and use a different word instead. This is not the case when writing for young readers, however. Especially when writing beginning readers, repetition is an essential ingredient because it helps young children gain confidence, build strong reading skills, and learn the intended sight vocabulary. Plus, kids love it!

There are various ways to incorporate repetition into your beginning readers. You can add a repeating refrain that appears regularly throughout the text whether you're writing in rhyme or in prose. For instance, if you're telling a story about an airplane, you can repeat a refrain each time the airplane takes off. Here is an example of a non-rhyming "refrain" you could repeat several times throughout the story:

Up into the air it flew.
It zoomed up into the sky.

Another way you can use repetition in your beginning reader manuscripts is to repeat a word three times in succession within the same sentence. This repetition also adds rhythm to your sentences, so you're incorporating two of the three R's at once! Here is an example of repetition of words within the same sentence:

Up, up, up into the air it flew,
zoom, zoom, zooming into the sky.

Another way to incorporate repetition in beginning readers is to repeat parts of sentences while completing the sentences with new words or groups of words. This repetition is a very effective tool to help young readers gain confidence in reading because since they already decoded part of the sentence earlier in the story, they can read this part more quickly and only have to decode the new words. Here is an example of using repetition in a reproducible beginning reader play from my book with Scholastic Professional Books, *15 Easy-to-Read Nursery Rhyme Mini-Book Plays* (used by permission of Scholastic Inc.).

The Story of Hey Diddle, Diddle

Child 1: I read a good story today!
   It's called "Hey Diddle, Diddle"
   by Mother Goose.
Child 2: Why did you like it?
Child 1: It had animals!
   The cat played a fiddle.
Child 2: Oh! I love stories with animals!
Child 1: It had adventure!
   The cow jumped
   over the moon.
Child 2: Oh! I love stories
   with adventure!
Child 1: It was funny!
   The little dog laughed.
Child 2: Oh! I love stories
   that are funny!
Child 1: It had a surprise ending!
   The dish ran away

with the spoon.

Child 2: Oh! I love stories
     with surprise endings!

Child 1: Why don't you read it, too?

Child 2: I will! I'll read it today!

The End

How many repetitions can you find in this example?

Here's one example of repetition (in bold):

Child 1: **It had** animals!

Child 1: **It had** adventure!

Child 1: **It** was funny!

Child 1: **It had** a surprise ending!

Here's a second example of repetition (in bold):

Child 2: **Oh! I love stories with** animals!

Child 2: **Oh! I love stories**
     with adventure!

Child 2: **Oh! I love stories**
     that are funny!

Child 2: **Oh! I love stories**
     with surprise endings!

Here's a third example of repetition (in bold):

Child 1: It had **animals!**

Child 2: Oh! I love stories with **animals**!

Child 1: It had **adventure!**

Child 2: Oh! I love stories
     with **adventure!**

Child 1: It was **funny!**

Child 2: Oh! I love stories
      that are **funny!**

Child 1: It had a **surprise ending!**

Child 2: Oh! I love stories
      with **surprise endings!**

Incorporating the three R's: *rhyme, rhythm*, and *repetition* into a beginning reader automatically strengthens the manuscript. There are also other elements you can include, such as humor, in order to increase the pizzazz factor and add kid-appeal.

Humor

Humor is always a plus. Everyone loves a chuckle, especially children. Kids love humor, and beginning readers are a great arena where you can include funny moments in your stories.

A note about using bathroom humor, however. Because beginning readers are aimed toward the educational market and teachers purchase them for use in their classroom, be aware that many teachers simply do not like encouraging this kind of humor. They spend all day correcting students who have a potty mouth and instructing them to speak politely in school. Many teachers and librarians therefore avoid intentionally bringing books with bathroom humor into the school environment. Sure, you'll find some educators who love it, but in general, stay away from using bathroom humor in your beginning readers manuscripts or you might endanger potential sales of your books to their main target audience.

If the idea of writing with humor comes naturally to you, then by all means, incorporate humor as often as possible and you'll write winning beginning readers. However, if the idea of writing with humor makes you feel clueless, one strategy to try is to think of a group of three items that go together such as a knife, fork, and spoon. Then replace one of those items with a totally unrelated item so that you now have a group of three items such as a knife, fork, and hairbrush. Can you see the instant potential for humor? How can a princess eat soup with a knife, fork, and hairbrush?

Try this technique with other groups of three items such as Jack, the Giant, and the Golden Harp. Replace one item with a totally unrelated item so that you now have a group of three such as Jack, the Giant, and the Big Bad Wolf. What an interesting and funny story that could make! When Disney used this technique, they came up with Mickey Mouse, the Giant, and the Golden Harp which made for a hilarious children's classic movie called *Mickey and the Beanstalk.*

A great resource to have for learning how to add humor to beginning readers is the book, *Ready…Set…Read—and Laugh! A Funny Treasury for Beginning Readers.* This treasury compiled by Joanna Cole and Stephanie Calmenson contains over 25 published beginning readers all in one book that are guaranteed to generate giggles and guffaws. Read and analyze these stories and poems on your journey to discover how to add a dose of zany zest to your own manuscripts.

Surprise Endings

Another way to add pizzazz and kid appeal to beginning readers is to incorporate predictability with a surprise at the end. Similar to repetition and often incorporating repeated words or sentences, predictability in a beginning reader story gives young readers the ability to build strong reading skills. Predictable text helps children decode words from the clues and therefore read new words with which they might be unfamiliar. Concluding predictable text with a surprise ending automatically takes a beginning reader up a notch.

Rozanne Lanczak Williams, author of nearly 200 beginning reader books, is a master of writing predictable text with a surprise at the end. Visit her Website at www.magicbookgarden.com to become familiar with her titles. Purchase copies of her books and study how she writes predictable text that helps children gain valuable reading skills and then adds a surprise ending that leaves them with a feeling of satisfaction and delight.

Here is an example of a predictable story that has a surprise at the end:

Good Morning on the Farm

I tell Brown Cow, "Good morning."
"Moo," Brown Cow tells me.
I tell Pink Pig, "Good morning."
"Oink," Pink Pig tells me.
I tell Black Sheep, "Good morning."
"Baa," Black Sheep tells me.
I tell Barn Owl, "Good morning."
"Good night," Barn Owl tells me.

The story I wrote here for an example is predictable because children recognize a pattern in the text and expect the same repeated words to repeat again in the next lines of the story. However, the surprise is at the end when a barn owl, who is awake during the night and sleeps during the day, says "Good night." Simple surprises at the end of beginning readers such as this example tickle children's funny bones and bring a smile to their faces.

Self-Editing Checklist

To double check that your manuscript for the beginning readers and chapter books market is sparkling with pizzazz, it's important to take it through rounds of self-editing after it's written. To help you evaluate your manuscript for the specific qualities needed in this market, use the following checklist as a guide. (To check that the format and sentence structure is geared to the target age and reading level, refer to Chapters 8 through 13.)

Self-Editing Checklist for
Beginning Readers and First Chapter Books

_____ Fresh and original story

_____ Strong universal childhood theme

_____ Rhyme

_____ Rhythm

_____ Repetition

_____ Humor

_____ Characters have kid-appeal

_____ Plot is geared for target age and reading level

_____ Surprise ending or satisfying ending

_____ Format geared to target age and reading level

_____ Sentence structure geared to target age and reading level

_____ Grammar

_____ Punctuation

Beginner's Tip

The Rule of Three is a common rule in writing and very effective to use when writing beginning readers and chapter books. The Rule of Three is a guide to use when incorporating repetition, humor, and kid appeal into your manuscripts. Basically, it suggests that writers should include *three* items in a list or repeat something *three* times to create the funniest, most satisfying, and most effective results.

Professional Track

Interview your editors and published children's writer friends on your blog, especially any who publish beginning readers and chapter books. In their interviews, ask them to explain how they incorporate the three R's into writing for children as well as share secrets for adding huge doses of kid appeal to their manuscripts.

Strengthen Your Writing Muscles

Create a point system to evaluate the pizzazz factor in published beginning readers. Award one to five stars, with one being the lowest vote and five being the highest vote, for the following attributes:

Rhyme
Rhythm
Repetition
Humor
Predictable Text
Surprise Ending

After you gain practice evaluating published stories for their pizzazz factor, use this point system to evaluate your own beginning reader manuscripts. If you score low in one or more areas, rework your manuscript to make it shine and get a better score.

Chapter 8

PRE-EMERGENT READERS

8.1 Sentence Structure and Vocabulary

In pre-emergent readers, the use of basic vocabulary and simple sentence structure is the rule. The age group for this reading level ranges from preschool to children in kindergarten or first grade. They are making important discoveries about letters, their shapes, and how they group together to form the written word. These children are just figuring out how to read, and the sentence structure and vocabulary used at this level is geared to guide their faltering steps in reading forward on a positive journey.

Pre-emergent Readers At-a-Glance

(Check with each publisher to determine specifics.)

Sample Titles:

God's Colors by Heather Gemmen and Mary McNeil (Rocket Readers: Pre-Level 1 Reader, FaithKidz)

Go, Go, Go (Read with Dick and Jane, Grosset & Dunlap)

See It, Say It, Hear It, Read It! (Sandcastle 1: Grades Pre-K to K, ABDO Publishing)

The Ball Game by David Packard (My First Hello Reader! With Flash Cards!™ Preschool-Grade 1: Ages 3-6, Scholastic)

Word Count:

   From one sentence to 250 words

Page Count:

   8 to 32 pages

Lines of Text:

   1 to 5 lines per page

   Up to 30 characters per line

The discoveries children in preschool through first grade make in the world of reading at the pre-emergent readers level can affect their entire life experience with reading, whether in a negative or positive way. You can join the ranks of writers who create reading material for these precious young minds and make it your goal to help launch little ones off on a lifetime journey with the hope of experiencing the joys and positive benefits of reading.

Children used to learn to read in first grade. Not so any more. With new legislative decisions and more strict State and National Standards including the Common Core State Standards, children are often taught basic reading skills in preschool, so that by the time they are in kindergarten, they are able to read portions of selected text independently.

Because material written for pre-emergent readers is used with children in preschool through first grade who are experiencing their first encounter with letters, groups of letters, and words read on a printed page, sometimes individual vocabulary words are first identified by themselves before forming them into sentences. Several series of leveled readers start this way with their pre-emergent reader level. Some books at this level include flash cards for parents and teachers to use to introduce each vocabulary word in the book and practice identifying them by sight.

Here is an example of how you can introduce words by themselves in a picture book or a reproducible mini-book to help pre-emergent readers first identify the vocabulary words and then read them altogether in a sentence:

At the Zoo
Pages 2-3: Tim
[Illustration: There is a picture of a boy. Underneath the picture is the word, "Tim." Children see both the picture and the word and learn to identify the word as the name of the boy in the picture.]

Pages 4-5: lion

[Illustration: There is a picture of a lion. Underneath the picture is the word, "lion." Children see both the picture and the word and learn to identify the word as the object in the picture.]

Pages 6-7: tiger

[Illustration: There is a picture of a tiger. Underneath the picture is the word, "tiger." Children see both the picture and the word and learn to identify the word as the object in the picture.]

Pages 8-9: zoo

[Illustration: There is a picture of a zoo. Underneath the picture is the word, "zoo." Children see both the picture and the word and learn to identify the word as the object in the picture.]

Pages 10-11: Tim sees a lion at the zoo.

[Illustration: For the first time, the words are formed into a sentence. There is a picture of Tim looking at a lion at the zoo. Because the reader has already identified the words Tim, lion, and zoo, the only new words encountered are: sees, a, at, the.]

Page 12: Tim sees a tiger, too.

[Illustration: More words are formed into another sentence. There is a picture of Tim looking at a tiger. Because the reader has already identified the words Tim, sees, a, and tiger, the only new word encountered is: too.]

Vocabulary words for pre-emergent readers usually focus on Edward W. Dolch's list of 220 high-frequency words and his list of 95 common nouns.

To learn more about this list of first vocabulary words taught to children in preschool through first grade at the earliest stages of learning to read, look at *Section 2.1 Before Beginning Readers*. Vocabulary words for pre-emergent readers can also come from phonics lists. You can refer to phonics lists found in books including those written by Wiley Blevins such as *Phonics from A to Z*. Other phonics lists can be found online at sites such as First School Years at www.firstschoolyears.com/literacy/word/word.htm.

Instead of introducing individual words by themselves, however, some material for pre-emergent readers introduces chunks, or parts of sentences, that eventually build to create one whole sentence over the course of the book. This is the strategy I employed when I wrote my bestselling book for Scholastic Teaching Resources, *25 Read & Write Mini-Books that Teach Word Families*. It's sold over 240,000 copies to date and is still selling strong, with two other titles in the series, *25 Read & Write Mini-Books that Teach Phonics* and *26 Read & Write Mini-Books: Beginning Sounds From A to Z*. The success of these three books is evidence that introducing chunks, or parts of sentences, along with individual word identification, is an effective use of sentence structure for helping pre-emergent readers acquire strong reading skills.

Young children in preschool through first grade who are at the pre-emergent level are working hard to learn to identify words as well as group them together into a sentence. Therefore sentence structure at this level is very basic and short. Often, short sentences with just two or three words are used such as: *Sam sat. The dog ran. Jim ate.* Longer sentences are usually broken into chunks over several lines of text.

Sentence structure and vocabulary words are very important in pre-emergent readers. So are the characters. To learn about the type of characters publishers want to see in stories for this reading level, continue on to the next section.

Beginner's Tip

Visit a teacher's supply store or online bookstore and look for supplemental books with activities and worksheets for students to learn all about sentence parts including nouns and verbs. Try to find one for kindergarten or first grade. Purchase it, take it home, and complete the exercises until you're a pro at identifying sentences.

Professional Track

Pair up with a literacy specialist to write for this reading level. Use your published credibility and her expertise in literacy to write pre-emergent readers as a team.

Strengthen Your Writing Muscles

Learn how to spell, pronounce, and read five simple vocabulary words in a foreign language that you've never studied before. This will help you better understand some of the feelings pre-emergent readers experience while learning new vocabulary words for the very first time. After you learn your five new words, spend 15 minutes doing a freewriting exercise that begins with the prompt, "When I learned to read five new words in a foreign language, I felt…"

8.2 Characters

The world of pre-emergent readers is based on everyday experiences. These experiences include parents, brothers and sisters, babies, friends, and animals. By choosing characters for writing pre-emergent readers that are based on the familiar world of a young child in preschool through first grade, you can experience success from the start.

Unlike books for older readers where animals with human attributes are discouraged as a choice for characters, anthropomorphic characters abound in pre-emergent readers. Little ones delight in seeing the antics of monkeys, dogs, and even ants who walk and talk just like people do.

Zoo animals, farm animals, pets, and dinosaurs as main characters in pre-emergent readers instantly attract the interest of young children in preschool through first grade. Even though children just beginning to sound out letters and recognize words by sight usually cannot sound out a complicated word such as *alligator*, they can easily identify the word by its picture. Therefore harder words such as *giraffe, zebra*, and *kitten* can be found on the Kindergarten Word List in Alijandra Mogilner's *Children's Writer's Word Book* because zoo animals, farm animals, and pets are a part of a young child's world. Animals become prime choices for creating delightful characters in stories you can write for this reading level.

The world of pre-emergent readers is a fantastic world of imagination and creative play for three-to-five year olds. In their world, lambs can go to school, elephants can play baseball, and sheep can drive a jeep. Characters can act and talk in ways that seem nonsensical to practical adults, yet appear very real and make perfect sense to pre-emergent readers.

For example, here is a story to show how three animal characters can interact in a pre-emergent reader:

Cover:
Three Ants

Page 1:
Three ants
and a bug...

Page 2:

[Art shows a picture of three ants and a ladybug standing up like people and wearing baseball uniforms. All have anthropomorphic qualities and appear to be human.]

Page 3:

Three ants

and a bug

play ball…

Page 4:

[Art shows the ants and ladybug holding a baseball, mitts, and a baseball bat.]

Page 5:

Three ants

and a bug

play ball

with their friends.

Page 6:

[Art shows the ants and ladybug with lots of other bugs who also appear anthropomorphic with human qualities. They are all playing a game of baseball.]

Not only can characters in pre-emergent readers be anthropomorphic, but you can also name your characters with old-fashioned, out-of-date names. Using names such as Bob or Tim for characters in a middle grade novel for today's market might get an automatic rejection from an editor, yet here in pre-emergent readers, every three letter or single syllable name possible can be used for your characters in an attempt to introduce a full range of the most basic vocabulary words to this target age of children in preschool through first grade.

There is an entire set of *Bob Books*® for pre-emergent readers written by Bobby Lynn Maslen and illustrated by John R. Maslen. This hugely successful series teaches young children the alphabet, phonics, word families, complex words and other reading skills through the use of characters with three-letter names such as Mat and Sam.

Pre-emergent readers introduce simple characters to children in preschool through first grade who are just learning to read. To explore a character's use of dialogue in pre-emergent readers, look at the next section.

Beginner's Tip

Purchase a one-volume encyclopedia about animals from a used bookstore. When developing an animal as a character, first read about it in the encyclopedia. Note any characteristics the animal has. Incorporate these natural traits into your character's personality.

Professional Track

If you love writing about anthropomorphic animals but your editors in other genre discourage it, jump right in and start creating adorable animal characters for the earliest reading levels in the beginning readers market. You'll have the time of your life!

Strengthen Your Writing Muscles

Write vocabulary words on index cards, one word per card. Use simple three- and four-letter words and single syllable words geared for this reading level. Sit down with a writing pal or take the cards to your writer's group and play a game called Simple Sentences. Place all the cards face down individually spread out on the table. The first player turns over three words. Set a timer for one minute. All players write down as many simple sentences as they can that use all three words and still make sense. Players score one point for each sentence they write. Turn the cards back over and the second player takes a turn, alternating turns until done. Discard vocabulary words that have been used twice. The player with the most points at the end wins the game.

8.3 Dialogue

There is little or no dialogue used in material for pre-emergent readers. Words and sentences for this level are very concrete and easily identified with a picture. It's hard to effectively illustrate what someone is saying in order to provide clues to the reader for decoding the text independently. When writing pre-emergent readers, you can craft stories without any dialogue at all!

If occasional dialogue is used, some publishers prefer not to use quotation marks. This is because children in preschool through first grade who are beginning to acquire reading skills can't distinguish easily between punctuation marks and letters at first. However, some publishers will use quotation marks. You can check their guidelines or books for pre-emergent readers to find out what different publishers prefer to do.

Here is an example of dialogue without the use of quotation marks:

Come with me,
said the bee.

Here is an example of dialogue that uses quotation marks:

"Come with me,"
said the bee.

Instead of using dialogue with this reading level, use lots of action words such as *ride, swim,* and *sit*. Provide clues through the illustrations that tell young readers in preschool through first grade what is being communicated between the characters in your story. Move the plot forward by having your characters move. To discover how to structure the plot in pre-emergent readers, continue on to the next section.

Beginner's Tip

Search online (or visit www.mrsperkins.com/dolch.htm) and print out Dolch's list of 220 high-frequency words and his list of 95 common nouns. Add this list of words to your own writer's notebook as a handy reference to use when writing pre-emergent readers.

Professional Track

If you've had difficulty developing dialogue in another genre, you might enjoy writing pre-emergent readers where dialogue isn't needed for a successful story.

Strengthen Your Writing Muscles

Animals cannot speak, yet they communicate very effectively. Take a notebook and pen and sit down to observe an animal for 15-30 minutes. It can be your pet dog or cat. It can be a bird in your backyard. It can be an orangutan at the zoo. Make notes on how you see this animal communicating without words. Write down what you think it would be saying if it could speak. Now write a short story for a pre-emergent reader with this animal as the main character.

8.4 Plot

Simple and predictable plots are enough when writing pre-emergent readers. Because little ones in preschool through first grade are concentrating hard on reading letters, words, and sentences independently, many for the very first time, complex plots are too confusing. You can create a simple plot that moves forward in a predictable pattern, and children this age will be delighted that they read the story from beginning to end!

At this reading level, a plot line can be effective when it uses repetition and a list or series of events that repeat every word except the introduction of one new word in each different scene. This repetition allows pre-emergent readers in preschool through first grade to only have to decode one new word each time, but each new word also serves to move the plot forward.

Even though working with the most basic of plots, you can still try to give your readers a surprise at the end, a simple twist to the plot, or some unexpected element that provides a very satisfying ending. Here is an example of a story that uses repetition to move the predictable plot forward and adds a surprise ending.

Bill Takes a Bath
Bill takes a bath
with his toy duck.
[Art shows Bill sitting in the bathtub playing with his rubber duckie. On the
rim of the tub is his cat, Mittens. Mittens is watching Bill take a bath.]

Bill takes a bath
with his toy fish.
[Art shows Bill now is also playing with a fish in the tub. Mittens is still
perched on the rim of the tub, watching.]

Bill takes a bath
with his toy boat.
[Art shows Bill now has his duck, a fish, *and* a boat. Mittens is still perched
on the rim of the tub, watching.]

Mittens takes a bath, too!
[Art shows on this last page that Mittens has slipped into the bathtub, too, by
mistake.]

Don't feel that you need to clarify the beginning, middle, and end of
your story through the text. Allow the art to convey the story arc, or plot.
You can include detailed art instructions in [brackets] on your manuscript so
that the illustrator can portray exactly what you intend to be happening in
each scene of the story.

To help brainstorm a predictable plot with a surprise ending, make a list
of similar items. For instance, a list of bath toys could include a duck, a fish,

a boat, and a starfish. Then add a totally unrelated item to your list. This unrelated item becomes your surprise ending.

Let's take a second look at this same story about Bill's bath, but this time we'll put *only* similar, related items in the tub:

Bill Takes a Bath
Bill takes a bath
with his toy duck.

Bill takes a bath
with his toy fish.

Bill takes a bath
with his toy boat.

Bill takes a bath
with his toy starfish, too.

Yes, the story comes to an end because now bath time is over for Bill. But because all four items in the bath are related, there is no surprise or twist to the plot. Simply by adding one *unrelated* item to the predictable plot, a cat who doesn't like to take baths, the ending becomes humorous and feels much more satisfying, especially to young readers in preschool through first grade.

Working to create plots with a surprise ending, even for pre-emergent readers, you can help instill a natural love for reading in the precious hearts of little ones who are experiencing for the very first time the magic and wonder of the written word. Every plot needs a setting, however, so continue reading to see how a setting is created for pre-emergent readers.

Beginner's Tip

The best way to learn the pace of repetitive and predictable plots is to read lots of them. The more examples you find to read, the more natural your own writing will become when you write stories with predictable plot structures.

Professional Track

Write a number of short pre-emergent readers with predictable plot patterns. Ask an illustrator friend to create simple art for each, or illustrate your own. Offer these for free on your blog or Website to draw educators and parents to your site.

Strengthen Your Writing Muscles

Did you ever eat a box of Cracker Jack® and find the prize inside? Or did you dig through a box of cereal and find the toy? If so, try to remember those feelings of delight and satisfaction when you found the surprise. It's this same feeling you want to capture when you write pre-emergent readers with a surprise ending. Do a 15-minute freewriting exercise starting with the prompt, "When I discovered the surprise, I felt…"

8.5 Setting

In pre-emergent readers, the setting is conveyed through art. You can create a sense of place that adds wonderful dimension to your story without ever describing it in the text. In fact, you do not ever have to mention the setting in the actual text at all. However, even though you are not describing the setting, it still plays an important role in your story.

Setting for this reading level should be very familiar to a three-to-five year old and a natural part of his or her world. The setting for your story can be a child's bedroom, a kitchen, a home, or a grandparent's house. Your story can take place at a park or on a playground or in a preschool classroom. The setting can be any number of familiar places in a community such as a store, fire station, or restaurant.

The setting needs to be easily identifiable. Little ones in preschool through first grade who are just being introduced to the joy of reading are working hard to identify letters and words. We don't want to make them work hard to identify a setting that is unfamiliar to them because they haven't yet traveled far from home.

When using animals as the characters of your story, you can place an animal in its natural setting. For instance, a penguin can be standing on a patch of floating ice. To add instant humor to your story, you can also choose to place an animal outside of its normal setting. For example, a penguin could be swimming in a pool in someone's back yard.

Settings should be very generalized. Your story can take place on a hill, in a barn, in the snow, or at a house. For this reading level for children in preschool through first grade, do not identify a specific setting such as the Arctic Ocean or Mount Everest. It's also not necessary to include intricate details of the setting. If the story takes place at the top of a hill, the hill is all that in needed in the art. A tree or bush or other item does not need to be added to the setting unless it is an important part of the story itself.

It is permissible and often required for writers to include detailed art instructions in [brackets] so that the illustrator understands the setting for each page of the story. Sometimes authors are also required to submit sketches of simple stick figures positioning the characters within the setting on each page. If you are required to do this and drawing isn't your special talent, don't worry! Editors know we writers aren't often very artistic. You can just draw stick figures in simple settings so the illustrator will know what to do. Here is an example of the art instructions you could include for a pre-emergent reader:

A Fun Day

A cat

[Art: Show cat wearing a dress and driving in a car.]

got a bag

[Art: Show cat standing inside a candy store buying a bag of candy.]

in the city

[Art: Show cat outside the candy store standing on the street with big city buildings all around her.]

for a dog.

[Art: Show cat giving the candy to a dog and there is a birthday cake and party balloons because it is the dog's birthday.]

Whatever setting you choose to use as a backdrop for your story in a pre-emergent reader, it will tie hand-in-hand with your topic, or theme. To learn more about choosing which topics and themes to write about for this reading level, continue on.

Beginner's Tip

Make a list of places in your neighborhood such as a park, a school, and a restaurant. Which sites are more familiar to young children? Which ones are more for adults? Choose from the list of kid-friendly places to create settings in your own stories.

Professional Track

Interview the illustrator of one of your children's magazine stories or books. In the interview, ask him to describe the process he went through to develop the art for the setting based on the manuscript you submitted. Post the interview on your blog.

Strengthen Your Writing Muscles

Create a scrapbook of places you lived in or visited before you turned six. Include photos if you have any. Write memories about specific places such as the sandbox you played in, the table where you ate breakfast, and the couch you sat on to read a book. Focus on a sense of place as a very young child, and use this as a reference while writing pre-emergent readers. (If you can't remember these early years, create a scrapbook for a child you know.)

8.6 Topics and Themes

Once again, the familiar world of young children in preschool through first grade sets the parameters when choosing topics and themes to write about for pre-emergent readers. Family relationships between parent and child, interactions between siblings, and visits with grandparents are common choices you can write about.

Even though words such as *Thanksgiving, Christmas,* and *Easter* are usually introduced in the actual text at the next higher level for emergent readers, stories for pre-emergent readers often feature a holiday theme. Special events such as a birthday parties or the birth of new puppies are also appropriate themes for this reading level.

Nursery rhymes are often used as the theme for pre-emergent readers. In the Christian market, Bible stories are retold using repetitive sentences and the simplest vocabulary words.

Familiar topics such as playing at the park, feeding a pet goldfish, and finding a ladybug provide lots of interest for children just learning to read who are in preschool through first grade. Their everyday world, though it might not seem very interesting to us at times, is filled with excitement and new discoveries to make each day. Look for topics and themes to write about for pre-emergent readers simply by becoming familiar and more aware of the world through the eyes of a three-to-five-year-old child.

Sports stories can be interesting themes for pre-emergent readers. Just be aware, however, that not many children at this age are enrolled in highly organized sports. Your story can feature kids having fun at a soccer game, for instance, but don't go into detail about competition between teams or the duties of the goalies. You can even choose the theme of soccer as the topic of your story, but just have the main character kicking around a soccer ball for fun rather than actually participating in a game.

It's best to stay away from scary topics at this reading level. Pre-kindergartners and kindergartners just learning to read often scare very easily. Sometimes even silly monsters can appear scary to a child at this reading level, but monster stories with a loveable monster such as Sesame Street's Tickle Me Elmo or Cookie Monster are usually okay. Also steer clear of sad stories. It's one thing for an adult to read a scary or sad story or watch a scary or sad movie with a young child. It's quite another issue for the same little one to try to read a story all on her own that is scary or sad. Try to give your story a happy ending for this reading level, no matter which theme or topic you choose.

Children at this tender age blossom in a safe environment with large doses of comfort and security. As they grasp solid footing reading their first stories independently within their own comfortable world that still includes blankies, cuddles on comfy laps, and hugs and kisses at naptime, they'll soon become confident enough and brave enough to advance to the next level of reading where stories with challenges such as losing a first tooth or learning to tie their shoelaces become a more natural part of their days.

Beginner's Tip

Search online for the term "kindergarten readiness." Read a variety of articles listing the developmental qualifications of children who are considered ready to start kindergarten. Jot down notes from these articles to help you understand the pre-emergent readers target age more fully.

Professional Track

Take your expertise as a writer to the next level by learning the lingo educators use when working with pre-emergent readers. Familiarize yourself with terms such as: decode, analogy, phonograms, spelling patterns, spelling-sound translations, letter-sound correspondence, blends, digraphs, word families, onset, rime, phonemes, sight words, guided reading, and reading fluency. Incorporate these words into your queries and cover letters as you pitch ideas to land contracts to write manuscripts for the pre-emergent readers level.

Strengthen Your Writing Muscles

Make a list of animals such as farm animals, zoo animals, and pets. Write down a second list of single syllable action verbs such as *drives, ran, jumps,* and *swims*. Next make as many two-word sentences that you can think of choosing one animal and one verb from each list. For example: *Fox ran. Bear drives. Duck swims.*

Use these examples to write a story for pre-emergent readers that only features two-word sentences throughout. Try to add a surprise ending. If you have any, include art directions in [brackets]. Here is an example:

Jumps

Fox jumps.

Bear jumps.

Duck jumps.

Kangaroo jumps.

[Art: Show in the last picture that Kangaroo jumps past them all!]

Chapter 9

EMERGENT READERS

9.1 Sentence Structure and Vocabulary

Classics such as *The Cat in the Hat* and *Green Eggs and Ham* by Dr. Seuss typify the sentence structure and vocabulary words found in emergent readers. Sometimes referred to as *beginning readers* or *Level 1 readers* or *beginning-to-read books*, these stories are for children in kindergarten through first grade although some are still used with preschoolers who have already acquired basic reading skills. It's hard to describe the excitement kids this age feel with each step of joyful discovery they make as they master new reading skills. You can tap into this joy and experience a similar measure of excitement as you write emergent reader manuscripts for this target age. Delightful, whimsical, and fanciful worlds of creativity that tap into the enchantment of a child's imagination await you each day you sit down to craft new stories for this reading level.

Emergent Readers At-a-Glance

(Check with each publisher to determine specifics.)

Sample Titles:

A Dozen Dogs: A Read-and-Count Story by Harriet Ziefert (Step into Reading™ A Step 1 Book: Preschool-Grade 1, Random House)

Mr. Noisy's Book of Patterns by Rozanne Lanczak Williams (Learn to Read, Read to Learn Math Series: Emergent Reader Level 1, Creative Teaching Press)

A Day in the Life of a Builder by Linda Hayward (Dorling Kindersley Readers, Level 1: Beginning to Read, Dorling Kindersley)

Itchy, Itchy Chicken Pox by Grace Maccarone (Hello Reader!™ Level 1: Preschool-Grade 1, Ages 3-6, Scholastic)

Word Count:

About 250 words

Page Count:

16 to 32 pages

Lines of Text:

Up to 100 lines per book

Up to 12 lines per two-page spread

Up to 36 characters per line

The main difference between pre-emergent readers and emergent readers is that pre-emergent readers often include vocabulary words all by themselves on one page of the book, or include some method such as flash cards at the back of the book for a teacher, parent, or other adult to introduce individual words to the child. Emergent readers usually do not present individual vocabulary words all by themselves, but instead feature complete sentences working together to create a story.

In most other ways, sentence structure and vocabulary words found in emergent readers can be very similar to pre-emergent readers. If a publisher has reading levels that include both pre-emergent readers and emergent readers, their series of emergent readers may have slightly more complex vocabulary words and slightly more complex sentences than the earlier level. Other than that, these two reading levels can be very much the same in regards to sentence structure and vocabulary words.

Sentence structure in emergent readers is simple. Two, three, and four-word sentences are common such as: *Jill swings. Go to sleep. I can swim. Pam and Rich run.* Longer sentences are broken into phrases at natural pauses and printed over several different lines of text. Sentences and phrases within sentences are often repeated to give children beginning to read confidence and fluency skills.

Here is an example of the sentence structure and repetition of sentences used in emergent readers. This sample is from the reproducible mini-book, "Patty's Pets" in my book for Scholastic Teaching Resources, *Cut & Paste*

Mini-Books: Math (used by permission of Scholastic Inc.).

Cover:
Patty's Pets

Page 1:
"We're hungry!" cried the pets.
"I'll feed everyone," Dog said.
Dog gave each bird a dog bone.
One for each!
"Yuck!" said the birds.

Page 2: illustration of two birds

Page 3:
Dog gave each turtle a dog bone.
One for each.
"Yuck!" said the turtles.

Page 4: illustration of three turtles

Page 5:
Dog gave each cat a dog bone.
One for each.
"Yuck!" said the cats.

Page 6: illustration of four cats

Page 7:
Dog gave each rabbit a dog bone.

One for each.

"Yuck!" said the rabbits.

Page 8: illustration of five rabbits

Page 9:

Just then Patty came in.

She put the rest of the

dog bones in the bag.

Then she got out the right food.

"Yummy!" cheered the pets.

Page 10: illustration of a bag of dog food

Page 11: illustration of a math activity

The use of repetition helps children practice reading familiar words several times. Note the repetition of the following three sentences on four of the pages of the mini-book.

Dog gave each _____ a dog bone.

One for each!

"Yuck!" said the _____.

Each of these pages also introduces a new vocabulary word: *birds, turtles, cats*, and *rabbits*. The illustrations of these animals provide picture clues to help children decode and figure out the new vocabulary words. However, unlike pre-emergent readers that sometimes introduce new vocabulary words all by themselves, here in this emergent reader example, the new vocabulary words are introduced within the actual sentences. Placing them as the only new word in a sentence that otherwise is repeated from the previous page helps young children focus on the new vocabulary word instead of having to learn every single word in a brand new sentence. This technique of introducing a new vocabulary word within a repeated sentence helps children increase confidence, build strong reading skills, and improve independent reading fluency.

As with pre-emergent readers, vocabulary words for emergent readers include words from Edward W. Dolch's list of 220 high-frequency words and his list of 95 common nouns. (To learn more about this list of first vocabulary words taught to children at the earliest stages of learning to read, look at *Section 2.1 Before Beginning Readers*.)

However, because topics and themes such as holidays and seasons are taught in kindergarten and first grade, seemingly complicated words such as *Christmas* and *Hanukkah* are also taught to emergent readers and have a viable place in stories written for this reading level. Likewise difficult words such as *butterfly, dinosaur*, and *elephant* can also be used in your emergent readers manuscripts because they are also topics taught to children in early elementary grades.

To help choose appropriate vocabulary words to use as you write emergent readers, refer to the Kindergarten Word List and the First Grade Word List in Alijandra Mogilner's *Children's Writer's Word Book.* Another excellent reference is found in *The Reading Teacher's Book of Lists.* "List 16: Instant Words" in this book features the most common words children will encounter when they read, and therefore should be able to recognize by sight. The first 300 words in List 16 are especially helpful to refer to when writing for this reading level.

Some publishers of emergent readers will provide you with their own lists of vocabulary words for authors to choose from. These lists have usually been carefully selected by literacy specialists for writers to follow. Receiving a ready-made list within a packet of writer's guidelines can make your job significantly easier, but if your publisher doesn't provide you with such a list, or you are writing emergent reader manuscripts before you land a contract with a publisher, referring to the lists in the *Children's Writer's Word Book* or in *The Reading Teacher's Book of Lists* will give you the tools you need.

Armed with these tools, you can begin to brainstorm ideas for characters in your stories. To learn more about developing characters for emergent readers, read the next section.

Beginner's Tip

Compare a pre-emergent reader and emergent reader from the same series side by side such as *I'm a Fire Fighter* by Mary Packard and *Pizza Party!* by Grace Maccarone. Note the difference you see between sentence structure and vocabulary words.

Professional Track

If you have published a holiday book for kids, write an emergent reader about that holiday as well. Educators and parents like to purchase other books by their favorite authors. Start building name recognition as an author of stories about that holiday. Just be careful with your competing works clause on your contracts. Work with your publisher to clarify the wording to state that your books aren't *competing* against each other, but are *complementing* each other to increase sales.

Strengthen Your Writing Muscles

Make a list of three-letter words that start with the letter *b*. Look over your list. Which words can easily be identified with a picture? Use as many of these words to write a simple story based on words beginning with the letter *b*. Try this exercise with other letters of the alphabet.

9.2 Characters

The world of children in kindergarten and first grade is starting to expand as they begin school and experience situations they've never before encountered in their young lives. However, characters in emergent readers are still based on familiar people in a little one's world such as parents, grandparents, siblings, and friends. Because children also move more freely around their neighborhood and community, their list of familiar people is expanding to include community helpers. You can therefore choose characters such as teachers, librarians, fire fighters, postal workers, and zookeepers as strong choices for this reading level.

Once again, anthropomorphic characters, or animals with human characteristics, are a big hit in emergent readers. Nearly any animal can become a winning character in your emergent reader as long as most children are familiar with it at this age. Koalas and kangaroos from Down Under, boa constrictors and toucans from the South American rainforest, and roadrunners and kangaroo rats from deserts in the American southwest all make quirky and enchanting casts of characters in emergent readers.

Children in kindergarten and first grade don't need a rhyme or reason for why a certain animal appears walking and talking in an emergent reader story. In other words, nonsense situations can seem perfectly acceptable and actually very appealing to kids this age. However, it's usually best to group animals from the same geographic location or in the same environment together in one story. For instance, you could have a cast of characters that includes forest animals such as Bear, Squirrel, Deer, and Skunk. All of these animals live in the same setting and appear together in a story very naturally. You would not want to write a story with forest animals and one zoo animal such as Bear, Squirrel, Skunk, and *Giraffe* unless you were specifically featuring this character in the story for a purpose such as adding an element of humor. If that is the case, your story would be driven by this odd and out-of-place character and should center around its problem trying to fit into a different world.

As Dr. Seuss has shown, even nonsense characters spark a child's imagination and can be created to star in your emergent reader story. If you have ideas for imaginary characters, follow the example Dr. Seuss gave us and name these imaginary characters with words or mix-matched combinations of words that use vocabulary geared for this reading level. For instance, the Grinch, the people living in Whoville, and the Who that Horton hears all have names that can be read successfully by emergent readers. Stay away from naming your imaginary characters with difficult invented names such as Aeridophila or Cleopatricia. Those names are great for older readers, but not as easy to encounter on a page for children who are just beginning to read.

Emergent readers can have just one character in the entire story. At the most, you can feature two main characters. You can include an entire cast of several supporting characters, however, who interact with the main character. Just be sure to focus on the main character. (To explore how one main character interacts with a supporting cast of characters in emergent readers, read my mini-book, "Patty's Pets" in *Section 9.1 Sentence Structure and Vocabulary*. Dog is the main character. Patty, birds, turtles, cats, and rabbits form the supporting cast.)

Whether you choose people or humans to take center stage in your emergent readers, your characters will draw young readers immediately into your story. Children will smile with pleasure and giggle with amusement as they follow your characters' adventures while learning important reading skills. They'll want to hear your characters speak, too, so continue to the following section to learn how to incorporate dialogue into this reading level.

Beginner's Tip

Characters can even be items such as cars or vegetables that are anthropomorphic. Think of the successful *Veggie Tales*® series by Big Idea® and Disney/Pixar's animated movie, *Cars*.

Professional Track

Pitch an idea for a story featuring a nonsense character to a magazine editor you've already published with. Keep all rights. If the editor likes your story and it gets published, give your character new life as an emergent reader.

Strengthen Your Writing Muscles

Watch a children's movie that features animals as the main characters. Practice writing for this reading level by retelling a scene from the movie as an emergent reader with less than 100 words.

9.3 Dialogue

In kindergarten and first grade, children learn how to use punctuation in sentences. This punctuation includes the use of quotation marks in dialogue.

In emergent readers, therefore, simple dialogue can be included. Not only does this teach young children how quotation marks are used correctly, dialogue can also add interest to stories. You can use simple dialogue in stories for this reading level to make your characters come alive to your readers.

Because teachers are specifically teaching the correct use of punctuation such as quotation marks, it's essential for us as writers to type quotation marks correctly in our manuscripts. Because I am involved with several writers' critique groups as well as provide manuscript critiques at various writers' conferences, I see a lot of children's manuscripts. One of the most common mistakes I find is the incorrect use of quotation marks when writing dialogue and with the use of dialogue tags. (A dialogue tag shows the reader who is speaking and includes phrases such as: *he said, she said, exclaimed Bear, shouted Rabbit.*)

Make it a point to learn the correct use of quotation marks, and your emergent reader manuscripts will look more professional than other manuscripts in an editor's submissions pile. There are various reference books you can refer to in order to learn the correct use of quotation marks. The *Chicago Manual of Style* provides the most detailed information about quotation marks. However, *Write Right!* by Jan Venolia and *The Elements of Style* by William Strunk, Jr. and E. B. White give more user-friendly, if not comprehensive, guidelines. Here in a nutshell are pointers to remember:

A period goes inside quotation marks at the end of a sentence when using dialogue.

Correct example: Turtle said, "Come to the pond with **me.**"

Incorrect example: Turtle said, "Come to the pond with **me**".

A comma goes inside quotation marks when the dialogue tag comes after the sentence.

Correct example: "Come to the pond with **me,**" Turtle said.

Incorrect example: "Come to the pond with **me**"**,** Turtle said.

Correct example: "Come to the pond with **me,**" said Turtle.

Incorrect example: "Come to the pond with **me**"**,** said Turtle.

A question mark goes inside the quotation marks when using dialogue.

Correct example: Turtle asked, "Will you come to the pond with **me?**"

Incorrect example: Turtle asked, "Will you come to the pond with **me**"**?**

A question mark goes inside the quotation marks when the dialogue tag comes after the sentence.

Correct example: "Will you come to the pond with **me?**" Turtle asked.

Incorrect example: "Will you come to the pond with **me**"**?** Turtle asked.

Correct example: "Will you come to the pond with **me?**" asked Turtle.

Incorrect example: "Will you come to the pond with **me**"**?** asked Turtle.

An exclamation point goes inside the quotation marks at the end of a sentence when using dialogue.

Correct example: Turtle shouted, "Come to the pond with **me!**"

Incorrect example: Turtle shouted, "Come to the pond with **me**"**!**

An exclamation point goes inside quotation marks when the dialogue tag comes after the sentence.

Correct example: "Come to the pond with **me!**" Turtle shouted.

Incorrect example: "Come to the pond with **me**"**!** Turtle shouted.

Correct example: "Come to the pond with **me!"** shouted Turtle.

Incorrect example: "Come to the pond with **me"!** shouted Turtle.

Another point to remember about writing dialogue for emergent readers is to always use a dialogue tag. Dialogue tags identify who says what. Children need to understand who speaks every single sentence of dialogue in a story. Don't worry about being repetitious. Repetition helps young readers build strong reading skills and is a key element of writing for this reading level.

If you write middle grade or young adult novels, you know that you don't always need to use dialogue tags to identify who is talking. However, for emergent readers, dialogue tags help children who are just beginning to read identify the use of quotation marks as a signal that someone is talking. Dialogue tags are essential to their reading success.

Here is an example of appropriate use of dialogue tags in a middle grade or young adult novel:

"I did not do it!" shouted Mary.

"Yes, you did!" cried Jen.

"Did not!"

"Did too!"

"Did not!"

"Did too!"

"Not!" shouted Mary.

Then it started to rain.

Here is an example of how this same passage of dialogue is written for an emergent reader:

"I did not do it!" shouted Mary.

"Yes, you did!" cried Jen.

"Did not!" said Mary.

"Did too!" said Jen.

"Did not!" said Mary.

"Did too!" said Jen.

"Not!" shouted Mary.

Then it started to rain.

Even though the repetitive use of dialogue tags may seem too much to us, for children struggling to read independently at this level, repetition is good, and identification of who says what through the use of dialogue tags is important. It also teaches emergent readers the word *said*. Always use dialogue tags when writing dialogue for emergent readers, and double check that you have used the quotation marks correctly as part of the punctuation of the complete sentence.

Not only is repetition helpful in the text itself in emergent readers, but repetitive plot patterns help children become stronger and more fluent readers. To explore various repetitive plot structures and how to create stories based on them, continue reading.

Beginner's Tip

In manuals of style, the rules for using quotation marks include examples of quotation marks being placed *inside* the punctuation. However, those types of sentences are too complex for emergent readers so you do not need to know those rules when writing for most beginning readers.

Professional Track

Pull one of your old manuscripts out of the file cabinet. Edit it for proper use of quotation marks.

Strengthen Your Writing Muscles

In your own personal writer's notebook, create a page for dialogue tags. List as many dialogue tags as you can think of and add to this list over time. Include words such as: *asked, said, shouted, exclaimed, explained, stated.*

9.4 Plot

Once again, simple and predictable plots are winners with emergent readers. Don't add too many elements to the plot structure that will cause young readers to pause to figure out what's happening. They're so focused on understanding each word and each sentence that adding complicated elements to the plot will overwhelm them and they will give up trying to read the story. You can help them focus even more on learning vocabulary and reading skills by choosing to structure your story in a predictable pattern.

As with pre-emergent readers, predictable plots that use repetition and a list or series of events to move the story forward can be very effective in emergent readers. A surprise at the end is always a plus and leaves young readers feeling very pleased and satisfied when the story is over.

There are various plot structures you can utilize when writing emergent readers with predictable plots.

Predictable Plots for Children's Stories

Cumulative stories follow a plot where each time a new event occurs, all previous events are repeated. Think of the folk tale, *This is the House that Jack Built.*

Decreasing structure stories start with more and end with less. *Five Little Monkeys Jumping on the Bed* is an example that is also a counting story.

Increasing structure stories such as *There was an Old Lady Who Swallowed a Fly* start small and build up to a grand and glorious ending.

Full circle stories follow a round pattern because they begin and end in a similar way. Laura Numeroff is a master at writing circular stories, as demonstrated with her endearing picture book, *If You Give a Mouse a Cookie,* and other books she has written in that series.

Journey stories follow the main character on a quest that takes him or her to new places. *The Lord of the Rings* trilogy is an example for older readers of this classic plot structure of myths.

Pattern stories such as *The Gingerbread Man* have each new scene repeat the previous ones with only slight variations.

Question and answer stories such as the picture book *Brown Bear, Brown Bear* by Bill Martin develop the plot by asking repetitive questions with slight variations of text accompanied by repetitive answers with slight variations of text as well.

Sequence stories develop the plot based on counting with numbers, the alphabet, the days of the week, the months of the year or other predictable and familiar sequences. My book, *D is for Drinking Gourd: An African American Alphabet* is a picture book that incorporates the sequence of the alphabet from A to Z as part of its plot structure.

Emergent readers in the trade book market, or books that can be purchased in a bookstore or borrowed from a library, are often the very first books children choose off a shelf by themselves and attempt to read without the help of an adult. With this in mind, publishers in the trade book market want emergent readers with plots that are delightful, whimsical, and grab the attention of kids in kindergarten and first grade. These publishers are not looking for books with plot lines or story arcs that have a beginning, middle, and end that feel like the story is didactic, educational, or teaching a lesson.

Some publishers have emergent readers that focus on science or math concepts such as Scholastic's *Hello Reader! Math Books!*™ series and *Hello Reader! Science*™ series. Because these series are still for the trade book market, however, they still need a plot that gives the story an overriding entertaining feel rather than an educational tone.

Stories written expressly for the educational market can have a much more educational slant to their plot structure. Even though these emergent readers are still appealing to a child's sense of wonder and delight, the plot can be more instructional in nature. Why? Because emergent readers published in the educational market are for teachers to purchase and use in their classrooms. Little children won't buy these for themselves. Emergent readers in the educational market must support the State and National Standards as well as the Common Core State Standards. (For more information about writing beginning readers that support the Standards, read *Section 3.2 State and National Standards*.)

As a simple example of the difference between developing the plot or story arc for an emergent reader in the trade book market versus developing the plot for an emergent reader in the educational market, let's start with Bear as our main character. Let's give Bear a problem to solve: Which shirt should Bear wear to his birthday party? Now we need to develop the plot, or give this story a beginning, a middle, and an end.

In the trade book market, the problem in the beginning would stay the same. Bear can't decide which shirt to wear to his birthday party. The middle, where Bear is trying to decide which one he should wear, should be totally sweet and charming. For instance, each time Bear tries on a new shirt, Squirrel could simply say Bear's shirt doesn't look "just right." The ending should be just as cute. Squirrel can hand Bear his pajama shirt to wear and they decide to have a pajama party for his birthday.

Here is a story that has an endearing plot that could be written as an emergent reader for the trade book market:

A Shirt for Bear
Today is Bear's birthday party.
Which shirt should he wear?
Bear puts on a shirt.
"Do you like my shirt?" Bear asks.
Squirrel says, "This shirt does not look
just right for a party."
Bear puts on another shirt.
"Do you like my shirt?" Bear asks.
Squirrel says, "This shirt does not look
just right for a party."
Bear puts on another shirt.
"Do you like my shirt?" Bear asks.
Squirrel says, "This shirt does not look
just right for a party."
Squirrel gives Bear a shirt.
"Put this one on," Squirrel says.
"But this is my pajama shirt!" Bear says.
"I know," Squirrel says.
"We will have a pajama party
for your birthday party today!"

Now, let's develop a different plot or story arc that is intended for an emergent reader in the educational market. We'll use both the same main character, Bear, and the same problem. The beginning can stay the same: Bear can't decide which shirt to wear to his birthday party. However, because we're developing a plot intended for the educational market such as reproducible mini-books or read aloud plays, we need to have the problem solved in such a way that an educational concept is taught. This time, even though we are still creating a sweet, endearing story, it will have more of a didactic feel and definite educational focus. For this story's middle, let's give Bear different colors of shirts to try on. In the end, Squirrel can still give Bear a pajama shirt to wear, but this time it will be a specific color.

Here is the same story I wrote for the first example, but this time I developed the plot to have the problem be solved in such a way that it can be published in the educational market. Its educational concept will be teaching about colors. Because the story now includes this focus, trade book publishers might not want it due to its didactic feel.

A Shirt for Bear
Today is Bear's birthday party.
Which shirt should he wear?
Bear puts on a blue shirt.
"Do you like my shirt?" Bear asks.
Squirrel says, "This blue shirt does not look
just right for a party."
Bear puts on a yellow shirt.
"Do you like my shirt?" Bear asks.
Squirrel says, "This yellow shirt does not look
just right for a party."
Bear puts on a red shirt.
"Do you like my shirt?" Bear asks.

Squirrel says, "This red shirt does not look
just right for a party."
Squirrel gives Bear a green shirt.
"Put this one on," Squirrel says.
"But this is my pajama shirt!" Bear says.
"I know," Squirrel says.
"We will have a pajama party
for your birthday party today!"

Whether totally entertaining or educational in nature, a simple plot or story arc with a clear beginning, middle, and end is just right for an emergent reader. Add a surprise or a twist in the end, and you'll create a winning manuscript for this reading level. Place it in the perfect setting, and your story will win its way into precious little hearts. Continue reading to learn more about crafting a setting for emergent readers.

Beginner's Tip

Predictable plots are a great way to practice writing emergent readers. These stories practically write themselves. Go ahead. Try one on for size!

Professional Track

Practice using predictable plot patterns to write magazine stories. Editors might love this fresh, new approach! I've written several stories with predictable plots for magazines and my editor keeps asking for more.

Strengthen Your Writing Muscles

Choose one fairy tale or tall tale. Rewrite it as an emergent reader using several different predictable plot patterns. Which worked the best? Which didn't work at all for that particular story?

9.5 Setting

Setting is not described in emergent readers. As with pre-emergent readers, the setting is conveyed through the illustrations. Art supports the text, and setting can be very basic at this reading level. However, no matter how basic the setting for your story might be, you can create a setting that spells success.

For instance, if the main character, Duck, is riding a bike, the art might only show a picture of Duck riding a bike. There might not be any background illustration at all. This simplicity of artwork helps children look at the pictures for clues to decode or figure out what the text is saying. If the art shows Duck riding a bike and an airplane is flying overhead and a boat is sailing down a river next to the path Duck is riding on, it makes it just a little bit more difficult for children to know whether the text is talking about the plane or a boat when they read: *Duck rides a bike*.

Setting for emergent readers should still be in the familiar world of a young child. Even though you might not mention the setting and definitely won't describe it in the actual text, the setting of your story is important. Your story can take place in a park, on a farm, or at the zoo. It can be in a house, even if the characters are animals. In this case, your characters would sit in chairs and sleep in beds just like people do. If animals are your main characters, the setting can also be an animal's home such as a cave, a burrow, or a nest. Keep the setting familiar, however, and don't make it be in some exotic animal home that most children are not yet familiar with at this young age.

When writing your emergent reader manuscript, describe detailed art instructions in [brackets]. If the illustration needs to be very specific, find a picture on the Internet and include a copy of the image along with your manuscript submission. For instance, if your main character wakes up each morning to an alarm clock because you are writing a story for the educational market that teaches children how to tell time, you might need an alarm clock that is an analog clock on one page and an alarm clock that is a digital clock on the next page. If there is any question about which type to use where, supply an actual image. Unlike picture book publishers, publishers of emergent readers expect authors to be very specific with their art instructions because the illustrations in emergent readers represent the text literally. These literal illustrations provide clues for young readers to use to read successfully, confidently, and more independently.

As with pre-emergent readers, the setting in this reading level works hand-in-hand with the topic or theme your story is about. To discover how to choose topics to write about for emergent readers, continue to the following section.

Beginner's Tip

Reread classic fairytales such as *Goldilocks and the Three Bears, Little Red Riding Hood*, and *The Three Little Pigs*. Note the importance of setting in each story but also note the lack of words used to describe each setting. It's the same with emergent readers.

Professional Track

Which verb tense do you like to write in the best—present or past tense? Write one story in present tense and one in past tense. Some authors, editors, and publishers like to use present tense because it draws readers instantly into the stories. Some prefer using past tense because it's a more natural voice to read. Which worked best for you when you wrote an emergent reader?

Strengthen Your Writing Muscles

Open your refrigerator. Study what it looks like inside. Then close the door. Using the inside of your refrigerator as the setting, write an emergent reader about an orange and an apple who are best friends and decide to explore their chilly world together.

9.6 Topics and Themes

Similar to the topics and themes for pre-emergent readers, the topics and themes for emergent readers are centered on the experiences and real world of young children. Family relationships, school days, and interacting with friends are great choices you can write about for this reading level.

Because children who read emergent readers are usually in kindergarten and first grade, topics taught in K-1 classrooms are also high on the list as potential themes you can choose when writing for this reading level. These include holidays, seasons, and science topics such as animals' homes, the life cycle of a butterfly, and seeds. Concepts taught at this grade level include the alphabet, colors, and counting skills. Calendar skills include the days of the week and the months of the year.

If you want to brainstorm ideas for topics and themes you can write about for emergent readers, go to your local teacher supply store and look at the table of contents for supplemental books teachers use in kindergarten and first grade. Supplemental books include books of reproducible worksheets, read-aloud plays, or emergent reader mini-books geared for K-1 students that teachers use in the classroom. If you don't have a teacher supply store near you, use the feature on Amazon where you can peek inside a book and view its table of contents. In the book I wrote with Sheryl Ann Crawford for Scholastic Professional Books, *15 Easy-to-Read Holiday & Seasonal Mini-Book Plays*, our table of contents includes three to five plays for each of the four seasons: fall, winter, spring, and summer. Look over tables of contents in K-1 or K-2 books such as this for handy lists of themes and topics you can choose from when you write material for this level.

Here is an example of the table of contents for my emergent readers mini-books for Scholastic Teaching Resources, *Cut & Paste Mini-Books: Around the Year* (used by permission of Scholastic Inc.). The first line in the table of contents shows the title of the mini-book and the second line explains which educational skill or concept that particular mini-book features. This sample will give you a starting point for knowing which holidays and seasons children at this reading level are learning about in school.

Cut & Paste Mini-Books: Around the Year
Table of Contents
Ready for School
 Context clues
Apples in the Tree
 Simple subtraction
Pumpkin Time!
 Size concepts
Thank You, Squanto
 Common nouns
Winter is Here!

Number words

A Colorful Holiday

Color words

New Year's Day Parade

Sequencing words

Dr. King Had a Dream

Skip counting

Presidential Pets

Animal names

My Special Valentines

shapes

Hello Spring!

Predictable text

It's Earth Day

Making inferences

If You Meet a Gull at the Beach

Sun safety

The Fourth of July

The five senses

Candles on the Cake

Counting

Children at this level also learn about neighborhoods and communities. They learn about people who work in their towns and cities such as doctors, postal workers, and firefighters. They learn about the places they can go in their neighborhood such as the library, school, stores, and the park. Maps and simple map skills are introduced to children in this age group.

More topics and themes you can write about for emergent readers include common learning experiences for children this age. Little ones in kindergarten and first grade start to lose their teeth. They experience their first day of kindergarten. Sometimes they connect with their very first special friend. They might get their very first pet of their own because they are now old enough to start helping to care for it. They might join an organized sport for the first time. All of these "firsts" provide great topics and themes you can choose to write about for emergent readers.

Beginner's Tip

Supplemental books make great resources to browse through while you're brainstorming ideas for your own stories. Collect used ones from thrift stores or a sampling from online used bookstores to add to your personal research library.

Professional Track

Pitch an idea to a publisher to write a supplemental book for the educational market for grades K-1. If you land the contract, use the research you dig up when you write that book to gather ideas for emergent readers and beginning readers.

Strengthen Your Writing Muscles

What was your favorite holiday as a child? Do a freewriting exercise where you describe a favorite childhood holiday memory (or that of a child you know). When finished, use this precious memory as a theme to write an emergent reader.

Chapter 10

EASY READERS

10.1 Sentence Structure and Vocabulary

Learning to read is a journey of discovery every child embarks upon. You can help make this a journey of success and positive achievement through the easy readers you write. Carefully crafted sentences with appropriate grade-level vocabulary words target children in first through third grade and provide the means to transport readers from their first attempts to sound out words to the place where they can read independently.

Easy Readers At-a-Glance

(Check with each publisher to determine specifics.)

Sample Titles:

Fluffy's School Bus Adventure by Kate McMullan (HelloReader!® Level 3: Grades 1 & 2, Ages 6-8, Scholastic)

Jonathan James Says "I Can Help" by Crystal Bowman (Learn to Read: For ages 4-8, Zondervan)

The Missing Tooth by Joanna Cole (Step into Reading™ Step 2 Book: Grades 1-3, Random House)

Betsy Ross and the Silver Thimble by Stephanie Greene (Ready-to-Read Level 2: Reading Independently, Aladdin Paperbacks)

Word Count:

     550 to 900 words

Page Count:

     32 to 48 pages

Lines of Text:

     Up to 12 lines per two-page spread

          Up to 36 characters per line

Different publishers use different terminology for easy readers. Some have them broken into various levels such as a Level 2 or a Level 3. Others use terms such as "reading alone" or "independent readers." Most students at this reading level are in first or second grade. Some are in third grade. Easy readers provide material for them to use the reading skills they have already acquired to read all on their own.

Sentences average between seven to ten words in length, with shorter sentences scattered in between. Occasionally, you might write a longer sentence, but only if it's absolutely necessary or if it's broken into segments such as through the use of dialogue where one chunk is inside the quotation marks and the other chunk is the dialogue tag.

Some common prefixes (*un-*) and suffixes (*-ing*) can be found in easy readers as can the simplest compound words. Apostrophes are used with words such as possessives (the *boy's* bear, *Meg's* paper, *Grandma's* glasses) and selected contractions such as *I'll, can't*, and *wasn't*.

Vocabulary words reflect the subjects taught in first through third grade. Some teachers post words up on a bulletin board called a Word Wall that lists groups of words supporting a similar theme. For instance, because basic math skills such as standard and metric measurement are introduced in these grades, a teacher might post a list of words on a Word Wall that include: inch, ounce, meter, and kilogram. Students are then encouraged to refer to the Word Wall while reading and writing about the featured topic. These same vocabulary words and words associated with other topics taught in first, second, and third grade are therefore appropriate to use when writing easy readers, even if they might seem too complicated to sound out or decode for children at this reading level. For instance, because the life cycle of a butterfly is taught at this age level, complicated words such as caterpillar, butterfly, and cocoon can be introduced.

Some publishers start to use paragraph format on the actual page of published easy readers. Others still use a vertical sentence structure where each sentence appears line by line with no paragraphs or indentations.

Some easy readers may be broken into very short chapters. Even though easy readers still fall under the picture book category and technically aren't classified as first chapter books because they have the appearance, format, and overall feel of fully illustrated beginning readers, some publishers do feature easy readers with chapters. (To learn more about first chapter books, read *Chapter 12: First Chapter Books*.) Easy readers are a transition to the more advanced readers that children will eventually enjoy along their journey of mastering the ability to read without help.

Even though easy readers work hard to help kids in first, second, and third grade learn how to read grade-level vocabulary with controlled sentence structure, easy readers are loads of fun! To learn how to develop characters who burst onto the scene with their own exciting adventures, continue to the next section.

Beginner's Tip

Make your own Word Wall or miniature bulletin board next to your desk or the place where you write. Post vocabulary words geared to your target reading level for a handy reference. If you switch reading levels, post a different list of words.

Professional Track

On a computer desktop publisher software program such as Inkscape, *Printmaster*® or the *Print Shop*®, create a mini-dictionary with vocabulary words for your beginning reader. Post it on your blog as a pdf file (portable document file) for teachers to download and use with their students. There are free pdf file converters online.

Strengthen Your Writing Muscles

Select several easy readers. Type them onto your computer, word for word from beginning to end. Be sure to type the sentences in the same format as the published text appears. Doing this exercise will train your brain to learn to know better where to break sentences into chunks on different lines.

10.2 Characters

Children who are just acquiring the reading skills to read independently are loyal fans of a favorite character. One story about this character is simply not enough. They want to read more! And even more! By understanding the dynamics of this devotion and the qualities that make a winning character, you can create strong characters in your own easy readers that this eager audience will delight in following along with through countless adventures.

I love to study fiction techniques produced for writers of older audiences. One of the fiction techniques I'm always enthusiastic about studying is character development. Even though the examples in these fiction classes I take or how-to books I read are not geared for writing easy readers, the principles of character development are much the same. One book I enjoy gleaning from is Elaine Marie Alphin's *Creating Characters Kids Will Love.*

Because children at this reading level are such devoted fans, we want to create strong characters who will instantly capture their affection. Even though not much literal character development is included in the actual text of easy readers, character traits are revealed through dialogue and actions. Taking time to create strong character traits in your main characters *before* you sit down to start writing your easy reader manuscripts will produce incredible results. For step-by-step guidance on developing strong characters for your easy readers, read *Section 7.2 Characters with Kid-Appeal.*

Many publishers only want characters who are actual people at this level. Some publishers are more open to using animals as characters. Especially in the educational market you might be able to sell a story concept with animals as the main characters versus in the trade book market for easy readers where many publishers insist the main characters be actual children.

If you choose to create a cast of animals for this reading level, however, be sure that they are not cute and babyish as in earlier levels. Children choosing easy readers off the shelves by themselves are experiencing a newly discovered sense of independence. They won't touch anything that appears babyish in their eyes. They want stories about characters who move around independently in a realistic world. If using animals as your main characters, make them move and talk just like people do.

Series are big hits in this reading level. The driving force behind the success of these series are the strong characters themselves. Therefore, when writing for this reading level and pitching ideas to editors for potential easy reader manuscripts, always think series. I don't recommend pitching an idea or submitting a completed manuscript for a stand-alone easy reader title or just one book about your character. Yes, you might land a contract for a stand-alone easy reader title. But your chances of landing an easy reader contract will increase if you present the concept as a series.

When my dear friend and writing buddy, Sheryl Ann Crawford and I were brainstorming ideas for a book of 15 reproducible math mini-books for children in kindergarten through second grade, we could have easily chosen to write 15 totally different stories with 15 totally different characters as we had written in our other books for Scholastic. However, because we knew that many students at this age are independent readers and choosing easy readers with strong characters, we decided to develop a pair of best friends who would appear in all the books. We chose animals as our main characters to appeal to our younger audience, but we worked to make them appear more mature to appeal to our older audience as well.

Here is an example of the characters Lion and Mouse that we developed in our book, *15 Easy & Irresistible Math Mini-Books: Reproducible, Easy-to-Read Stories and Activities That Invite Kids to Add, Subtract, Measure, Tell Time, and Practice Other Important Early Math Skills* (used by permission of Scholastic Inc.). This sample is from the mini-book, "Subtraction Cookies."

Subtraction Cookies
Page 2:
"Today is Bird's birthday," Mouse said. "I will bake a cake for the party."
Lion said, "I will bake 10 cookies."
[Art shows Lion wearing oven mitts and a chef's hat and putting a sheet of cookies in the oven, a very grown-up thing to do.]

Page 3:
Mouse asked, "Did you bake 10 cookies?"
"Yes, I did!" Lion said. "But I ate 3."
[Art shows Mouse and Lion talking on the phone to each other from their own homes. Lion has cookie crumbs all over his face and just seven cookies left on his cookie sheet.]

Page 4:
"I think 7 cookies are enough for the party," Mouse said.
"Do not eat any more!"
[Art shows Mouse and Lion still talking on the phone.]

Page 5:
"What is that crunching noise?" asked Mouse.
"Did you eat more cookies?"
"I ate 5 more," Lion said. "I am a great cook!"

[Art shows Mouse arriving at Lion's house and carrying a big cake. Lion has cookie crumbs all over his face and just two cookies left on his cookie sheet.]

Page 6:
"Two cookies are not enough for Bird's party," Lion said.
[Art shows Lion looking very worried.]

Page 7:
"That's okay," Mouse said. "I have enough cake for everyone."
"Hooray!" said Lion. "And I have enough cookies for 2 friends."
[Art shows Mouse and Lion each happily eating a cookie together.]

Page 8:
[Art includes two math problems.]

Because this mini-book focuses on math skills, we kept most of the vocabulary words very simple. We used actual numerals such as 5 and 7 instead of spelling out the words, because in a math book geared for beginning readers, most publishers want children to identify and work with numerals rather than identify the number words. We used contractions such as *that's*, very little repetition, and longer sentences that appear all on one line of text rather than broken up over several different lines. These are key components of easy reader manuscripts. The 15 easy-to-read mini-books in our book were the perfect vehicle for developing a series of strong characters kids would find irresistible. And since strong characters need a strong voice, continue to the next section to explore ways to create effective dialogue for this reading level.

Beginner's Tip

Make a Christmas list of presents your main character would want. Then write a scene of mostly dialogue where your main character sits on Santa's lap and tells him what's on the list.

Professional Track

Create a report card for each of your characters. What grades would they get? What are their strengths and their weaknesses? What kind of comments would they get from their teachers?

Strengthen Your Writing Muscles

Evaluate Lion and Mouse, the characters in "Subtraction Cookies." Which character was the more practical one? Which character was more of the "adult" voice? Which character was messy? Which character made endearing mistakes? Which character was a problem solver? What other character traits did you see in each one?

After your evaluation, use these same characters, Lion and Mouse, to star in a short easy reader of your own. Be sure to give them the same character traits in your new story as they had in "Subtraction Cookies."

10.3 Dialogue

Easy readers are driven by dialogue. This means that instead of a lot of narrative that describes emotion, character traits, or thoughts, the characters use dialogue and state most things clearly and directly to each other. You can give each of your characters their own strong voice by developing dialogue that brings life to each scene of your story.

The use of dialogue tags in easy readers is still important to provide information about who is saying what. The proper use of punctuation and quotations marks with dialogue is essential to prepare a professional manuscript for submission to a publisher or agent. For the basic rules about using quotations marks, turn back to *Section 9.3 Dialogue.*

If you were to count the number of sentences in almost any easy reader you might select as an example, you would see that dialogue is a very common story ingredient for this level. Let your characters speak and you'll instantly engage your readers. Use dialogue to develop strong character traits in your main character. Use dialogue to add vivid and lively dynamics to your story. Use dialogue when you write easy readers to show, not tell.

Here is an example that helps clarify the positive difference the use of dialogue can make and the power it has to show what's happening in a scene versus just using narrative text to tell about the scene.

Example of narrative text without dialogue:
Karla took her pet hamster to her friend's house. Patti was happy to see Twinky.
Karla told Patti that Twinky did tricks.
Both girls watched Twinky do a trick. Then they taught him a new one.

Example of text that uses dialogue:
Karla took her pet hamster to her friend's house.
"Hi Twinky!" Patti said.
"I taught Twinky a new trick," Karla said. "Watch what Twinky can do."
Karla put Twinky down on the rug.
"Twinky," Karla said. "Disappear."
Twinky ran under the bed. Now the girls could not see him.
Patti laughed. "Let's teach Twinky a new trick," she said.

In the first example, the narrative "tells" what is happening but doesn't make the scene come alive because there is no dialogue. It is flat and boring.

In the second example, dialogue is used to develop the scene. Now we can see what is happening ourselves and don't have to be told. The story is shown to us as it unfolds before our eyes.

The main difference between the two examples is the use of dialogue. You can use dialogue effectively when you write easy readers to show, not tell. Dialogue makes a scene come alive. Dialogue draws young readers immediately into the story. Dialogue is a key ingredient to use when writing easy readers. Developing a strong plot is also important. To learn how to structure the plot of easy readers, go to the next section.

Beginner's Tip

Take a field trip. Sit at a children's play area in the mall. Or take a picnic lunch to the park and sit near the swings. Go anywhere small children are playing and sit with your writer's notebook and pen. Write down snippets of actual dialogue you overhear.

Professional Track

Invite two or three published writer friends to a chat session or conference call. Ask each to come as a favorite easy reader character. Then ask a variety of questions and let each one respond in their own character's unique voice. When finished, discuss what you learned.

Strengthen Your Writing Muscles

Find a passage of narrative in a favorite middle grade or young adult novel. Rewrite the passage as an easy reader using mostly dialogue.

10.4 Plot

The plot thickens in easy readers. No longer limited to simple, basic plots, the plot structure for this reading level can be more complex. Children in first through third grade are very busy exploring the world in their newly-found independence. They find excitement in adventuring into new situations, and the plot structure you can create reflects the new levels of complexity they experience at this age.

For fiction, most publishers at this reading level do not want stories with predictable plot patterns. (For more information about predictable plots for children's stories, see *Section 9.4 Plot*.) The story arc in an easy reader should have a clearly defined beginning, middle, and end. As with writing fiction in all reading levels, the beginning of the story is where you introduce the main character, the main problem, and the setting.

The middle of an easy reader story is where things get more complicated than in pre-emergent readers and emergent readers. This adds more tension and more interest to the story and appeals to older kids. Instead of having just one main problem to solve as a character might have in a pre-emergent reader or an emergent reader, here in easy readers smaller problems can surface within the main problem. Usually, these smaller problems occur in a set of three, and each time the main character attempts to solve them, things just get worse.

By the last attempt to solve the third smaller problem, the main character is in a mess. The main character is therefore forced to make a pivotal decision. This decision propels the main character to take action and thus the main problem presented at the beginning is now resolved in the end of the story.

To help develop a more complex plot structure for the easy reader manuscripts you write, create a Plot Structure Chart:

Plot Structure Chart

Title of Easy Reader:

Beginning:

  Main character:

  Main problem:

  Setting:

Middle:

  Small problem #1:

    Main character's attempt to solve #1:

  Small problem #2:

    Main character's attempt to solve #2:

  Small problem #3:

    Main character's attempt to solve #3:

End:

  Pivotal decision:

  Main character's resulting action:

  Resolution of the main problem, which also solves the smaller problems:

Sitting down to brainstorm ideas for the ingredients of your story's plot structure *before* you start writing your story will automatically give you a stronger story. Use the above sample to design your own Plot Structure Chart by hand or on a computer desktop publisher software program such as Inkscape, *Printmaster*® or the *Print Shop*®. Photocopy blank copies of it and keep these in a handy file folder to fill in for each of your easy reader manuscripts.

In first, second, and third grade, children are also reading nonfiction. Even though everything in a nonfiction easy reader is fact, however, don't just list facts. That's boring even if the facts are interesting in and of themselves. Tell young readers fascinating facts in such a way that gives them a sense of story. How can this be accomplished? Through developing the structure of your nonfiction manuscript in a way similar to developing the plot structure when writing fiction.

When writing easy readers that are nonfiction biographies, you can create the plot structure to be similar to the plot structure used with fiction. However, everything in a nonfiction biography must be true. Even the dialogue must be actual words the main character said as found in primary sources such a diaries, speeches, newspaper interviews, or articles the person wrote.

Other nonfiction is based on the structure of a familiar pattern, a sequence of events, a chronological progression, or a logical presentation of information that takes the reader from starting at Point A to Point B to concluding with Point C. For instance, if you're writing a *how-to* piece, you would structure your manuscript starting with the first step and moving forward step-by-step until the last step completes the project.

Nonfiction needs an *introduction*, a *body,* and a *closing.* The introduction is the beginning of the manuscript. The body includes the supporting details, step-by-step instruction, or presentation of information that flows logically from the first fact to the last. The closing is where the manuscript is wrapped up with a conclusion that leaves the reader feeling a high level of satisfaction.

Whether writing nonfiction or fiction, however, your story has to take place somewhere. To help develop your story's setting, continue reading.

Beginner's Tip

Use the five W's to help brainstorm ideas for your easy reader plot. Who? What? When? Where? Why?

Professional Track

Is there a favorite story you've written but haven't yet published? Restructure the plot following the Plot Structure Chart. Rewrite your story as an easy reader and make it have a stronger plot.

Strengthen Your Writing Muscles

Fill in your Plot Structure Chart for a new easy reader story. Create a puppet stage on a TV tray and make stick puppets of each of your characters by cutting out pictures and gluing them to Popsicle or craft sticks. Have your puppets perform the story before you ever write the first word, following the Plot Structure Chart as a guide. When finished with the play, sit down and write the first draft of your easy reader.

10.5 Setting

As in the earlier reading levels, setting is usually not mentioned in the text in an easy reader. Because easy readers are still fully illustrated, the setting does not need to be described or even mentioned. Children can look at the setting right in the picture on the page. Art is still very literal in easy readers and shows exactly where the story is taking place. Armed with this knowledge, you can create a setting, however, that sticks in the hearts and minds of kids and makes them want to visit this place and follow the further escapades of these characters again and again.

Unlike earlier reading levels where there might not be any background illustration but just a picture showing the key vocabulary words, art in easy readers can have a lot of details within each picture. For instance, in an emergent reader, the sentence on the page might be: Juan kicks the ball. The accompanying illustration might only be a picture of Juan and a soccer ball. There might not be any background to the scene. In an easy reader, however, the scene would be developed behind the picture of Juan and the soccer ball. We might see him playing on a team on a soccer field with a crowd of people watching on the side.

The art and therefore the setting are still very literal, but are more developed than in earlier reading levels. The reason for this change between reading levels is because children who read easy readers are independent readers. They have acquired a substantial number of vocabulary words they can recognize by sight or attempt to read by themselves by sounding out the words and looking at the pictures for clues. They are not learning new vocabulary words when they read at this level as much as they are developing reading fluency and the ability to read smoothly and with comprehension.

Because a child's world is expanding in first through third grade, the setting can include places that might be unfamiliar. Also, adventures that take place in a setting such as a child's home, school, or neighborhood are of keen interest to this target age because they are eager to explore the real world.

Unless it isn't obvious where your story is taking place, there is no longer a need to include detailed art instructions about the setting in brackets. Easy readers usually incorporate enough text and take place in familiar enough surroundings that you don't have to include directions for the illustrator to follow. In fact, now that the background can feature realistic scenes and a variety of details, many illustrators of easy readers add fresh and endearing elements to the setting that they create themselves! In many easy readers the author and the artist truly become a team, especially in a series of easy readers where they develop the whole story concept together over a number of books.

Since easy readers are all about series, there are also a variety of topics and themes you can choose from for each different book in your series. Read the following to learn more.

Beginner's Tip

Look at a picture in an easy reader, but don't read the text on that page. Brainstorm ideas for a brand new story based only on the setting you see in that illustration. Sometimes establishing a setting for a story first helps our creative juices flow.

Professional Track

On your blog, host a Wordless Wednesday. Take a picture of a place in a child's world such as a child's bedroom, a tree house, or a swing set. Post this picture on your blog but don't tell your readers where it is. Ask readers to post comments, describe the setting, and share what the picture means to them. Use these ideas to write an easy reader.

Strengthen Your Writing Muscles

Examine an easy reader. Look carefully at the art on one page. What do you see in the setting that is not ever mentioned in the text? Evaluate whether or not you think this detail was suggested by the author or added because it was the illustrator's own idea.

10.6 Topics and Themes

Because children reading at this level are exploring more and more outside their familiar world, you can choose from a much larger variety of topics and themes while writing easy readers than in earlier reading levels.

Relationships between family members, friends, and community helpers such as teachers and librarians can be more complicated. Unfamiliar settings and more exotic locales can form the backdrop of your story, opening up an even larger selection of topics and themes to choose from. A wide variety of genre can be introduced as an engaging vehicle to convey your story, broadening your choice of topics and themes even more. Here are some examples of popular genres for this reading level:

Humor

What child doesn't find it amusing to have his or her funny bone tickled? Humorous easy readers are always winners. There are numerous ways to incorporate humor into your story. Laugh your way through piles of funny easy reader books while researching this genre and note pointers on what made you chuckle the most. Again, because teachers are a viable target audience for this level, try to avoid bathroom humor.

Mysteries

Kids love mysteries. Kids' puzzle-solving skills are challenged as they try to find clues in the story to solve the problem. A red herring or clue that temporarily misleads the reader is always a favorite. There are potential suspects, each of them guilty until the main character discovers the true culprit. In the world of easy readers, engaging mysteries keep young readers on the edge of their seats from beginning to end.

Historical Fiction

Take your readers back in time along journeys of discovery that are based on real people, real places, and real events. Historical fiction places make-believe characters in history. These easy readers make history come alive to young readers with vivid colors and bold adventures.

Fantasy

Anything can happen in this genre! There are no limits to the imagination of a child, and fantasy sparks new possibilities with every new story that's written. Entire new worlds never heard of before are trademarks of this genre.

Science Fiction

Kids eagerly hop on board to be transported to imaginary worlds in totally different dimensions. Similar to fantasy, there is one main difference. Everything fantastical in this genre is based on actual scientific fact. In this modern age of computers and cell phones, youngsters love these hi-tech easy readers.

Adventure

Ready…set…go! Action-packed adventure grips readers as they follow their favorite heroes and heroines racing to overcome extreme challenges through the pages of these books. Easy readers filled with treasure maps, swashbuckling pirates, modern spies, and hi-scale adventure make this genre a favorite at this age.

Nonfiction

Knowledge is power, and children this age eat up fascinating facts as fast as we can dish them out. If you love researching cold, hard facts, then dig through treasure troves of information and present gold nuggets to young readers in nonfiction easy reader manuscripts.

Have fun exploring different genres published for easy readers. Read lots and lots of examples. If you don't find many titles published in one of your favorite genres, brainstorm ideas for titles of your own. Kids this age love reading lively and engaging easy readers in a variety of genres. You can write stories that win their way into kids' hearts.

Beginner's Tip

Browse through a stack of easy readers. Identify which genre each story is. Group titles of similar genre together. Compare and contrast their similarities and differences as you gain a better understanding of each genre.

Professional Track

Have you been published in each of the above genres? If not, choose one of them to explore. Branch out and write an easy reader for a new genre. You never know how it will "fit" you until you try.

Strengthen Your Writing Muscles

Write down a list of five to ten actual hi-tech gadgets such as a cell phone and a laser pointer. Next, mix and match two gadgets to invent a new one such as a laser pointer that can also send a text message. Brainstorm ideas for a way to use this new gadget in a sci-fi easy reader.

Chapter 11

ADVANCED READERS

11.1 Sentence Structure and Vocabulary

Many children in second and third grade are mastering the skills to read fluently. They are eager and often able to read all on their own, but shy away from middle grade novels because they are daunted by the page length and text-heavy appearance of those books. They feel much more comfortable picking up advanced readers. The page length is shorter, each page is fully illustrated, and the themes are topics they like. Kids this age instinctively know that these advanced readers are written just for them. As a writer for this target audience, you can bring a smile to their hearts. You can light up their world. You can give them books that will become some of their dearest friends.

Advanced Readers At-a-Glance
(Check with each publisher to determine specifics.)
Sample Titles:
Five Brilliant Scientists by Lynda Jones (Hello Reader!® Level 4: Grades 2
   & 3 Nonfiction, Scholastic)
Clara Barton: Spirit of the American Red Cross by Patricia Lakin (Ready-
   to-Read: Level 3 Reading Proficiently, Aladdin Paperbacks)
The Case of the Shrunken Allowance by Joanne Rocklin (Hello Math
   Reader™ Level 4: Grades 2 & 3, Scholastic)
Space Station: Accident on Mir by Angela Royston (Dorling Kindersley
   Readers: Level 4 Proficient Readers, Dorling Kindersley)
Word Count:
   About 1500 words
Page Count:
   32 to 48 pages

Lines of Text:

   Lines per two-page spread not restricted at this level

   Characters per line not restricted at this level

Advanced readers are also labeled as "reading proficiently" or "accelerated readers." Advanced readers can be classified as a Level 3 or Level 4, depending on which system a publisher uses.

Advanced readers are formatted in short standard paragraphs. This is the first reading level where many publishers do not break sentences up into phrases over different lines of text as in earlier reading levels. Most publishers also do not clarify the number of characters per line at this level. Instead, advanced readers format sentences into paragraphs in the same way you'll see in middle grade and young adult novels with font a similar size. Here is an example of the paragraph format used in advanced readers. This sample is from "The Number Detectives and the Case of the Hungry Hikers" in the book for grades 2 to 4 that Sheryl Ann Crawford and I wrote for Scholastic Professional Books, *15 Math Mystery Mini-Books* (used by permission of Scholastic Inc.):

"How many hikers are in your hiking club?" Casey asked.

"Twenty," answered Derek. "I already got a juice box for each person. Next on my list are marshmallows."

"Here's a bag of marshmallows," Casey offered. "I wonder how many marshmallows are in there?"

Sentences are still short in advanced readers and can average 10 words in length. Even shorter sentences appear frequently in the text as well. Alternating long and short sentences helps children gain stronger reading skills while continuing to build confidence in reading on their own.

New vocabulary words are introduced within the context of familiar words. When writing advanced readers, introduce a new vocabulary word carefully. You can either clarify the meaning of the word as part of the context of the entire paragraph, or include the actual definition of the word, or do a combination of both. For vocabulary words at this level, refer to the Second Grade Word List and the Third Grade Word List in the *Children's Writer's Word Book* by Alijandra Mogilner.

As with other reading levels, vocabulary words for advanced readers support the topics and themes taught in second and third grade. As you become more familiar with the State and National Standards along with the Common Core State Standards for these grade levels, you'll gain a firmer grasp of which vocabulary words not found on some word lists can be used successfully in your stories for this reading level because they support the material students are learning about in the classroom. (For more information about the State and National Standards as well as the Common Core State Standards, see *Section 3.2 State and National* Standards.) A general rule of thumb is that you can include more difficult words that are theme-related to this age group as long as these words can still be sounded out by young readers without asking an adult for help.

Advanced readers have short chapters. Because the overall goal of advanced readers is to help children in second and third grade transition from the world of easy readers into the world of novels, a shift is made in structure to break away from the format found in earlier reading levels. Paragraph format and short chapters make advanced readers appear and feel more like novels. Advanced readers such as *How Much is That Guinea Pig in the Window?* and *Finding the Titanic* are the bridge between beginning readers and chapter books.

Sentence structure, vocabulary words, and paragraph format can be similar in advanced readers and first chapter books in both the educational market and the trade book market. The main difference between the two reading levels in the trade book market, however, is the appearance of each published book. Advanced readers usually have full color illustrations and still retain the shape and cover size of other beginning readers levels. First chapter books, on the other hand, only have a few black-and-white illustrations and are the same shape and cover size as a novel. Both, however, feature casts of engaging and lively characters that instantly catch the hearts of young readers. Continue to the next section for tips and strategies on creating characters with big doses of kid-appeal.

Beginner's Tip

Look for published examples of how a new vocabulary word is introduced in an advanced reader for children in second and third grade. Write these examples as a reference in your personal writer's notebook.

Professional Track

Ask your publisher for permission to create coloring pages based on your advanced reader that have black and white outlines of pictures with short excerpts of text. (Some computer desktop publisher software programs similar to Inkscape, *Printmaster*® or the *Print Shop*® can generate a coloring page from any picture with the click of a button.) Distribute these pages during author visits or book signings to help market your book.

Strengthen Your Writing Muscles

Choose any middle grade or young adult novel. Don't worry about vocabulary level. Focus only on sentence structure. Type two or three paragraphs from the novel onto your computer. Now look for every sentence that is longer than 10 words. Break each of these sentences into at least two sentences so that each sentence in this passage is less than 10 words in length. Use this same technique to shorten sentences in your own advanced readers.

11.2 Characters

Unique and quirky characters frolic through the pages of fiction stories in advanced readers. Kids delight in their one-of-a-kind personalities and out-of-this-world escapades. As a writer, you can experience as much fun writing advanced readers as kids do reading them. Developing lively characters is the secret key that will open up a treasure house of enchanting adventures for both of you.

Naming your characters is so much fun! You can choose goofy, corny, and crazy names for your characters at this level, and you'll invent an instant magnet that attracts kids in second and third grade to your stories for advanced readers. For example, when Sheryl Ann Crawford and I were developing the concept for our book, *15 Math Mystery Mini-Books* for Scholastic Professional Books, we had a wacky time picking the names for our main characters and their sidekick, a smart detective dog who knows his math!

We started by creating a math detective team that included one boy and one girl. This makes the stories equally appealing to both boys and girls to read, an important factor when writing for second and third graders where publishers are always on the look-out for advanced readers that boys want to read, too.

We brainstormed a variety of different names and tried them on for size. Finally, we named the girl Sue McClue and the boy Casey Counts. The name of the detective dog? Sherlock, of course!

Because these three characters appeared in all 15 of the mini-books in this reproducible book for teachers, they were the main characters. In each different story, however, different minor characters came and went with different mysteries to solve. In contrast to the catchy names of the main characters, the minor characters had regular names and represented a variety of ethnicities such as Deon, Jessica, and Mario. Here's an example of this contrast between the names of major and minor characters that's from our story "The Number Detectives and the Case of the Missing Eggs," (used by permission of Scholastic Inc.):

> "Someone stole pennies from my piggy bank!" Deon cried.
> "How do you know there are pennies missing?" Sue McClue asked.
> "My piggy bank isn't as heavy as it was yesterday," Deon explained.
> "We'll find the thief," Casey Counts said.

Note that their sidekick, the smart detective dog, was not identified in this portion of text. He's not ever mentioned in the dialogue. No need to. He's in the art along with the kids. He wears a dog tag in the shape of a dog bone that has his name printed on it: Sherlock. Kids know Sherlock's name and see his personality conveyed through the art.

When writing advanced readers, you do not need to introduce your characters. Just let them jump onto the first page of the story and start talking. Their personality is revealed through their dialogue and their names are revealed through the use of dialogue tags.

When Sheryl and I developed Sue McClue, Casey Counts, and Sherlock the math detective dog, we also gave them unique character traits. These traits surfaced throughout the stories in each of the books. We worked hard to make them a natural part of the story and used these character traits to move the stories forward. Because each story was about solving a mystery, these character traits helped gather clues and figure out the math.

Sue McClue always wore a backpack. True to her name, she found lots of clues to help solve the mystery.

Casey Counts always carried a notebook in his hand. Throughout the pages of each story, he could be seen writing down the math problems and taking notes.

Sherlock never said anything in the story's actual text, but in the art, he was always thinking things in thought bubbles. His main focus in every story was trying to find a dog bone to eat! For example in the story, "The Number Detectives and the Case of the Puzzling Pizza," Sherlock is looking at a pizza and thinking in his thought bubble, "Dog biscuits would make good topping."

To help brainstorm ideas for your own cast of characters and develop engaging characters of your own with their own snazzy names and quirky personality traits, take time to create a Top Secret Detective File for each main character. To learn how to make a Top Secret Detective File and develop winning characters, read *Section 7.2 Characters with Kid-Appeal.*

After you develop your own cast of quirky and engaging characters, it's time to start giving them each a voice of their own. Read the next section to explore how to craft winning dialogue for advanced readers.

Beginner's Tip

Purchase a yearbook from your neighborhood elementary school. It will be chock full of current and popular children's names. You can use it as a great reference for a number of years!

Professional Track

Call up a writer friend and offer to swap character interviews. You can interview her main character and she can interview yours. (Of course, you'll each be answering for your own characters!) After you ask each other the interview questions, discuss what you like most about each other's characters. Offer constructive ideas for improvement.

Strengthen Your Writing Muscles

Write a normal schedule for your main character, One Day in the Life of My MC. (MC stands for Main Character.) From the minute your MC wakes up to the time your MC goes to bed, write down what your MC is doing each hour of a normal day.

11.3 Dialogue

Take a walk to your neighborhood elementary school. Try to arrive during recess. Stand just outside the fence and listen to the sounds of children playing. You'll hear a hundred little voices shouting out all at once, "Let's play tag!" "I'll race you to the swings!" and "I'm first at bat!" Without even looking at the kids, you can picture in your mind what's happening. That's how effective dialogue can be.

In advanced readers written for kids in second and third grade, action takes place in dialogue. Information is presented in dialogue. The plot moves forward through dialogue. In other words, dialogue is key.

You will find some advanced readers that are written nearly one hundred percent with dialogue. This is mostly in fiction, however. Nonfiction, a genre that has established a strong identity in this reading level, is often mostly narrative. (To learn more about writing nonfiction advanced readers, see *Section 11.6 Topics and Themes*.)

Here is an example I wrote of using dialogue to show action:

"Recess!" Carlos cried. "Let's play tag."

"You're *It*," Jennifer shouted, running away from him. "But you know how Mr. Sams said we'd get in trouble if we play tag."

"Maybe we won't get in trouble if we play freeze," Lee suggested, hopping out of Carlos's reach. "If Carlos touches you, you freeze."

"Freeze!" Carlos shouted, tagging Jennifer.

"But how do I unfreeze?" Jennifer asked as she skidded to a stop. "I forget."

"Like this!" Lee cried, running up and tagging Jennifer. "You're not frozen anymore."

Just look at all the information that was presented, all through dialogue! We know who the characters are in the story. We know the problem: the kids aren't supposed to play tag. We know the setting because it's recess at school. All this has been conveyed within the dialogue. That's how dialogue works effectively in advanced readers.

Because advanced readers are written in paragraph format, it's important to know the rules when using dialogue. Each time a different character speaks, a new paragraph is started. Each new paragraph is indented. This can seem confusing as you look at a page that has different characters speaking *short* lines of dialogue. It can appear to have the sentences each on their own line of text without any indented paragraphs. It can have the appearance of earlier reading levels that use that format, but actually, it's not. Advanced readers for second and third graders use paragraph format, even when the text is all dialogue.

To clarify what I'm talking about, first let's look at text where two different characters are talking but they're only saying short sentences. Here is how this dialogue will appear on the published page:

"It's my birthday today," Taj announced.
"Can I come to your party?" Candy asked.
"Of course!" Taj said.
"I can't wait," Candy said.

Note that the example does not line up at the extreme left of the page. Even though it might not look like it, each new line of dialogue is actually starting a new paragraph that is indented like the first line of every paragraph is when using paragraph format. You just can't tell this at first glance because all of the sentences are very short and don't carry naturally on over to the next line.

Here is another example of the same text with new text added to show you how this same dialogue would appear in paragraph format if it had longer sentences:

"It's my birthday today," Taj announced. "I'm having a birthday party today and am inviting all my friends."

"Can I come to your party?" Candy asked. "I was supposed to help my brother clean his room but we can do that later."

"Of course!" Taj said. "You're my best friend! Here's the invitation to my party. It's just after lunch."

"I can't wait," Candy said. "I already know what present I'm going to get you. Don't try to guess, though, or it might spoil the fun."

Here is another example. This uses the first text example but makes the mistake of putting everyone's dialogue all in the same paragraph. This is a common mistake many writers make because it feels like it should all be in the same paragraph since it's all talking about the same thing.

Example of the wrong format:

"It's my birthday today," Taj announced. "Can I come to your party?" Candy asked. "Of course!" Taj said. "I can't wait," Candy said.

Just try to remember that each time a new character speaks, a new paragraph should start. Even if it looks strange in your eyes, just start a new paragraph and indent the first line each time a different person says anything, even if it's only one word.

As each character speaks in the dialogue you write, the plot is moving forward step-by-step. Continue reading to learn more about structuring effective plots in advanced readers.

Beginner's Tip

Always practice reading the dialogue portions of your manuscript aloud. Tweak these passages until they sound more like natural conversation to your ear.

Professional Track

Take one character from one of your published manuscripts and one character from another published manuscript. Have these two characters meet in a scene you create and talk with their own unique voices. Write their dialogue in advanced reader format.

Strengthen Your Writing Muscles

Stop and evaluate your own personal writing habits. Are you most productive early in the morning, at mid-afternoon, or late at night? Schedule tomorrow's writing session on your calendar at your most productive time. Sit down and work on your dialogue passages. Note the improvement in your writing just from working at your best time of day.

11.4 Plot

Upping the stakes and increasing the tension results in more complicated plots with a stronger story arc here in advanced readers than in easy readers, just one reading level lower. You can add bigger doses of excitement, heighten the suspense, increase the sense of adventure—all through developing a slightly more complex plot than for the earlier reading level.

Once again, publishers at this reading level for kids in second and third grade do not want stories with predictable plots. (For a list of "Predictable Plots for Children's Stories," see *Section 9.4 Plot*.) Fiction stories in advanced readers should have a structured story arc that includes a strong beginning, conflicting middle, and satisfying end.

The conflicting middle is where you can increase the thrill and suspense. Using the classic rule of three, instead of just presenting three small problems that the main character attempts to solve, you can have the main character make three different attempts to solve each of those problems along the quest to solve the main problem presented at the beginning of the story. Each attempt should result in a bigger disaster than the first.

This heightens the sense of urgency for the main character to make a decision. It effectively builds the story arc. (This is the opposite of stories with predictable plots that develop using a predictable pattern but often lack a steady increase in tension.) At the end of the story arc, the main character is forced into making the big decision that spurs a resulting action and therefore solves the main problem presented in the first place. The ending quickly wraps up after this action, leaving the reader with a feeling of satisfaction.

Once again, a chart is very helpful to use as you're brainstorming ideas for more complicated plot structures in advanced readers. You can create a more complex Plot Structure Chart based on the one you created for easy readers. (See *Section 10.4 Plot* for comparison.)

Plot Structure Chart

Title of Advanced Reader:

Beginning:

   Main character:

   Main problem:

   Setting:

Middle:

   Small problem #1:

      Main character's first attempt to solve #1:

      Main character's second attempt to solve #1:

      Main character's third attempt to solve #1:

   Small problem #2:

      Main character's first attempt to solve #2:

      Main character's second attempt to solve #2:

      Main character's third attempt to solve #2:

   Small problem #3:

      Main character's first attempt to solve #3:

      Main character's second attempt to solve #3:

Main character's third attempt to solve #3:
End:
Pivotal decision:
Main character's resulting action:
Resolution of the main problem:

Create your own Plot Structure Chart for advanced readers. Use my example as a guide to draw one by hand or on a computer desktop publisher software program such as Inkscape, *Printmaster*® or the *Print Shop*®. Photocopy or print out extra blank copies to keep on hand for each advanced reader you write.

Brainstorm a variety of actions your main character can take to attempt to solve each small problem that surfaces as the main problem is being worked through. Try not to repeat any action more than once unless you have a specific purpose for doing so.

If you run out of ideas, take your Plot Structure Chart to your critique group. Ask them to help brainstorm ideas for your story. Have fun thinking of creative and exciting situations together with your writing buddies! I've seen some exciting results when people hold brainstorming sessions with their peers during their turn at a writer's group.

Also enlist the help of kids you know. Children are eager to share their input when they know it might be used in an actual book. Plus, by this age, they are also familiar with the basic concept of how to write a story. Explain that you are writing a story and working to develop the plot. Discuss the main story problem and each of the smaller problems that surface while the main character is trying to solve it. Then ask them for suggestions on how they think this particular character might attempt to solve each particular problem. Add each suggestion to your brainstorming list, no matter how bizarre or off-topic it may seem. You could be surprised how something might work its way into your story as a result of these brainstorming sessions.

Nonfiction for Advanced Readers

If you are writing nonfiction for advanced readers that will be read by kids in second and third grade, you can use this same Plot Structure Chart to develop nonfiction biographies. If you're presenting information about a certain topic, however, be sure to structure the plot to include an introduction, a body, and a closing. The introduction should introduce the main topic or theme of your manuscript. The body should contain supporting facts about your topic, fascinating details, or step-by-step methods of how to do something. The closing should offer a short summary of what was learned about the topic.

Beginner's Tip

You don't need to create an entirely new scene each time your main character attempts to solve one of the small problems. Each new attempt to solve a problem can be described in just one sentence that shows what the main character does without going into unnecessary elaborate detail. For example, if your main character is trying to housesit while her best friend is on vacation, the first small problem that arises could be she discovers her friend's cat is missing. She can call the Animal Rescue Shelter. She can make a flyer and hang it in her neighborhood park. She can set a can of cat food outside the back door. Each of these attempts to solve her problem can be stated in one sentence without developing an entire scene. And then, when you want to focus on a scene for a pivotal point in the story, you can use dialogue to flesh it out.

Professional Track

Fill in the Plot Structure Chart for a manuscript you already wrote. Now add a sense of urgency to your plot line by adding in a deadline of some sort. For example, what if your main character is house sitting for just 24 hours? How would this affect your main character's actions if she discovers the cat is missing? Go back and tweak the Plot Structure Chart to reflect this new tension. Then compare the two different plots. Which do you like better?

Strengthen Your Writing Muscles

Select an advanced reader that is published in the trade book market. Fill in the Plot Structure Chart for this advanced reader's plot. Evaluate the plot of this story. What changes could be made to strengthen the plot? Rewrite the story to reflect these changes, keeping the rest of the storyline intact.

11.5 Setting

A sense of place is essential to every story. In advanced readers targeted to children in second and third grade, successfully creating a sense of place transports your readers into another world. As a writer, you can enjoy the delicious experience of dishing up huge portions of delectable adventures to young readers by learning how to effectively establish the setting in which your story takes place.

Whether your story's setting is in familiar surroundings or unfamiliar and exotic locations, adding sensory details will instantly make young readers feel like they're inside the world you've created, walking and talking alongside your characters. Adding sensory details can actually be one of the simplest tasks you accomplish with your manuscript. How, you ask?

First of all, don't stress out about adding sensory details while you're writing the first draft of your advanced reader. If something jumps out of your brain and suddenly announces itself as part of the story and just happens to be something you can taste, touch, smell, see, or hear, then fantastic! You've added a sensory detail as a natural part of your story. Otherwise, don't worry about it while you're writing. Writing advanced readers still takes a lot of concentration to keep the sentence structure, word length, and vocabulary choice at the correct reading level. You don't need other distractions to draw you away from getting the story down on paper.

After you have written your first draft, however, now it's time to roll up your sleeves and get to work. Write down a list of the five senses. Read through your story. Identify the first scene. Can you choose one sensory detail to add to that scene in one sentence? Try to fit it in as a natural part of the text.

Move forward and examine the next scene of your story. Once again, choose one sensory detail to add to that scene in one sentence. Try to use a different sense in this second scene than you did in the first, and see if that works well.

In a similar manner, progress scene by scene through your advanced reader. Look for places you can plug into one more sentence in each scene that includes a sensory detail and makes the story come alive. If kids in second and third grade can taste the cookies, smell the onions frying, hear the pop of firecrackers, see the flash of lightning, and feel the scratchy robe against their skin, they'll automatically feel like they're in the story. The setting comes alive.

Here are two examples. One is a passage of text without any sensory details. The second example is the same passage of text, only this time one sentence has been added that includes a reference to one of the five senses. Which example gives a more exciting feel to the setting?

Example A

"Hurry!" Sophie cried.

"I'm running as fast as I can," Sam said, out of breath.

"We don't want the bloodhounds to catch us," Sophie said. She pushed her way into a bush.

"Will they find our hiding spot here?" Sam asked. He crouched down beside her.

Example B

"Hurry!" Sophie cried.

"I'm running as fast as I can," Sam said, out of breath.

"We don't want the bloodhounds to catch us," Sophie said. She pushed her way into a bush. The branches scratched her face, stinging her cheeks

"Will they find our hiding spot here?" Sam asked. He crouched down beside her.

As with all other levels of beginning readers and chapter books, there will not be long narrative passages that describe the setting. Beginning readers and chapter books are filled with action and dialogue, but not long passages of narrative.

Instead of including detailed descriptions about the setting, provide just enough bits and pieces of information to create a *sense* or feel of where the story is taking place. Work to give just enough details to establish the world your characters are moving around in. When writing advanced readers, even though the setting can be more detailed and more involved than in earlier reading levels, don't slow down the plot progression or stop the action by describing the setting. Save that for middle grade novels and young adult novels where the only illustration in the entire book usually is the picture on the cover. It's not necessary to describe the setting in detail in advanced readers because these stories are fully illustrated. Children can already see what the setting looks like every time they turn the page.

Let's take a look at that same passage again. This time, let's stop and describe the setting. Note how it slows down the forward movement of the story and drains away the tension that's building in the scene.

"Hurry!" Sophie cried. The woods were beautiful this time of year, but she didn't really notice the happy yellow daffodils blooming at her feet. A fawn and its mother were standing in the shadows of a tree.

"I'm running as fast as I can," Sam said, out of breath.

"We don't want the bloodhounds to catch us," Sophie said. She pushed her way into a bush. The branches scratched her face, stinging her cheeks.

"Will they find our hiding spot here?" Sam asked. The trees were tall and loomed darkly over them. He crouched down beside her.

In advanced readers, children don't need to be told all the details of the setting because they can see them in the picture. If the illustrator draws daffodils in the woods and a fawn with its mother, young readers can automatically see that in the illustrations. Keep the setting simple in the text in advanced readers, and work instead to create a sense of place rather than include a lengthy description of narrative. Be sure that your setting supports the theme you're writing about. To learn more about the topics and themes publishers, educators, parents (and kids!) want to see in advanced readers, continue to the following section.

Beginner's Tip

It's important to create a sense of place in your own mind so you can write the story more effectively. However, when your advanced reader is delivered into the hands of the illustrator, it will now undergo an entirely new development of the setting. Learn to let go at this point and look forward to the new concepts an illustrator adds. Learn to view the publication of a children's story as a team effort and you'll enjoy the process even more.

Professional Track

Establish positive relationships with your illustrators. Even if you never personally communicate with them, ask your editor to convey your appreciation and delight for the positive elements the art ads to your published manuscripts.

Strengthen Your Writing Muscles

Every neighborhood has its own personality. Take time to get to know your main character's neighborhood. Even though these details won't be described in the story itself, it will help you create a sense of place for your advanced reader. Write a description of the neighborhood's personality. Does it feel safe? Does it feel family-oriented or is it home to mostly elderly people because most young families have moved away? Is it a lonely place for your main character or a place where your main character knows lots of friends? Does it feel big and exciting, or small and cozy? Explore the emotions your main character experiences living in this neighborhood.

11.6 Topics and Themes

By the time children are in second and third grade, they are studying a lot of facts about the great big world we live in. They learn about famous Americans and world leaders. They examine nature more closely and study how things grow. Many of them are on sports teams where they are taught specific rules of the games. Children at this age are like a sponge, soaking up an amazing and vast amount of knowledge that ranges in size from learning about the tiniest seed they can hold in their hands to seeing pictures of the gigantic universe. Books are in demand to teach early elementary students these facts at their own reading level. You can tap into this open-ended market by writing advanced readers.

As with easy readers, a wide variety of genre can be found at this reading level. However, because of the ever-increasing need for resource material for students in second and third grade, nonfiction really comes into its own in advanced readers. You will find nonfiction titles even in the earliest reading levels. Here in advanced readers, though, entire series of nonfiction themes are developed.

Nonfiction Topics and Themes

For instance, series of nonfiction biographies are listed in the catalogues of most advanced readers for trade book publishers. Reproducible mini-books and Readers Theatre plays that feature nonfiction biographies are found in the educational market. If you want to write nonfiction biographies or other nonfiction topics such as sports for advanced readers and have experience writing for the beginning readers and chapter books market, I recommend trying to land the contract before you write the book. Here are the steps you can take:

Break into the Nonfiction Advanced Readers Market

1. Explore existing series of nonfiction topics at this reading level.
2. Target one publisher who has a series of nonfiction advanced readers and accepts queries.
3. Make a list of nonfiction advanced readers in that series your target publisher has already published.
4. Brainstorm and write down a list of topics that have not yet been published by this publisher and that would fit into their series.
5. Contact the publisher and pitch three to five topics of potential nonfiction advanced readers you could write for their series. Ask the publisher if they'd like to see a proposal for any of these ideas.
6. If the publisher requests a proposal for one or more of your ideas, respond and say that you will submit a proposal within about a month.
7. Prepare your proposal and submit it to the publisher. Include the following:
   a. Write a cover letter reminding the publisher that you had previous contact with her and she requested a proposal. State how your topic would fit into their advanced readers series of nonfiction titles.
   b. Include a chapter-by-chapter outline of the entire book.
   c. Write three to five pages of sample text.

To learn more about how to pitch ideas to publishers in order to try to land a contract before you write the manuscript, read my first book in this series, *Yes! You Can Learn How to Write Children's Books, Get Them Published, and Build a Successful Writing Career.* Because nonfiction topics geared for this reading level require a certain amount of research and time to write, various publishers of nonfiction sign contracts with their authors before these books are written. Learn to pitch ideas and land a contract first, especially when writing nonfiction, so that you're earning income while you write.

Research and Bibliographies

If you have not written much nonfiction yet or don't yet have published credits in the beginning readers and chapter books market, it's to your advantage to try your hand at writing a complete manuscript first. As you gather notes and resources about your topic, keep careful track of all the sources you use. Books are still the required main sources for most research. Create an alphabetical list based on the author's last name with a bibliography for each title you refer to since many nonfiction publishers require you to submit one with your completed manuscript. Some authors like to use the online source, EasyBib at www.easybib.com, to create their bibliographies.

Here is a sample of the standard format with the exact punctuation that most publishers expect to see in a bibliography of book titles:

Last name of author, First name. *Title of Book in Italics.* City book was published: Publisher's Name, Date of copyright.

Or:

Writer, Wanda. *Five Famous Children's Writers.* New York: Sensational Writers Press, 2010.

You can use Internet resources to supplement the research you dig up in books. However, not all Internet sites are equal. Learn to distinguish reputable sites from amateur sites that post information without checking that their sources are reliable and actually true. Also, because Internet sites are updated or deleted frequently, always print out a copy on the day you visit a site and gather research. Keep this copy in your files and add a reference for each site to your bibliography. There are various different formats publishers like to use, but here is a sample of the standard format with the exact punctuation that many publishers expect to see in a bibliography that includes Internet sources:

"Title of Internet Article." www.WebsiteWhereItWasFound.com. (Date of week you visited the site, Month, Year).

Or:

"Great Children's Writers." www.WeWrite4Kids.com. (1 May 2010).

I recommend purchasing three to five key books on your topic to use as your main sources for research. In your personal research library, include at least one book written for adults on this topic and one book written for children. The books for adults you own on this topic will give you in-depth facts at your fingertips. The books for children you own on this topic will give you a quick reference for how to present each fact at a child's level of understanding.

The basic rule for research is this: **If you use one source as a reference, it's plagiarism. If you use three sources as a reference, it's research.** In other words, be sure to find three sources to support each fact you decide to use in your nonfiction advanced reader. This shows that fact is common knowledge and is supported by enough documented research sources for you to state in your manuscript.

Specialize in Nonfiction Topics or Themes

If you want to write nonfiction advanced readers, I also recommend making it your goal to specialize. For instance, if you're fascinated with Clara Barton and want to write an advanced reader nonfiction biography about this amazing woman, after you finish the book, look for other topics to write about in the same era or on a common theme. For example, you could try to land contracts to write advanced reader nonfiction biographies on other heroes during the Civil War. Or you could try to land contracts to write advanced reader nonfiction biographies on other influential women in history. Or, you could try to land contracts to write advanced reader nonfiction biographies on other people who shaped the medical field in America.

The more you can start to specialize in specific topics or themes as you write nonfiction advanced readers, the less time and money you'll spend on research. Plus, publishers are keenly interested in working with writers who specialize in certain nonfiction topics. Because of their proven track record and published credits on this topic, publishers trust the reputations of these authors for accuracy and skill in presenting facts to kids.

I've experienced a wonderful measure of success by specializing in several key topics over my career. Each time I write on the same topic or theme again for a brand new book or magazine article, I feel more confident about my own research and level of expertise. Specializing in certain topics has also led to contracts with publishers I've never worked with when they contact me out of the blue to write about a topic I've been published in before. You can reap similar benefits as a writer if you make it one of your goals to specialize in a certain topic that interests you, too.

Beginner's Tip

It's often easier to break into the nonfiction market. Fewer writers submit nonfiction manuscripts and more nonfiction titles are needed each year. Even if it's not your main interest, try to break into writing nonfiction advanced readers. If you do, you'll increase your chances of getting your fiction manuscripts published, as well.

Professional Track

Write your own biography as an advanced reader. Include your first rejection, your first sale, and your first published work. Write your biography up to the current day. Include photos for added fun! Who knows? It just might get published one day.

Strengthen Your Writing Muscles

Each week for the next month, or until you land a contract, send a short query to an editor pitching three to five nonfiction topics that would fit into their existing product line of advanced readers for children in second and third grade. Target a different publisher each week.

Chapter 12

FIRST CHAPTER BOOKS

12.1 Sentence Structure and Vocabulary

Little kids love to feel grown-up. When they're preschoolers, they play dress-up and parade through the house in high heels or fire fighter boots. As they grow older, they play "mommy and daddy," "store," or "school." One of the ways children in first, second, or third grade like to feel more grown-up is by the books they choose to read all on their own. For many, it's a very rewarding experience to pick up and read their very own first chapter books that have a similar feel and look to the books they see grown-ups reading. You can be a part of this "growing up" journey by learning how to write first chapter books that they will want to read.

First Chapter Books At-a-Glance
(Check with each publisher to determine specifics.)
Sample Titles:
Nate the Great series by Marjorie Weinman Sharmat (A Dell Young
    Yearling: Dell Publishing)
Marshal Matt: Mysteries with a Value series by Nancy I. Sanders
    (Concordia Publishing House)
Junie B. Jones series by Barbara Park (Random House)
Magic Tree House® series by Mary Pope Osborne (Random House)
Word Count:
    From 1500 to 10,000 words
Page Count:
    48 to 80 pages

Different publishers have different definitions of first chapter books. Some call them junior chapter books. Some lump them together with advanced readers. Others group them in the lower end of middle grade novels. For our purposes here in this book, I will set the parameters for first chapter books to be books we discuss in the trade book market with the following qualifications:

Slightly smaller trim size (cover size) than most beginning readers

Total word count of entire book can be about the same word count in one single chapter of an adult-length novel, although many are longer

Written for early elementary target age from first to third grade with vocabulary and topics geared to this age

Black and white illustrations of fewer number instead of full-color art throughout the book on every page

Longer first chapter books can be broken into separate chapters and shorter first chapter books can have no chapter breaks at all

First chapter books are written in paragraph format, just like a novel. The sentence structure and vocabulary words in first chapter books are similar to advanced readers which are geared to second and third graders. (See *Section 11.1 Sentence Structure and Vocabulary*.) This is in contrast to the earliest middle grade novels that use more complicated sentence structure and vocabulary words taught in the middle grades beginning in upper elementary school at fourth grade.

The best way to clarify which level to incorporate into your own first chapter books is to examine the books your target publisher publishes. Follow their submission guidelines for sentence structure and vocabulary words. If they do not have official submission guidelines for first chapter books, look at the books they publish and write yours at the same reading level.

Probably one of the most popular first chapter book series is Mary Pope Osborne's *Magic Tree House*® series. Become familiar with and read lots of successful published first chapter books to get a better sense of the sentence structure and vocabulary words that publishers want to see at this reading level for children in first through third grade.

I wrote two first chapter book series for Concordia Publishing House, the *Marshal Matt: Mysteries with a Value* series and the *Parables in Action* series. At that time they did not have submission guidelines to follow for this genre. However, they did already have a series of first chapter books they wanted me to follow, so I based the books I wrote on the sentence structure, vocabulary words, format, page length, and total word count of those.

I also developed my own set of characters for these two series of first chapter books. To learn more about creating characters for the first chapter books you write, continue reading.

Beginner's Tip

Make a list of action verbs from the second and third grade vocabulary lists in the *Children's Writer's Word Book* by Alijandra Mogilner. Use lots of these vocabulary words in your first chapter book to add interest and action.

Professional Track

Compile a list of current first chapter books. Try to find out which editor oversees these at which publishing house by looking in market guides, visiting the publisher's website, examining their submission guidelines, and noting the names of the various acquisitions editors they list on their sites. Search the Internet to see if any of these editors keep a blog. When you find one that does, follow her posts. Watch for tips or ask questions about which vocabulary levels, sentence length, and format this editor prefers.

Strengthen Your Writing Muscles

Choose a target publisher who publishes first chapter books like ones you want to write. Get their submission guidelines. These can usually be found on their Website under tabs such as "About us" or "Contact us." If they don't have any submission guidelines, study their line of first chapter books and create your own guidelines to follow as you write.

12.2 Characters

Some of the most enjoyable experiences I have had as a writer were the times I developed the characters for the two first chapter book series I wrote for Concordia Publishing House. You can enjoy the thrill and delight along this enchanting journey as well when you create your own characters for this reading level.

Characters in first chapter books can be like splashes of bold and vivid colors across the pages of a book that for the first time in a young reader's life are illustrated in black and white. Characters in first chapter books can be whimsical, endearing, lively and engaging.

It took me several months to develop the cast of characters in my first chapter book series, *Marshal Matt: Mysteries with a Value.* Before I started the process of character development, first I pitched an idea for a new series of first chapter books to my editor at Concordia. She was interested, so I brainstormed ideas for this series while I was busy working on a different book deadline. (To learn more about how I brainstormed for the characters in my *Marshal Matt* series, see *Section 4.4 Writing for the Trade Market.*)

When I worked with my co-author, Susan Titus Osborn, to write our *Parables in Action* series, it took time for us to develop the cast of characters, as well. We brainstormed a unique and enchanting character trait for each that would easily identify them from book to book in the series. Here is a list of the quirky and fun characters that we created:

Parables in Action series
Cast of Characters
Suzie: This is the main character whose voice tells each story. She always prays when the situation gets sticky. Each story and each character is seen through her eyes.

Bubbles: This is Suzie's best friend. Bubbles' real name is Nan. She is a child actress on TV and appears in a different costume in each book because she is always practicing for her next new TV role.

Mario: Suzie's friend, Mario, likes to collect things. He's very resourceful and comes up with all sorts of ways to raise money and fix problems.

Woof: Mario's dog is named Woof. Woof is always running into a scene and barking, "WOOF!" at a key moment of the scene.

The Spy: He's always writing spy notes in his spy notebook. The Spy's real name is Larry. He always talks in secret code. For instance, "Iggle, iggle, snoogle, snoogle" means "yes." When he says, "Ark, ark! Bam, bam!" he's really saying, "Wow!"

Mr. Zinger: This is the classroom teacher of all the kids in this series. He has a beard, wears a baseball cap, plays the guitar, and sings with the kids. Mr.

Zinger's character traits are based on my husband, Jeff, who teaches fourth grade and plays guitar while singing with his students!

As you can see, characters in first chapter books can be over-the-top funtastic! Kids in first through third grade love reading about characters like these. Now you know why I had such a great time working to developing them. Characters in middle grade novels can't be quite as fun since those books for older upper elementary and junior high students feature more realistic characters.

So go ahead—have loads and loads of fun! Create a super duper scrump-dilly-icious cast of characters for your own first chapter book series and you'll have just as much fun inventing them as kids in first through third grade will have reading about them. Then give them a fantastic voice that keeps kids begging for them to speak again…and again! To learn more about writing dialogue for first chapter books, continue to the next section.

Beginner's Tip

Take a field trip to places kids hang out and write down a character profile of half a dozen. Assign character tags, or unique quirks to identify each character, in their dress, mannerisms, and speech.

Professional Track

Who is your favorite main character you've ever created? Make a list of his personality traits. Can you breathe new life into your character, give him a new name, and have him star in a first chapter book series?

Strengthen Your Writing Muscles

Keep a journal for your main character. Write in it every day you're working on your first chapter book. Journal in the voice and through the eyes of your main character. This will help you get inside your main character's head and heart.

12.3 Dialogue

As in advanced readers, dialogue is key in first chapter books. Dialogue speaks directly to kids in first through third grade who are reading first chapter books and draws them into each scene. You can create effective dialogue in the first chapter books you write that has the power to draw young readers into the world you're creating.

Because first chapter books are really more a part of the world of novels and not as much a part of the world of beginning readers, you can introduce more narrative along with dialogue in the scenes you create. It's still important to use dialogue as a key vehicle to move the plot forward, present information, and create action, but it's not as essential now as in earlier reading levels.

Your use of dialogue can now be intermixed with narrative more freely as you create the scenes your characters move around in. Here is an example of dialogue and narrative working together to create a scene in the book Susan Titus Osborn and I co-wrote, *Comet Campout: #3* in the *Parables in Action* series:

Just then Bubbles joined us. She had on a pink tutu. She looked like a ballerina. "You're wearing THAT on our campout?" I asked in surprise.

"Yes," Bubbles said. "I'm practicing for my next TV ad. I'm a ballerina."

Bubbles handed me her pink backpack. She twirled and did a pirouette.

Because each of the characters in a first chapter book is very unique, it's important to give each one of them their own unique voice. A character's voice can naturally be heard when they speak. The dialogue each character speaks in a first chapter book should be uniquely his or her own way of speaking.

For instance, in my *Marshal Matt: Mystery with a Value* series, the main character, Matt, always says the same thing when he has found a new mystery to solve. This is accompanied by the same action he always does when he says it. Here is an example of his character's voice that can be found in each book in the series:

I reached into my shirt pocket. I pulled out my badge. I pinned my badge to my shirt. "I, Marshal Matt, will solve this mystery."

In the same way, Janie, Marshal Matt's friend, is the character in each book of the series who has a mystery that needs to be solved. She always asks Marshal Matt for help. That bit of dialogue in each book of the series is part of her unique voice. Blinky, Janie's pet parrot that rides on her shoulder and follows her wherever she goes, always repeats key words or phrases Janie has said to add humor to a scene. This repetition of words as part of his dialogue is the trademark of Blinky's voice.

Here is an example from my first chapter book *Marshal Matt and the Case of the Secret Code* that shows how both Janie's and Blinky's unique personalities come through their voices as depicted by each of their own distinct and one-of-a-kind dialogue:

"I think there is a mystery going on," Janie said. "I want to know what these secret codes mean. Will you help me, Marshal Matt?"

Blinky blinked. "Help! Help! Help!" he squawked.

To help invent your own character's unique voice that will be manifested through dialogue, create a Top Secret Detective File that really showcases their very own personality and character traits. (To learn how to make a Top Secret Detective File and develop winning characters, read *Section 7.2 Characters with Kid-Appeal.*) In each character's Top Secret Detective File, make a list of unique words or phrases they say in their dialogue that instantly identifies them and distinguishes them from your other characters.

When you sit down to develop a new scene in your first chapter book, refer to this list. Have each character speak in that new scene and act or react through dialogue by incorporating their own unique words, phrases, or way of speaking.

After you have written a scene, stop and evaluate each character's dialogue. Did you make them each speak in their own unique way? Or do some of them sound similar? Keep working and tweaking until each one of them speaks with their own unique voice.

Let's examine two portions of dialogue so that you can practice evaluating whether or not your own characters' use of dialogue represents their specific character traits.

Example A: Actual text in the published book that gives each character a unique voice in his or her own dialogue:

"I think there is a mystery going on," Janie said. "I want to know what these secret codes mean. Will you help me, Marshal Matt?"

Blinky blinked. "Help! Help! Help!" he squawked.

I reached into my shirt pocket. I pulled out my badge. I pinned my badge to my shirt. "I, Marshal Matt, will solve this mystery."

Example B: Text that shows where every character has a similar voice and none of their dialogue reflects their unique personality or character traits:

"I think there is a mystery going on," Janie said. "I want to know what these secret codes mean. Will you help me, Matt?"

Blinky blinked. "Will you help?" he squawked.

"Sure," I said. "I'll help you solve this mystery."

Can you see how every character's dialogue is the same voice in Example B? All three characters talk just like Janie talks. This creates boring dialogue and a flat story.

By keeping a list in each character's Top Secret Detective File of key words or phrases they say or how they speak in a unique voice, you will have a handy reference while writing dialogue in each new scene. The dialogue will better convey each character's unique personalities and character traits. This makes for a much more lively and engaging first chapter book series that readers will want to keep reading, book after book after book.

A character's Top Secret Detective File is also a great place to write down notes about the plot and develop a story's beginning, middle, and end. To learn more about the plot structure of first chapter books, read the next section.

Beginner's Tip

Double check that your dialogue has a purpose. If it doesn't move the plot forward or develop your character's personality, tweak it until it does.

Professional Track

Create an account on Twitter or Facebook based on one of your main characters in a book that has already been published. Identify your character, the title of your book, and yourself as the author. Post frequently in the voice of your character. This helps give practice talking in short bits in someone else's voice—a great exercise for strengthening dialogue skills. It also is a great way to help market your book!

Strengthen Your Writing Muscles

Write down what each of the following people would say if they were told their best friend was moving away: a five-year-old girl, a police officer, a squirrel named Acorn, a teenage girl who likes to paint, a thief, a grandmother, a nine-year-old boy, a nurse.

12.4 Plot

Reading a first chapter book on their own is the first step children in first through third grade take to enter the world of novels. A middle grade or young adult novel weaves a web and builds an infrastructure of plots and subplots that add layers and 3-D dimension to a story. As a writer of first chapter books, you can start adding layers to the main plot to add more interest to your story, too.

There are entire books about plot development for fiction that you can glean from. Explore a variety and study the strategies of plot development that are used when crafting middle grade and young adult novels as well as novels for adults. Based on your findings, you can start adding very simple layers to the main plot you're working on in your first chapter book. Just keep things simple and not too complicated or young readers might feel overwhelmed.

To help you track your first chapter book's plot development, create a timeline that your main plot will follow. Start by drawing a horizontal line across the top of a blank piece of paper and label it "Main Plot." If the main plot in your first chapter book is to solve a mystery such as a missing library book, mark the key points in the story on that horizontal line such as when the book was lost, when each clue was collected, and when the book was found.

Underneath that line, draw a second, third, or fourth horizontal line. Label each one Subplot #1, Subplot #2, Subplot #3, and so on. Next, mark the key points in the story on each horizontal line for each subplot. For instance, if the first subplot is about the kids attending summer camp, mark when they go on a hike, when they get chased by a raccoon, and when they toast marshmallows at the campfire.

Make sure that each of the subplots works to move the main plot forward. For example, the raccoon that chases them at camp could actually be the thief who stole the missing library book. Tracking your main plot and subplots on a timeline helps guarantee your plots all work together successfully to help solve the main story problem.

Cliffhangers

With first chapter books that actually contain chapters, you can also incorporate a tried and true strategy of novel writing that will structure your plot to keep your readers on the edge of their seats and turning pages instead of abandoning the book due to boredom. Cliffhangers at the end of each chapter are always a winner in every genre.

Most of us have heard about cliffhangers and the key role they play to make a book a page-turner. Yet so often, we write our chapter and wrap up all the details before we start the next because deep down inside we feel uncomfortable starting a new chapter until the first one reaches a significant pause.

To help alleviate this weakness in my own manuscripts, I like to create chapter breaks right in the exact middle of a scene where tension is at its height! The reader can't help turning the page to see what happens next. Then, I wrap up a scene in the middle of the chapter and start a new scene right there without creating a chapter break. I wait until the middle of that new scene when I stop. Then I start a new chapter.

Here's an example of how to create a cliffhanger at the end of a chapter by creating a chapter break at the most important moment of the scene:

Chapter 3

…The pirates climbed off their ship and got into a small boat.

"Look," Brandon whispered from his hideout behind the rock. "They left one pirate on the ship. They probably want him to guard their treasure chest."

"How are we going to get their treasure now?" Carlo asked. "We can't swim out to the ship now. It's no use. We'll never get the treasure."

The two friends were quiet. They watched the pirates row their boat toward the small island where they were.

"I don't know what we're going to do," Brandon said. He sat down and looked at Carlo. "I want to get that treasure. It belonged to my father. Now it belongs to me. We have to figure out a way."

Just then, Brandon heard a noise. He looked out behind the rock. It was the pirates! They had landed on the beach.

The pirate captain saw Brandon. He shouted something Brandon couldn't hear. All the pirates started running toward them.

Brandon jumped up. "Come on!" he cried. "We can't let them catch us!"

Chapter 4

Brandon and Carlo raced across the sand. Carlo tripped. Brandon stopped to help him up.

"We've got to hurry!" Brandon exclaimed. "They're coming closer…

Another way to create a cliffhanger at the end of a chapter is to have something unexpected suddenly happen that immediately presents a new sense of conflict. By placing this new plot twist at the end of one chapter, the reader can't help it. He must turn the page immediately and start reading the next chapter to see how this new problem is solved.

Make sure each chapter in your first chapter book ends with a cliffhanger. Go back and double check that each one does. If it doesn't, move the chapter break to occur in the middle of a scene instead of at the end of it. Try it! You'll see how much more exciting your first chapter book suddenly becomes.

Beginner's Tip

After you finish writing each chapter, go back and self-edit it before starting on the next chapter. Use the Self-Editing Checklist in *Section 7.5 The Pizzazz Factor* as a guide. Be sure to add to your list that you check for a cliffhanger at the end of the chapter.

Professional Track

Start or join a critique group for first chapter books. These special books are so different from others! Your writing will benefit with feedback from writing peers who are focusing on the same market.

Strengthen Your Writing Muscles

Think of an exciting moment in your life. Spend 15 minutes writing down the memory. Then go back and look for a great place to make a chapter break with a thrilling cliffhanger. Be sure to mark the place where the tension has built up to its utmost degree.

12.5 Setting

A cast of bold and fascinating characters practically beg for a vivid and imaginative setting for their escapades to take place in. You can invent a setting that's worthy of your characters and that children will be delighted to visit in their imagination.

First of all, brainstorm for ideas for your story's grand setting, or large picture behind the story you're painting with your words. It can be a universe you create, an actual place set in a specific era of history, or the everyday neighborhood of today's child.

Once you choose the backdrop of your story, you'll work to create the individual small settings where each scene takes place. These small settings can take place in the kitchen, at the park, or on a beach. The details of the small settings can include furniture or items in nature for your characters to sit on, hide behind, jump over, or race across.

As your characters move from one small setting to another within the larger world you've placed them in, it's helpful to draw a map to keep everything organized. Especially because most first chapter books are series, you want to know what item is where so everything stays in the right place book after book after book.

For instance, in a first chapter book I have been working on, the main character and supporting character, a boy and a girl, are best friends who happen to also be next-door neighbors. When they walk out of the boy's house together, they turn to the right and enter a path into the woods. After they walk out of the woods, there is an abandoned barn in a field. Their spaceship is stored in the abandoned barn where nobody can find it. Drawing all these items on a simple map helps me keep these details straight so I don't have them walk out of the boy's house in the first book of the series and turn right to enter the path but by mistake in the second book, have them turn left to enter the same path.

Even if you are not an artist, have fun creating a map of the world your characters move around in. Mark on the map where buildings are, where different streets are, and where key landmarks are placed. Most of these details won't be described in your text. Descriptions still aren't a big ingredient in first chapter books for children in first through third grade.

However, these specific details will be important as your characters retrace their steps during new adventures in new books. Creating a map to refer to and marking important landmarks in their world will help you move them in the right direction.

Beginner's Tip

Purchase a set of colored pencils and a tablet of art paper. Since you're a children's writer, you get to have fun! Enjoy the journey in as many ways as you can. Take time to create maps and diagrams of scenes you're imagining in each of your stories.

Professional Track

When you attend your next writer's conference, draw a map of the facility. Take lots of photos of each place and each of the buildings. Ask someone to take several photographs of *you* in this place. When you get home, use this information as a springboard to create a setting for a new first chapter book where the main character attends a big convention for a child-related theme such as a gem and rock show.

Strengthen Your Writing Muscles

Think of a main character you are creating. Where will she go to college when she grows up? Explore that college's Website. Then create an adventure your main character can have if she visits her future college while she's still in third grade. Write a scene about what happens.

12.6 Topics and Themes

As with other levels of beginning readers, the topics and themes in first chapter books are the topics and themes children are studying in school at this age. Because first chapter books are mainly targeted to students in first through third grade, you can choose nearly any topic to write about that you find in a first, second, or third grade classroom.

The State and National Standards along with the Common Core State Standards are great resources to explore for a comprehensive list of topics and themes taught in first, second, and third grade. The National Standards are more generalized. The Common Core State Standards and State Standards are more specific. Even more specific and often more helpful are the Standards your local school district has adopted. To learn more about using State and National Standards as well as Common Core State Standards when you write for the beginning readers and chapter books market, see *Section 3.2 State and National Standards.*

Genre-related Topics and Themes

Due to the important role first chapter books play in the school classroom, these books often have an educational feel even though they are published in the trade book market. Historical fiction is a common genre because these stories teach children what life was like during certain eras of history. Even fantasy often features some educational slant in first chapter books.

If you choose to write topics and themes related to historical fiction, minimize your efforts with maximum results by choosing to specialize in a certain era or topic. For instance, if you decide to specialize on writing about the era of the American Revolution, you can write historical fiction based on topics such as the Revolutionary War, the founding mothers, the First Rhode Island Regiment, and the signers of the Declaration. Because a lot of your research will overlap among the different topics, you'll spend less time on research and less money on purchasing reference books. An important added benefit is that you'll gain confidence writing widely on different topics all surrounding this era.

Because historical fiction is based on research in a similar way that writing nonfiction is, it can feel overwhelming to write for this genre, especially if you're not used to doing research. (To learn more about writing nonfiction for the beginning readers and chapter books market, see *Section*

11.6 Topics and Themes.) It is even more overwhelming to jump from one era in history to another in each different first chapter book you write because you have to start at square one with your research topic for each new manuscript. That is why I recommend making it your goal to specialize in one era or topic if you want to tap into the market of writing a historical fiction first chapter book series.

Historical fiction first chapter books usually have a cast of fictional characters who live and move around during a certain period of history, experiencing key events and meeting famous people. These books usually don't feature an actual person as the main character. The story contains a lot of elements of make-believe because it centers on the imaginary lives of fictional characters placed within an historic setting.

Some first chapter books are biographies. Even though these biographies can contain fictionalized elements in them to help give the feel of a story, these books really center on fact and shouldn't stray as far away from what actually happened as historical fiction can. Some people refer to books such as fictionalized biographies as *faction.* This term can mean that the information presented in the story is completely true but realistic sounding dialogue or transitional information has been added to make the story come alive in the same way that fiction does for young readers. If the biography is classified as nonfiction, even the dialogue would have to be quoted from actual primary sources such as journals, letters, or interviews. Nothing can be invented when writing nonfiction biographies or else it isn't nonfiction after all.

First chapter books are delightful opportunities for us as writers to invite children into imaginary worlds we created or to experience real historic events. The topics and themes we can choose from are rich with a variety of options.

Beginner's Tip

As you're learning about writing topics and themes for different genre, be sure to learn the rules and parameters of writing for each. A great resource to use that also shows what students are learning in the classroom about genre is the teacher's reproducible workbook by Tamara B. Miller, *Pop-up Activities to Teach Genre* (Scholastic Teaching Resources).

Professional Track

If you've written about topics and themes that have been published in a variety of genre, consider the possibility of creating a new genre of your own! Mix and match your favorite elements from different genre, give the new genre a unique name, and pitch your concept to your editor. It's fun to experiment and see if an editor likes your fresh approach. You never know what might be the next new voice in children's literature—it could be yours!

Strengthen Your Writing Muscles

Explore writing historical fiction as a first chapter book. Consider an era of history you are fascinated with. Imagine that you lived during this time and met the famous people who lived in this era. Spend 15 minutes doing a freewriting exercise that starts with the prompt, "If I lived during the era of…"

Chapter 13

HI-LO READERS

13.1 Sentence Structure and Vocabulary

More and more children are diagnosed each day with learning disabilities. More and more junior high and high school educators are working with struggling students in intervention programs that include strengthening reading skills. More and more adults are signing up for classes around the world to learn proficiency in English as their second language. You can become part of this educational phenomenon and write hi-lo readers, material written with a high-interest level at a low-readability level. You can help give the gift of reading to those who did not become fluent readers during their early elementary years.

Hi-Lo Readers At-a-Glance

(Check with each publisher to determine specifics.)

Sample Titles:

True Stories in the News: A Beginning Reader by Sandra Heyer (Pearson ESL)

Side by Side series by Steven J. Molinsky and Bill Bliss (Pearson ESL)

Hello Hi-Lo: Readers Theatre Math by Jeff and Nancy I. Sanders (Libraries Unlimited)

The World's Wildest Roller Coasters by Michael Burgan (Capstone Press)

Word Count:

    Varies with publisher

    Trade books range from 400 to 1200 words

Page Count:

    Varies with publisher

    Trade books range from 32 to 48 pages

Hi-lo readers are stories, both fiction and nonfiction, that feature a high-interest topic relevant to upper elementary through high school age students and even adults. These high-interest topics, however, are written with a carefully chosen sentence structure and vocabulary words selected from word lists geared for grades lower than the reader's actual age level. For instance, the high-interest topic might be a current event in world news. Such a manuscript might be written at a first grade reading level, however, with short sentences and simple vocabulary words.

There is a wide open market for writing hi-lo readers that includes the trade book market, the educational market, and magazines and periodicals. Any material that is published with content aimed toward older students or adults that is written for a lower reading level falls loosely under the category of hi-lo readers.

Students probably can't easily identify a hi-lo reader just from looking at the title of the book. There usually isn't a glaring label on these products that might embarrass the reader. However, the publisher knows which titles they are publishing as hi-lo readers. Educators know which material is classified as hi-lo readers. Authors know which manuscripts they're writing for this market. One of the easiest ways for you to identify a hi-lo reader is to pick up a book and look at it. Ask yourself if the topic it covers matches the readability level. In other words, is it about a topic that might interest older kids or adults yet written with simple sentence structure and basic vocabulary words?

Here is an example of the simple sentence structure and vocabulary words geared for lower reading levels found in hi-lo readers as compared to the topic which is geared for the interest of students in a higher grade level or even adults.

Stopped by Smoke

Smoke came out of a volcano. The volcano was in Iceland. The smoke filled the air. Planes could not fly in the smoke. People could not fly on trips. Some people on trips could not fly home. Many workers lost a lot of money.

Here is an example of how that same current news event might be written for an adult reading audience instead of as a hi-lo reader:

Eyjafjallajokull Volcano Eruption

The Eyjafjallajokull volcano continued to spew nearly 50 tons of magma per second for days even after its first explosive eruption. This Icelandic volcano's sudden and violent eruption has brought airline travel to an abrupt halt. Due to potential and tragic danger if planes attempt to fly through the plume of volcanic ash, flights are being cancelled between airports in Europe and America. Tourists are stranded and unable to reschedule flights home. Businesses are losing thousands of dollars each day even though eruption levels are diminishing.

Hi-lo readers written for English Language Learners, or ELL, start as early as a first grade reading level and increase to a level of reading proficiency. (For more information about writing for the ELL market, see *Section 6.4 English Language Learners*.)

For struggling students, hi-lo readers can be geared to an interest level targeted to upper elementary students in grades four through six. You can also find material targeted to older students in junior high and on up through high school. Once again, the topics are geared to older students and the readability level is lower and can start at any level an educator needs to use.

Here is an example of the sentence structure and vocabulary level my husband, Jeff, and I used in our book *Hello Hi-Lo: Readers Theatre Math* (Libraries Unlimited). The reproducible Readers Theatre plays in this book reinforce math concepts for students in fourth through eighth grade. However, each play has characters' parts assigned to different reading levels. Some characters in each play have a readability level of fourth grade or earlier. Some characters in each play have a readability level of fifth and sixth grade vocabulary words and sentence structure. Some characters in each play have a readability level of seventh to eighth grade or higher. A chart in the book clarifies which character in each play is assigned to which readability level. The teacher knows which level is assigned to each character, but students do not. This helps students all in the same classroom gain confidence with reading fluency at their own reading level without the embarrassment of being singled out and labeled.

A Colossal Surprise

Postal Worker:
Special delivery! I have a letter that just arrived from France, and it's marked urgent.

Government Worker 1:
Thanks for the mail. I appreciate your rush to get this here.

Postal Worker:
You're welcome. Have a good day and I hope to see you again, soon.

Postal Worker exits.

Government Worker 1:

I guess I should open this letter right away. It must be important.

Government Worker 2:

What does it say? And why would France be writing to us in America?

Government Worker 1:

You'll never believe it! The letter says there's going to be a fantastic celebration. France has decided to give America a present. It's a great big giant colossal Statue of Liberty!

Government Worker 2:

What a surprise! How big is the statue? What else does the letter say?

In this example, the characters each have been carefully assigned different readability levels. *Government Worker 2* speaks at a fourth grade or lower readability level. The *Postal Worker* speaks at a fifth to sixth grade readability level. *Government Worker 1* speaks at a seventh to eighth grade and higher readability level. The vocabulary words and sentence structure in each part varies according to its assigned reading level.

The sentence structure and vocabulary words vary from one hi-lo reader to the next, according to their target audience. The best way to understand which to use in your own manuscripts is to study your target publisher's line of hi-lo readers and familiarize yourself with their submission guidelines.

Beginner's Tip

When writing a hi-lo reader, there might be several key words that you want to include in your manuscript even though they are above the reading level you're targeting. You can introduce these words carefully into the context of your text along with their definitions. Be sure to repeat each one several times in close succession so your readers can learn to identify it.

Professional Track

Which market have you been published in? The tradebook market? The educational market? The ELL market? Spread your wings and pitch an idea to write a hi-lo reader in a market different from one you've been published in before.

Strengthen Your Writing Muscles

Choose one current event in the news. Find an article written about it. Select several paragraphs of text from that article and rewrite them with shorter sentences and simple vocabulary words geared to a third grade reading level.

13.2 Characters

Characters in hi-lo readers can be as varied as the audience who reads them. They are different, however, than the characters found in beginning readers and chapter books. This is because beginning readers and chapter books are targeted to children in preschool through third grade, whereas hi-lo readers are targeted to students in upper elementary school and on up through adults. Beginning readers and chapter books can have cutesy and charming characters that appeal to younger kids, but characters in hi-lo readers are more sophisticated and appeal to an older audience. You can create winning characters in hi-lo readers by targeting the age of the reader rather than the age of the reading level you're incorporating.

When writing nonfiction hi-lo readers, characters are real. Sports heroes, movie stars, and world leaders make fascinating subjects to write about. Some publishers produce series of hi-lo readers with titles based on a list of biographies. If you're interested in writing biographies, look at the list of names already published in a publisher's catalog. Pitch an idea to the editor for a list of three to five names that they haven't yet published that would fit into this list. Even if other publishers have published similar titles, this publisher hasn't and will probably be interested in adding one or more of these new titles to their own list of biographies for hi-lo readers. Try to land a contract before you write a manuscript that fits into a series of nonfiction hi-lo readers like this so you're earning income while you write. (To learn more about landing a contract before you write the manuscript, read my first book in this series, *Yes! You Can Learn How to Write Children's Books, Get Them Published, and Build a Successful Writing Career*.)

If writing fiction for students in upper elementary through high school, choose characters who are slightly older than your target audience. Most kids like to read about characters who appear a little bit more grown-up than they are. Especially at this reading level, you do not want to make main characters appear babyish or less mature than the kids who read these stories. Otherwise, they'll feel embarrassed by the story and won't read it.

Characters should be mostly human, but if you're writing fantasy or sci-fi, you can create characters as animals, creatures, or robots. As long as these characters feel sophisticated and act like adults, they'll fit well into a hi-lo reader.

If writing fiction for the ELL market, characters should be adults. These characters can appear in a variety of genre such as romance, mystery, and science fiction. Adult English Language Learners do not want to read stories with kids as the main characters. Create adult characters who move about in a real world for this audience. Also, any time you can create an international cast of characters who travel all over the world on their adventures, especially in countries where your manuscripts will be published, it broadens the appeal even more.

Your characters each have their own voice. To explore how to create dialogue for hi-lo readers so each of your characters can speak in their own, one-of-a-kind voice, continue to the next section.

Beginner's Tip

Plan a fake trip to a country you'd like to write material for in the ELL market. Gather travel brochures, plan key stops in a variety of cities, and look up all your travel details. This will give you a better sense of what the characters in your story will experience.

Professional Track

Now that you've got writing experience under your belt, always be working to improve your craft. That's part of the joy of writing! Study books such as Angela Ackerman and Becca Puglisi's *The Emotion Thesaurus* to learn how to create characters that experience real emotions. This will help your readers identify with your characters on a deeper level.

Strengthen Your Writing Muscles

Think of two people you know who have very unique personalities. Make a list of three to five of each of their quirky traits. Brainstorm a brand new character with some of the most fascinating traits of both.

13.3 Dialogue

When dialogue is used effectively, it creates an interesting and exciting scene. You can make your own hi-lo readers come alive to students or adults who are reading them by incorporating dialogue into the text. There are a few pointers to remember as you are crafting your manuscripts for this target audience.

Even though dialogue is key when writing beginning readers for the first and second grade reading levels, it's not as important when writing hi-lo readers even when using the sentence structure and vocabulary words geared for the second grade reading levels. This is because older students are able to think at a higher level even if they cannot yet read at this level. They can follow longer passages of narrative and understand what is happening in a story. They therefore do not need dialogue to drive the plot forward or develop character traits as much as younger children do.

This is especially true when writing hi-lo readers for the nonfiction market. For instance, a hi-lo book on Extreme Hockey does not need any dialogue at all! It can be totally narrative without dialogue even though it might be written at a first and second grade readability level. This is because older readers can think in more abstract terms than younger readers who need everything to be concrete and literal.

Because dialogue is an ordinary element of fiction for middle grade, young adult, and adults, it can be a natural part of your hi-lo reader. Study how to write dialogue effectively in fiction by referring to the wide variety of published materials available for this genre. Incorporate dialogue into your hi-lo readers in a similar manner, but use sentence structure and vocabulary words that correspond to the reading level you are targeting.

In hi-lo readers for English Language Learners (ELL), however, dialogue takes on a new responsibility that it has in no other beginning reader or chapter book. Because students in ELL programs are learning how to speak conversationally as well as how to read, there needs to be a lot of concrete examples of how to say common phrases or how to speak correctly in a variety of situations. For instance, if a character in a hi-lo reader for the ELL market visits a restaurant, it is helpful to include a small scene where that character needs to find the bathroom. Dialogue should be included so that the ELL student can learn the correct way to speak. Here is an example:

Carmen gave the waiter her money and paid the bill.
"Where is the restroom?" Carmen asked.
"It's in the back next to the kitchen," the waiter answered.

Whether creating hi-lo readers for the ELL market or for students in upper elementary through high school, incorporate realistic dialogue. Work to make dialogue feel like a natural conversation is taking place and you'll be well on your way to using it effectively.

The plot structure is also important when writing hi-lo readers. Continue reading to learn more.

Beginner's Tip

Don't write in dialect by using strange spellings of words. Students learning to read can't decipher it. Instead, make dialogue "feel" like a dialect by using words or phrases that are common to the region where your character lives.

Professional Track

If you're putting in long hours of writing hi-lo readers each day, be sure to take frequent, short breaks. Stand up from your desk, stretch, and walk around at least once each hour. Use these breaks to polish the dialogue in your hi-lo reader manuscript. One way to do this is to connect with a library that offers volunteer assistance to patrons who are trying to learn English. Establish a relationship with an ELL student and ask her to help you by reading aloud the dialogue portions you are writing.

Strengthen Your Writing Muscles

Imagine you are visiting a foreign country. Write down a list of questions that would be essential for you to know such as, "How much does this cost?" and "Where is the train station?" and "What time is it?" Write a scene for a hi-lo reader story geared for ELL students that uses at least two of these questions from your list to show correct examples of how to ask these questions in English.

13.4 Plot

Even though the sentence structure and vocabulary words may appear simple in hi-lo readers, these books can have very complicated stories with plots and subplots that add intrigue and build suspense. This is because hi-lo readers are targeted to students ages nine and older on up through adults. No longer needing to keep the plot simple, you can create as interesting a plot as you can think of to entice struggling readers into the imaginary world you're creating, so they will feel a measure of success as they build confidence and fluency in reading.

Rather than just one main plot line or story arc where the main character attempts to solve the main problem in the story, you can create subplots that add depth and tension. Work to make everything have a purpose, however, whether to move the plot forward or develop your characters. Don't just have random events occurring in your story that don't have an important influence on the advancement of the plot.

Because you're targeting an audience whose peers are reading middle grade novels such as *Charlotte's Web* or young adult novels such as *To Kill a Mockingbird* or adult novels such as *The Grapes of Wrath*, you can create hi-lo readers with just as many plot twists and subplots, but at a much lower reading level. Study strategies for building effective plots in how-to-write books such as my personal favorite, Todd A. Stone's *Novelist's Boot Camp: 101 Ways to Take Your Book from Boring to Bestseller*.

Study hi-lo readers your target publisher currently publishes. If these are trade books, map out the plot structure. Note the beginning, middle, and end. Include subplots. Mark the turning point or climax of the story. Create a timeline and note when each event happened and how it worked to move the plot forward. Evaluating current published books will help you develop the plot structure of your own.

If your target publisher publishes nonfiction, Readers Theatre, material for ELL students, graphic novels, or other types of hi-lo readers, take time to evaluate the plot structure of these published materials as well. Using published examples as your guide gives you a pattern to follow that an author has already used with success to get published in today's market. It will give you solid footing as you work on the plot to develop your own manuscripts.

Beginner's Tip

Taking time to develop the plot structure of your story before you begin to write will automatically give you a stronger story. As you begin to write, however, allow yourself to change the plot if the story "asks" for it.

Professional Track

If you don't like to create outlines before you write a story, teach yourself a new habit. Outlines are essential to submit to editors if you want to send in a proposal first and try to land a contract before you write so you're earning income while you write. Motivate yourself to start creating outlines by giving yourself small rewards each time you do.

Strengthen Your Writing Muscles

Write down five to ten key events that happened in your own life this past year. Then create a simple timeline that shows a chronological progression of these events. Practice creating a timeline of your own life, and then make one for the manuscript you're working on.

13.5 Setting

Whichever topic you're writing about, try to experience the setting. For instance, if you're writing about a story that takes place during the Civil War, you can watch a reenactment of a battle scene on YouTube at www.YouTube.com, or watch a movie that is set in this era. Better yet, attend a live reenactment done on an actual battlefield! While you watch, open all your senses to soak up the setting. What do you see? Is the grass blowing gently in the breeze while troops are marching into place? What noises do you hear? Is a bird singing peacefully in a nearby tree before the first shot is fired? What do you smell? Is the acrid smell of gunpowder hanging in the air? What do you touch? Is the wood of the log fence rough with splinters that you lean against? What do you taste? Is your mouth dry from the hot summer day and the water sweet and cool that you drink to quench your thirst?

As you experience all your senses in this place you are visiting or watching, imagine what your characters would see, hear, smell, touch, and taste in this setting. Write down what you're feeling and thinking during this experience. Then write down what the setting might be like from the viewpoint of your characters. As you write, don't try to write sentences you'll actually use in your hi-lo readers. Just write freely, without inhibition, to create a sense of the place you will be writing about in your manuscript.

Later, when you sit down to create the setting and develop the scenes in your hi-lo readers, you can use these notes as a reference.

If you're writing hi-lo readers for the ELL market, try to experience settings in your stories as well. For instance, if you're writing a mystery and the setting is in Hong Kong, watch video clips on YouTube or a movie that takes place in this bustling and overcrowded city. Once again, take time to become aware of the sensory details about this setting. Jot down notes about the sights, sounds, tastes, smells, and textures. Spend time writing freely about how you feel watching these scenes and also how your characters might feel moving about in this place. Use the notes you take as a reference when you are developing your setting for your hi-lo readers in the ELL market.

Even when writing nonfiction hi-lo readers, trying to experience the setting for your manuscript will help give you the tools to write your manuscripts and incorporate sensory details for a "you-are-there" type of feel. Developing the setting and adding sensory details to nonfiction helps draw readers into the action.

Beginner's Tip

To move from one setting to the next in hi-lo readers as well as in any story, a *transition* is needed. A transition shows how the character gets from here to there. You can use transition words such as: next, later, or eventually. Or, you can use transition phrases such as: the following morning, after he finished breakfast, or whenever she came home. Craft sentences to move your character between two scenes so your reader can move, too.

Professional Track

Play a Five Senses Game at your writers group. To prepare, place five to ten small objects or children's toys in brown lunch bags, one per bag. Select objects or toys that make a sound, have an unusual shape or texture, have a fragrance, or flash a beam of light. To play the game, let your friends try to guess what is in one of the bags. Give them clues. Let them touch the object with their eyes closed, smell it, or close their eyes and listen to its sound. Each time you give a clue, instruct them to write down what they think the object is and explain their reasons. Compare everyone's notes when an object is identified correctly. Use this experience to help you write better descriptions in your hi-lo readers manuscripts.

Strengthen Your Writing Muscles

Imagine that one of your main character's senses does not work. For instance, your main character could be deaf. How would the sensory details in your scene differ if this were so? Describe a scene as a hi-lo reader from your main character's new viewpoint.

13.6 Topics and Themes

Topics and themes that wouldn't be suitable for other beginning readers and chapter books find their place in hi-lo readers. For instance, romance is never an ingredient in a beginning reader or chapter book unless it is a fairy tale romance between Sleeping Beauty and Prince Charming or a silly romance between characters such as a loveable pair of two hippos. However, you can write a serious romance for hi-lo readers targeted to junior high or high school students, or for the ELL market where adults learning English enjoy reading about adult characters experiencing real-life situations.

If teens like to read about a topic in middle grade or young adult novels, it can be a topic or theme of a hi-lo reader geared for this target age. Google or search the Internet for lists of hi-lo books and you'll find a variety of reading lists available that are rich resources to help you choose themes or brainstorm ideas to write about for this market.

When writing hi-lo readers for the educational market, turn to the State and National Standards as well as Common Core State Standards for comprehensive lists of topics and themes that are taught in different grade levels. Once again, be sure to target the *age range* of your audience, and not the reading level, when choosing your topics and themes.

When my husband Jeff and I wrote our book of reproducible Readers Theatre plays, *Hello Hi-Lo: Readers Theatre Math*, we first checked the Standards for math topics taught in fourth through eighth grade, our target audience. Here are some of the math topics covered in this age range: *order of operations*, *measurements*, *circles*, *solid figures*, *fractions*, and *graphing on a coordinate plane.*

To create our list of themes that we chose to feature in our book, first we referred to the Standards and selected math topics taught at these grade levels. Next, to develop the theme for each math concept's story, we brainstormed lists of topics our target age would be interested in such as video games, sci-fi adventure, and sports. Taking this one level further, we explored common themes and topics educators used to teach various math concepts. For instance, examining textbooks and Internet sources, we discovered that a common theme teachers use for teaching positive and negative numbers in the middle grades is comparing temperatures in extreme places of the world by using a thermometer to gather the data. Based on this research, we chose the theme of solving a mystery by following clues to both the Arctic and Antarctica.

A great way to brainstorm topics and themes to feature in your hi-lo readers is to examine what's already published. Especially if you have selected or connected with one publisher to pitch an idea to or write a manuscript for, study their product line. Then research the State and National Standards as well as the Common Core State Standards for the grade level you'll be writing for. You'll be amazed at the number of fresh, new ideas for topics and themes that pop into your head simply by exploring what's already available for this reading level.

Beginner's Tip

Textbooks are great resources when brainstorming ideas for topics and themes to write about for hi-lo readers. Purchase used textbooks at low prices to add to your personal reference library.

Professional Track

"Swap" kids with your writing peers. Ask each writer to survey their own kids and write down their ages and each child's favorite topics or themes to read about. Compile all the information into one list and separate it according to age level. Then choose a topic that appeals to an older kid and write a hi-lo reader story for a younger reading level.

Strengthen Your Writing Muscles

Identify a fear that you have. Do a 10-minute freewriting exercise starting with the prompt, "The day I face my fear, I will…" Use this topic as a theme to write a hi-lo reader geared to students who are seniors in high school, but write the manuscript targeted to a fifth or sixth grade vocabulary level.

AFTERWARD

As you come to the end of this book, you might feel like a clumsy caterpillar, unsure of whether or not the beginning readers and chapter books market is the market for you. Just like a caterpillar who munches his way day after day from leaf to leaf, you've been learning a lot of material about State and National Standards, Common Core State Standards, leveled reading material, and hi-lo readers. It's a lot of information to swallow!

But just like a caterpillar eventually designs a cocoon in order to metamorphosize, take time to wrap yourself up in a cozy and comfy spot to digest all this information you've been acquiring. Enjoy completing the various exercises in this book. Explore the different reading levels and publishing opportunities that spark your interest.

If you do, one day you'll realize something inside of you has changed. You've developed new skills as a writer. It's as if you've grown wings. Suddenly, you'll know it's time to stretch your wings and fly! You'll have learned key elements of how to write beginning readers and chapter books. You can soar into this delightful world and join other children's authors who write for this wonderful market ripe with opportunities for success.

PART IV

Appendices

APPENDIX I

GLOSSARY

Accelerated Readers:
Another name for advanced readers.

Acquisitions Editor:
Editor at a publishing house who accepts manuscript submissions from authors.

Activity Book:
Children's book featuring crafts, games, puzzles, or other activities.

Advance:
Money paid to an author before the book is published. Half of the advance is usually paid upon signing the contract, with the second half of the advance paid after the publisher receives and approves the completed manuscript. The advance is subtracted from the royalties once the book starts to sell. After sales earn enough to cover the advance, then the author starts to receive royalty checks.

Advanced Readers:
Beginning readers or books for children in second or third grade who have already mastered basic reading skills and are reading at an advanced level.

Agent:
In the book industry, agents represent their authors, or clients, as they submit each client's manuscripts to potential publishers.

Alliteration:

Two or more words having the same beginning sound in the same sentence or phrase.

All Rights:

If you sell all rights to a publisher, this means that they completely own the copyright to your article or book and can use it however they wish.

Anthropomorphic:

Animals or objects having human characteristics.

Art specs:

Illustration samples prepared during the development of a book or article, sometimes sent to the author for approval before final publication.

Author's Packet:

A planner sent by some publishers to their authors to provide information on preparing the manuscript for submission.

Beginning Readers:

Also known as early, easy, or emergent readers, these books are written for children who are learning to read in pre-kindergarten up through third grade. Some publishers extend their beginning readers series up through sixth grade.

Bibliography:

A list of references used for research.

Blog:

Term used to describe a weblog, or website updated frequently like an online diary or news commentary.

Book Map:

A layout planner or thumbnail sketch for authors to fill out to show the content on each page of a manuscript.

Booksellers Conventions:

Large conventions where owners of bookstores (also known in this industry as booksellers) gather to meet with publishing houses and purchase the newest titles to sell in their stores. Various conventions meet each year such as BookExpo America (BEA) and Christian Booksellers Association (CBA). Similar conventions are held for literacy professionals including the International Reading Association (IRA) and the American Library Association (ALA).

Byline:

Short sentence or phrase at the end of a published article sharing a tidbit of information about the author such as the author's name, title of her book, and website.

Chapter Books:

Books with controlled vocabulary and short chapters that form the bridge between beginning readers and novels.

Characters (font):

The letters, spaces between sentences, and punctuation typed in a line of text.

Chunk:

A block of text from one sentence that has been divided over several lines on the printed page to help young children learn to read.

Classroom Resources:

Activities, games, worksheets, and other material teachers can use in their classroom.

Cliffhanger:

A suspenseful spot in the middle of a high-action scene that comes at the end of one chapter so the reader will want to continue reading the next chapter.

Common Core State Standards (CCSS):

Standards for curriculum goals that provide teachers with a clear understanding of what students are expected to learn. These standards relate learning to the real world to equip students for future success in college and careers.

Competing Book Clause:

Clause on a book contract that states the author cannot write a similar book that will compete for sales of original book.

Comprehension:

When students demonstrate that they understand the content of what they are reading.

Concept Books:

These books teach one or more concepts such as colors, numbers, or the alphabet.

Concrete Noun:

Nouns that can be easily illustrated with pictures such as bear, desk, and bike.

Context Clue:

Sentences or words that provide clues to define a word or concept in other parts of the text.

Contract:

The legal document or agreement between an author and a publisher about the rights and terms concerning a manuscript. Both the author and the publisher usually sign a contract.

Controlled Vocabulary:

Carefully chosen vocabulary words used in material for a specific grade or reading level.

Copyright:

The right to create and distribute your work. Every word an author writes is automatically protected under current copyright law until a contract or agreement is signed to sell rights to a publisher.

Cover Letter:

Similar to a query letter, this letter is written to an editor and sent along with a manuscript proposal or submission.

Cover Size:

The actual measurements of a book's cover, also known as the trim size.

Critique Group:

A group of writers that meets to read over and discuss each other's manuscripts, offering helpful and constructive feedback for improvement or potential markets.

Cross-curricular:

Activities, lessons, or reading material that can be used to teach skills in different areas of curriculum such as math, language arts, and science.

Deadline:

Date set by publishers on a contract to submit a completed manuscript.

Decoding:

Process where children sound out a new word or read a new word based on clues from pictures or the surrounding text.

Dialogue Tag:

Phrases such as *he said* or *she said* that show who is speaking what portion of dialogue.

Dummy:

A mock-up of a picture book, usually prepared by the author, that shows the projected layout of the text or illustrations of the book.

Easy Readers:

Level of beginning readers geared for children in first through third grade who have already acquired some reading skills.

e-book:

Digitized book that can be downloaded and read on electronic devises, cell phones, or computers.

Educational Market:

Books or materials published for teachers to use in the classroom.

Educational Publishers:

Publishers who produce material for teachers and the educational market.

Emergent Readers:

Level of beginning readers geared for children in kindergarten through third grade who have already acquired basic reading skills.

English Language Learners (ELL):

Students whose primary language is not English.

First Chapter Books:

A book with the look, feel, and cover size of a middle grade (MG) novel but its length can be the same as one single chapter in a novel. First chapter books bridge the gap between beginning readers and middle grade novels.

Flat fee:

A one-time payment offered by a publisher to the author for a manuscript.

Flesch-Kincaid Grade Level:

A program in Microsoft® Word that shows the reading level of a designated portion of text.

Flesch Reading Ease:

A program in Microsoft® Word that shows the reading level of a designated portion of text.

Fluent Readers:

Children who are reading at grade level and have mastered reading material that is written for their students in their grade.

Freelancer:

Also known as a freelance author or freelance writer, freelancers work independently with a publisher on a contract-by-contract basis and are not employed or on a salaried position with the publisher.

Geisel Award:

Award given out annually in memory of Theodore Geisel (Dr. Seuss), to honor author(s) and illustrator(s) of the most distinguished book for beginning readers published the previous year.

Genre:

A category such as science fiction, mystery, or adventure.

Graphic Novel:

A highly-illustrated novel that has the feel of a comic-book.

High-frequency words:

A group of words compiled in a list by Edward W. Dolch which children encounter frequently when they read.

Hi-lo Books:

These unique books are geared to meet the needs of struggling readers in upper elementary school through adult. Hi-lo books have a high level of interest but require a low level of reading skills.

Leveled Reader:

Reading material that uses carefully chosen vocabulary words and short sentences that are geared to children in a specific grade level.

Literacy Advocate:

Person who supports and endorses teaching children to read and experience the world of literature.

Lexile® Measure:

Rating system that rates the reading level of a book's text and also measures a student's reading ability.

Main Character:

The star of the story, this character is the main person the story is all about.

Manipulatives:

Objects such as special blocks that children can hold in their hands and work with to learn different skills such as counting.

Manuscript:

The work a writer is preparing on a word-processing program. The writer prints out this work to share with a critique group or mail to an editor.

Market Analysis:

A comparison of three to five current published books that are similar to the book an author is proposing, and a description of how the author's new book will be different from these.

Market Guides:

List of publishers that includes contact information along with pertinent details about each one's unique product line and policies for dealing with authors.

Middle Grade (MG):

Targeted to readers in upper elementary and sometimes through junior high.

Mock-up:

A dummy or actual sample the author makes of a book.

Name Recognition:

When authors are so famous that people purchase their books or read their articles based on the recognition of their name.

Narrative:

Text that tells what is happening as compared to a scene that shows what is happening often through the use of dialogue.

National Standards:

Standards for curriculum goals that teachers in every state are required to teach in their classroom.

No-pay/low-pay Market:

Publications that pay very little for an author's manuscript or don't pay anything at all. This market is a great opportunity to build published credits and gain experience as a writer.

Novelty Books:

These books have a gimmick or interactive element such as lift-the-flap or touch-and-feel.

On Spec:

When a publisher agrees to assign an author the task of writing a manuscript on speculation, but does not plan to offer a contract until after the manuscript is completed and approved.

Oral Reading:

The ability of children to read stories out loud.

Out of Print:

After a publisher determines not to print any more copies of a title, that book goes out of print when the publisher decides to stop publishing it.

Packager:

A type of company that produces books such as board books or novelty books and then sells the books to a publisher.

Periodical:

A publication such as a magazine or newsletter that is published at regular intervals.

Phonics:

A method of teaching children to read by sounding out the letters in a word.

Picture Book (PB):

Books for young children comprising mostly illustrations or pictures.

Picture Clues:

Illustrations that accompany a story that show what the text is saying. Picture clues help children figure out how to read new words all on their own.

Plot twist:

An unexpected change of events that occurs in a story plot.

Portable Document File (PDF file):

A type of universal file that can usually be read easily on most computers. The internet has free conversion programs that turn most documents into PDF files.

Predictable Plot:

A story plot that develops in a predictable manner by using a certain pattern such as the days of the week or repetition of scenes.

Predictable Text:

Words in a story that a child can read and automatically guess what comes next. Often accomplished by use of repetition or rhyme.

Pre-emergent Readers:

Children in preschool, kindergarten, and first grade who do not yet know how to read a complete sentence.

Print Run:

The number of copies a publisher decides to print at one time, usually of a new book.

Project Editor:

An editor used by some publishers who is assigned to work with an author after a manuscript has been submitted and accepted under contract. The Project Editor works with the author to edit, revise, and prepare the manuscript for publication.

Proofs:

A copy of the manuscript that usually has the artwork intact and is ready to be shipped to the printer. Authors are sometimes sent the proofs for one final check for typos or mistakes before the book is printed.

Proposal:

A submission sent to a publisher that generally consists of a cover letter explaining a projected manuscript, along with sample text of the project or a sample of the author's published work.

Prose:

Narrative text or text that is not poetry.

Published Credits:

The number of articles or books an author has had published. Most publishers require published credits to be published by traditional publishers and not self-published.

Publishing House:

A corporation or business that publishes books, magazines, or other materials.

Query Letter:

Similar to a cover letter, this letter is sent by itself to a publisher to ask if the publisher would like to receive a proposal or completed manuscript submission.

Readability:

The grade level at which an article or book can be read.

Readability Lists:

Lists of vocabulary words divided up into grade level.

Readability Statistics:

Programs are used to evaluate a portion of text and tell you the readability statistics, or grade level the vocabulary words and sentence structure are suitable for.

Readers Theatre:

Play scripts meant to be read aloud by children in order to practice oral reading skills.

Reading Curriculum:

Lessons developed for teachers to use in the classroom to teach reading to their students.

Reading Fluency:

The ability of children to read successfully at the grade level they are in school.

Reading Level:

The grade level most children are in when they can read a certain list of vocabulary words and sentences of a certain length.

Reading Specialist:

Person who understands which reading skills children should have in each grade level in school.

Rebus:

A story that substitutes pictures for some of the words.

Rejection Letter:

Letter sent to authors stating that the publisher will not be accepting their manuscript for publication.

Reprint Rights:

This means that your article has been published elsewhere already, and you're giving permission for a different periodical to publish it once more.

Reproducibles:

Worksheets that teachers can photocopy and distribute to their students.

Rights:

Authors sell a variety of rights to publishers, giving the publishers permission to publish and sell their manuscripts according to which rights are sold.

Royalty:

The percentage of income from a book that is paid to the author by the publisher.

SASE or Self-Addressed, Stamped Envelope:

Some publishers ask that a self-addressed, stamped envelope, or SASE, be included with a manuscript submission for their reply or for returning your manuscript if it's rejected.

Scope and Sequence:

Another term for an outline, often preferred by an educational publisher. The scope and sequence often includes the educational skills a book will teach as well as an outline of the topics presented.

Sensory Detail:

Adding examples of taste, touch, sight, hearing, and smell to a manuscript.

Sentence structure:

The sentence length as well as how complex a sentence is. For instance, more complex sentences include commas and phrases or clauses. More simple sentences include only a subject and a verb.

Sight Recognition:

The ability of children to recognize a word simply by looking at it.

Sight Words:

A list of pronouns, adjectives, and prepositions prepared by Edward W.

Dolch that children should know when they see them, even before they learn how to read other words.

Simultaneous Submission:

A manuscript sent to several publishers at the same time. Authors are required to always tell a publisher if they are sending a simultaneous submission.

Slush pile:

Term for the stack or pile of unsolicited manuscript submissions an editor receives.

Spread:

A term commonly used in the picture book market. A spread comprises two pages of the book, that when opened up, can be seen at the same time. A spread always has an even page number on the left-hand page and an odd page number on the right-hand page.

State Standards:

Standards for curriculum goals that teachers in each state are required to teach in their classroom. Standards vary from state to state, but most follow Texas or California's standards as a guide.

Story Arc:

The build-up of tension in a story's plot that increases from the beginning, through the middle, and comes to a climax at the end.

Story Bible:

Set of specific instructions prepared by the publisher to be followed by the author when writing a new title for an established series of books.

Style Guide:

Information a publisher provides to the author in an Author's Packet that tells how to format the text, what to name the saved files, which spellings or abbreviations are preferred for certain words, and how to prepare a bibliography or index.

Submission:

Manuscript sent by an author to a publisher or agent.

Submission Guidelines:

Also known as Writer's Guidelines. Often found on a publisher's website under "About us" or "Contact us," these guidelines spell out the publisher's interests and how an author should submit a query, proposal, or completed manuscript to the publisher. Each publisher's guidelines are uniquely suited to its individual needs and product line.

Synopsis:

Overview of a projected or completed manuscript that is often requested as part of a proposal.

Target Age:

The age of the child who will be reading the published article or book.

Target Audience:

The specific audience who will be purchasing a book such as teachers, librarians, or homeschooling parents.

Thumbnail Sketch:

A layout planner or book map for authors to fill out to show the content on each page of a manuscript.

Trade Book Market:

The books that sell to the general public in a standard bookstore. This market does not include books sold to teachers that include worksheets to photocopy for their classroom.

Trade Picture Book:

Picture books sold in a standard bookstore that are published by traditional publishers rather than self-published.

Transition:

A word, phrase, or sentence to help move the reader from one setting to the next, from one scene to the next, or from one paragraph to the next.

Trim Size:

The actual measurements of a book's cover, also known as the cover size.

Universal Childhood Theme:

A topic or theme that every child experiences such as losing a first tooth.

Unsolicited Submission:

Manuscript sent to a publisher without an editor's request.

Word Family:

A group of simple words that have the same ending such as –*ay, -in,* or -*op.*

Work-for-hire Market:

Publishers in this market purchase all rights from the author and usually pay a one-time, flat fee for the completed manuscript.

Young Adult (YA):

Targeted to readers 12 to 16 or even 18 years old.

Appendix II

RECOMMENDED BOOKS FOR CHILDREN'S WRITERS

Market Guides

Book Markets for Children's Writers (Writer's Institute Publications ™)

Children's Writer's & Illustrator's Market (Writer's Digest Books)

Christian Writers' Market Guide (Christian Writers Guild)

Magazine Markets for Children's Writers (Writer's Institute Publications ™)

Writer's Market (Writer's Digest Books)

Resources for Writing Beginning Readers and Chapter Books

Children's Writer's Word Book by Alijandra Mogilner

Merriam Webster's Intermediate Dictionary

The Reading Teacher's Book of Lists by Edward B. Fry and Jacqueline E. Kress.

Phonics from A to Z by Wiley Blevins

Building Fluency: Lessons and Strategies for Reading Success by Wiley Blevins

Teaching Phonics and Word Study in the Intermediate Grades: A Complete SourceBook by Wiley Blevins

Children's Writers' Books

The Complete Idiot's Guide® to Publishing Children's Books by Harold D. Underdown

Creating Characters Kids Will Love by Elaine Marie Alphin

The Everything® Guide to Writing Children's Books by Lesley Bolton

How to Write a Children's Book and Get it Published by Barbara Seuling

How to Write a Children's Picture Book, Volume I: Structure by Eve Heidi Bine-Stock

How to Write a Children's Picture Book, Volume II: Word, Sentence, Scene, Story by Eve Heidi Bine-Stock

How to Write a Children's Picture Book, Volume III: Figures of Speech by Eve Heidi Bine-Stock

Picture Writing by Anastasia Suen

Writing Children's Books for Dummies® by Lisa Rojany Buccieri and Peter Economy

Writing for Children & Teenagers by Lee Wyndham

Writing Juvenile Stories and Novels by Phyllis A. Whitney

Writing Picture Books by Ann Whitford Paul

Yes! You Can Learn How to Write Children's Books, Get Them Published, and Build a Successful Writing Career by Nancy I. Sanders

You Can Write Children's Books by Tracey E. Dils

You Can Write Children's Books Workbook by Tracey E. Dils

Of Special Interest

Anyone Can Get Published—You Can, Too! A Practical Guide for the Christian Who Writes by Nancy I. Sanders

35000+ Baby Names by Bruce Lansky

Book in a Month: The Fool-proof System for Writing a Novel in 30 Days by Victoria Lynn Schmidt

Chase's Calendar of Events (McGraw-Hill)

Children's Writer® Guide (Writer's Institute Publications ™)

The Complete Idiot's Guide® to Writing Poetry by Nikki Moustaki

The Complete Rhyming Dictionary by Clement Wood

The Emotion Thesaurus by Angela Ackerman and Becca Puglisi

Guide to Fiction Writing by Phyllis A. Whitney

Novelist's Boot Camp: 101 Ways to Take Your Book From Boring to Bestseller by Todd A. Stone

Pop-Up Activities to Teach Genre by Tamara Miller

Plug Your Book! Online Book Marketing for Authors by Steve Weber

Red Hot Internet Publicity: An Insider's Guide to Marketing Your Book on the Internet by Penny C. Sansevieri

Secrets of a Freelance Writer: How to Make $100,000 a Year or More by Robert W. Bly

The Timetables of History by Bernard Grun

The Train-of-Thought Writing Method: Practical, User-Friendly Help for Beginning Writers by Kathi Macias

Writing Skills Made Fun series by Karen Kellaher: *Capitalization, Punctuation, and Spelling; Parts of Speech; Sentences and Paragraphs*

Guides on Grammar and Style

The Blue Book of Grammar and Punctuation: An Easy-to-Use Guide with Clear Rules, Real-World Examples, and Reproducible Quizzes by Jane Straus

The Chicago Manual of Style (The University of Chicago Press)

The Christian Writer's Manual of Style by Robert Hudson, General Editor

The Elements of Style by Strunk and White

Nitty-Gritty Grammar: A Not-So-Serious Guide to Clear Communication by Edith H. Fine and Judith P. Josephson

More Nitty-Gritty Grammar: Another Not-So-Serious Guide to Clear Communication by Edith H. Fine and Judith P. Josephson

Rewrite Right! By Jan Venolia

Write Right! by Jan Venolia

Appendix III

ABOUT THE AUTHOR

Nancy I. Sanders is the author of over 80 books including the award-winning picture book *D is for Drinking Gourd: An African American Alphabet* and the bestseller for Scholastic Teaching Resources *25 Read and Write Mini-Books that Teach Word Families* with over 250,000 copies sold. Nancy has been published by such houses as Scholastic Teaching Resources, Reader's Digest Children's Books, Chicago Review Press, Sleeping Bear Press, Tyndale, and Standard. She has also written several books for teachers with her husband, Jeff, who teaches elementary school. They live in southern California and have two grown sons, Dan and Ben.

Nancy grew up in Everett, Pennsylvania on a dairy farm, the youngest of seven children. She milked the cows, baled the hay, drove the tractor, and spent all her spare time reading. Favorite memories include reading *Little Women* perched high up in the branches of a tree and *Pride and Prejudice* while floating on a raft in the middle of their pond. Now she loves to write and has had a successful writing career with books and numerous magazine articles published by publishers both big and small.

Nancy's passion is to teach others how to write as well as break into the world of publishing and experience success as a published author. She led writers groups for over 15 years as well as hosts small writers' mentoring workshops in her home. Her column for children's writers has appeared in the *Writer's* online magazine, the *Christian Communicator*, and in the Institute of Children's Literature *Children's Writers eNews*. She was on faculty with the Working Writers' Club where she taught tele-classes and tele-workshops for children's writers. In her award-winning first book of the series, *Yes! You Can Learn How to Write Children's Books, Get Them Published, and Build a Successful Writing Career,* she shares insider's tips and practical strategies to help writers realize their dreams.

Please visit the author's website at www.nancyisanders.com.

BOOKS BY THE AUTHOR

Books for Writers

Yes! You Can Learn How to Write Children's Books, Get Them Published, and Build a Successful Writing Career

Yes! You Can Learn How to Write Beginning Readers and Chapter Books

Anyone Can Get Published—You Can, Too! A Practical Strategy for the Christian Who Writes

Picture Books

D is for Drinking Gourd: An African American Alphabet

Easter (A True Book)

Passover (A True Book)

Earth Day (A True Book)

Independence Day (A True Book)

The Fall into Sin (Arch Book)

Jesus Walks on Water (Arch Book)

Board Books and Novelty Books

The Pet I'll Get

My Many Hats

My Special Things

Can't Catch Me

Off to the Fair!

Noah (Kingdom Kidz Bible)

King Solomon (Kingdom Kidz Bible)

Zacchaeus (Kingdom Kidz Bible)

Martha and Mary (Kingdom Kidz Bible)

Moses (A Bible Touch Book)

Jonah (A Bible Touch Book)

Beginning Readers and Chapter Books

Parables in Action Series: ***

#1 Lost and Found

#2 Hidden Treasure

#3 Comet Campout

#4 Moon Rocks and Dinosaur Bones

#5 Cooks, Cakes, and Chocolate Milk Shakes

#6 The Super Duper Seed Surprise

Marshal Matt Series:

#1 Marshal Matt and the Slippery Snacks Mystery

#2 Marshal Matt and the Case of the Secret Code

#3 Marshal Matt and the Topsy-Turvy Trail Mystery

#4 Marshal Matt and the Puzzling Prints Mystery

#5 Marshal Matt and the Case of the Freezing Fingers

Nonfiction for Kids

Frederick Douglass for Kids: His Life and Times with 21 Activities

America's Black Founders: Revolutionary Heroes and Leaders with 21
    Activities

A Kid's Guide to African American History

Old Testament Days

Black Abolitionists: Lighting the Way to Freedom

Educational Market

Readers Theatre for African American History*

Hello Hi-Lo: Readers Theatre Math*

WriteShop® Primary: An Incremental Writing Program—Books A, B, and C

WriteShop® Junior: An Incremental Writing Program—Books D, E, and F

Cut & Paste Mini-Books: Math

Cut & Paste Mini-Books: Science

Cut & Paste Mini-Books: Around the Year

26 Read and Write Mini-Books that Teach the Alphabet

25 Read and Write Mini-Books that Teach Phonics

25 Read and Write Mini-Books that Teach Word Families

Grammar Manipulatives Kids Love

Munch and Learn Math Storymats

Easy-to-Read Nursery Rhyme Plays

15 American History Mini-Books*

25 Science Plays for Emergent Readers**

Math Mystery Mini-Books**

15 Easy-to-Read Neighborhood and Community Mini-Book Plays**

15 Easy-to-Read Holiday and Seasonal Mini-Book Plays**

15 Easy and Irresistible Math Mini-Books**

15 Easy-to-Read Mini-Book Plays**

15 Irresistible Mini-Plays for Teaching Math**

Fresh and Fun: November

Engage the Brain: Games: Grade Four*

Brain-Compatible Math Activities: Grade Four*

Craft and Activity Books

Unforgettable Edible Bible Crafts****
Archy's Adventures: Colors, Numbers, Letters
Red Hot Bible Puzzles
Way Cool Bible Puzzles
Cents-ible Bible Crafts
My Book about Ben and Me
My Book about Sara and Me
Amazing Bible Puzzles: NT, OT
Bible Crafts and More
Jumbo Bible Bulletin Boards: More Bible Stories Preschool & Primary
Jumbo Bible Bulletin Boards: Fall & Winter Preschool & Primary
Favorite Bible Heroes for Ages 4 & 5
Bible Crafts on a Shoestring Budget Grades 3 & 4

*Co-author Jeff L. Sanders
**Co-author Sheryl Ann Crawford
***Co-author Susan Titus Osborn
****Co-author Nan Williams

Praise for *Yes! You Can Learn How To Write Children's Books, Get Them Published, and Build a Successful Writing Career*

Like no other how-to children's writers' book out there. An honest, realistic guide for anyone aspiring to become a career writer, Nancy I. Sanders demystifies the process from pen to paycheck. *Yes! You Can* is like having your own personal writing coach at your side.
-Aimee Jackson, former Senior Editor, Sleeping Bear Press

I bet I would have been a full-time writer many years sooner if *Yes! You Can* had been published when I was starting my writing career. It's full of practical advice, clear explanations, step-by-step plans, and plenty of encouragement. I especially love the way specific tips are offered depending on whether the reader is a full-time or low-time writer, as well as tips for both new writers and file-cabinets-full-of-unpublished-manuscripts writers. The Triple Crown of Success approach is fantastic! It helps me clarify, even at this stage, the balancing act I struggle with as a writer who loves to write but who also must make a livable income. *Yes! You Can* is a must-have for any writer trying to build a bona fide writing career! I'll be recommending it to all my writing students.
-Laura Purdie Salas, *Stampede! Poems to Celebrate the Wild Side of School* and more than 80 other books for kids, www.laurasalas.com

I'm 100% behind the idea of an alternate approach to the publication journey as my own publishing road has been anything but normal. This book offers a solid guide to publication for any writer looking for an eventual career in writing and willing to try a road slightly less traveled.
-Jan Fields, Editor of the Children's Writers eNews

Fresh. Practical. Honest. These are the terms which best describe Nancy's book on writing for children. It's unlike any other book on this topic that I've seen. If you don't succeed as a children's writer after studying this book and doing what it says, you probably need to stick with some other genre. The content in this book is awesome!

-Sandy Brooks, Former Director, Christian Writers Fellowship International

If you want to learn how to write, sell, and market a blockbuster, you should read this book. If you also want to produce a body of work, build a solid career, and make a living as a writer, you *must* read this book. It is a goldmine of information on every aspect of the writing craft. With plenty of insider tips and examples, the author demystifies manuscript preparation, queries, proposals, age range, controlled vocabulary, ghostwriting, work-for-hire, literary contracts and much, much more. In *Yes! You Can*, Nancy I. Sanders provides a road map that will help a writer take control of his or her career, get out of the slush pile, and turn the dream into reality.

-Q. L. Pearce, Author of more than 150 books for children

I highly recommend *Yes! You Can* to writers of all levels. Nancy I. Sanders' commonsense techniques and helpful tips can turn any writer into a success. How do I know? I landed my first picture book contract by applying her methods. If I can, you can, too!

-Catherine L. Osornio, Children's book author and freelance writer
www.catherinelosornio.wordpress.com

INDEX

Made in the USA
Middletown, DE
08 September 2019